iPod +
iTunes

Starter Kit

Brad Miser
Tim Robertson

800 East 96th Street,
Indianapolis, Indiana 46240

iPod + iTunes Starter Kit

International Standard Book Number: 0-7897-3278-5

Library of Congress Catalog Card Number: 2004110331

Printed in the United States of America

First Printing: October 2004

07   06   05   04   4   3   2   1

Trademarks

All terms mentioned in this book that are known to be trademarks or service marks have been appropriately capitalized. Que Publishing cannot attest to the accuracy of this information. Use of a term in this book should not be regarded as affecting the validity of any trademark or service mark.

Warning and Disclaimer

Every effort has been made to make this book as complete and as accurate as possible, but no warranty or fitness is implied. The information provided is on an "as is" basis. The author and the publisher shall have neither liability nor responsibility to any person or entity with respect to any loss or damages arising from the information contained in this book or from the use of the CD or programs accompanying it.

Bulk Sales

Que Publishing offers excellent discounts on this book when ordered in quantity for bulk purchases or special sales. For more information, please contact

U.S. Corporate and Government Sales
1-800-382-3419
corpsales@pearsontechgroup.com

For sales outside of the U.S., please contact

International Sales
international@pearsoned.com

Associate Publisher
Greg Wiegand

Acquisitions Editor
Stephanie J. McComb

Development Editor
Kevin Howard

Managing Editor
Charlotte Clapp

Indexer
Ken Johnson

Technical Editor
Brian Hubbard
John Nemerovski

User Reviewer
Rick Ehrhardt

Publishing Coordinator
Sharry Lee Gregory

Interior Designer
Dan Armstrong

Cover Designer
Anne Jones

Page Layout
Brad Chinn
Heather Klopfenstein

Contents at a Glance

Table of Contents

About the Authors

Brad Miser has written extensively about computers and related technology, with his favorite topics being anything that starts with a lowercase *i*, such as the iPod and iTunes. In addition to *Absolute Beginner's Guide to the iPod and iTunes*, Brad has written many other books, including *Special Edition Using Mac OS X, v10.3 Panther*; *Mac OS X and iLife: Using iTunes, iPhoto, iMovie, and iDVD*; *iDVD 3 Fast & Easy*; *Special Edition Using Mac OS X v10.2, Mac OS X and the Digital Lifestyle*; and *Using Mac OS 8.5*. He has also been an author, development editor, or technical editor on more than 50 other titles. He has been a featured speaker on various computer-related topics at Macworld Expo, at user group meetings, and in other venues.

Brad is the senior technical communicator for an Indianapolis-based software development company. Here, Brad is responsible for all product documentation, training materials, online help, and other communication materials. He also manages the customer support operations for the company and provides training and account management services to its customers. Previously, he was the lead engineering proposal specialist for an aircraft engine manufacturer, a development editor for a computer book publisher, and a civilian aviation test officer/engineer for the U.S. Army. Brad holds a Bachelor of Science degree in mechanical engineering from California Polytechnic State University at San Luis Obispo (1986) and has received advanced education in maintainability engineering, business, and other topics.

In addition to his passion for computers and technology, Brad likes to run and play racquetball; playing with home theater technology is also a favorite pastime.

Once a native of California, Brad now lives in Brownsburg, Indiana with his wife Amy; their three daughters, Jill, Emily, and Grace; and their guinea pig, Buddy.

Brad would love to hear about your experiences with this book (the good, the bad, and the ugly). You can write to him at bradmacosx@mac.com.

Tim Robertson has been publishing MyMac.com for a decade, and can be often found pretending to write a product review while actually playing with iTunes. Married and the father of three daughters, Tim spends most of his working hours in front of his Mac, pretending to write articles, reviews, or editing others, when in actuality he is probably surfing eBay. He has also been the focus and guest of computer related radio talk shows in New York, Boston, San Francisco, and Los Angeles, as well as being part of internet-based broadcasts. He has been interviewed for his opinion on Apple and the computer world in general. He spends much of his time evaluating new programs and hardware for product review. He spends a lot of his time at MyMac.com looking for new writers and other talent, as well as editing all site content before publication.

Dedication

From Brad:

I leave you, hoping that the lamp of liberty will burn in your bosoms until there shall no longer be a doubt that all men are created free and equal.

—*Abraham Lincoln*

From Tim:

My contribution to this book is dedicated to my wife, Julie, and our three kids, Raechel, Brooke, and Brittaney.

Acknowledgments

From Brad:

To the following people on the *ABG iPod and iTunes* project team, my sincere appreciation for your hard work on this book:

Stephanie McComb, my acquisitions editor, who made this project possible and convinced the right people that this was a good idea and that I was the right one to write it. **Marta Justak** of Justak Literary Services, my agent, for getting me signed up for this project and providing advice and encouragement along the way. **Kevin Howard**, my development editor, who helped make the contents and organization of this book much better. **Rick Ehrhardt**, my user reviewer, who made the jump to an iPod and iTunes at just the right time and provided lots of invaluable feedback that made this book much better.

Thanks to the following companies that provided some of the excellent iPod accessories that are covered in this book. **Dr. Bott "Distribution Macintosh Style,"** www.drbott.com, 9720 SW Hillman Court, Suite 840, Wilsonville, OR 97070. The team at **XtremeMac**, www.xtrememac.com, 15751 SW 41st Street, Suite 100, Fort Lauderdale, FL 33331. **TEN Technology**, www.tentechnology.com, 310-765-4834. **Griffin Technology**, www.griffintechnology.com, 615-399-7000. **Marware**, www.marware.com, 954-927-6031.

And now for some people who weren't on the project team, but who were essential to me personally. **Amy Miser**, my wonderful wife, for supporting me while I wrote this book; living with an author under tight deadlines isn't always lots of fun, but Amy does so with grace, understanding, and acceptance of my need to write. **Jill**, **Emily**, and **Grace Miser**, my delightful daughters, for helping me stay focused on what is important in life. While an iPod can play beautiful music, these precious people are beautiful music given form! (And, a special thanks to **Buddy** the guinea pig for his early-morning visits to cheer me up while I was working!)

From Tim:

This is my first book, which I only wrote a small part. I want to thank the great folks at Que publishing, particularly **Stephanie McComb** and **Kevin Howard**, for their understanding and patience, as well as guiding me in this new endeavor.

We Want to Hear from You!

As the reader of this book, *you* are our most important critic and commentator. We value your opinion and want to know what we're doing right, what we could do better, what areas you'd like to see us publish in, and any other words of wisdom you're willing to pass our way.

As an associate publisher for Que Publishing, I welcome your comments. You can email or write me directly to let me know what you did or didn't like about this book[md]as well as what we can do to make our books better.

Please note that I cannot help you with technical problems related to the topic of this book. We do have a User Services group, however, where I will forward specific technical questions related to the book.

When you write, please be sure to include this book's title and author as well as your name, email address, and phone number. I will carefully review your comments and share them with the author and editors who worked on the book.

Email: feedback@quepublishing.com

Mail: Greg Wiegand
            Associate Publisher
            Que Publishing
            800 East 96th Street
            Indianapolis, IN 46240 USA

For more information about this book or another Que Publishing title, visit our Web site at www.quepublishing.com. Type the ISBN (excluding hyphens) or the title of a book in the Search field to find the page you're looking for.

Introduction

If you have been toying with the idea of getting into digital music…. If you have an iPod and aren't sure what to do with it…. If you wish you had a good way to stop messing around with a bunch of CDs when you want to listen to music…. If you've heard great things about iPods, have seen the commercials for the iTunes Music Store, and want to know what all the fuss is about, then welcome to the *Absolute Beginner's Guide to iPod and iTunes*!

Meet the Digital Music Triumvirate

In this book, you'll learn about three of the most amazing things to happen to music since the first time someone decided that banging a stick on a rock had an appealing sound. These are the iPod, iTunes, and the iTunes Music Store.

The iPod Rocks

Apple's iPod has taken the portable digital device market by storm—and for good reason. Because the iPod includes a hard drive with up to 40GB of space, it is possible for you to take your music collection wherever you go. The iPod's tools enable you to organize, customize, and listen to your music in many ways while you are on the move—in your car, at home, or working at your computer. With its tight integration with iTunes and the iTunes Music Store, managing your music is both fun and easy. Your trusty iPod can also be used as a portable hard drive (for example, you can use it to carry files from your home to your office), to capture sound, and to store pictures; there are numerous peripheral devices that expand its amazing capabilities even further. And, iPods are just plain cool (see Figure I.1).

If you have never used an iPod before, this book is perfect for you and will help you learn everything you need to know. If you have some experience with an iPod, this book will still help you take your iPod skills to the next level. (If you are already an iPod expert, well, you aren't likely to be picking up a book called *Absolute Beginner's Guide to iPod and iTunes* now are you!)

iTunes Jams

With iTunes, you can create, organize, and listen to your entire music library from your computer (see Figure I.2). iTunes enables you to build as large a Library as you have the space on your computer's hard drive to store it. Then, you can customize music playback through playlists and smart playlists as well as create custom audio CDs in a variety of formats. It also provides other useful features, such as custom labeling and information tools, the ability to share your music on a local network, an Equalizer, and more. Because Apple's iTunes Music Store is integrated into iTunes, you can easily purchase and add music to your Library from within the application. Moreover, iTunes is the best software tool available for managing the music on an iPod.

FIGURE I.1

Whether you choose an iPod or an iPod mini, it will rock your world.

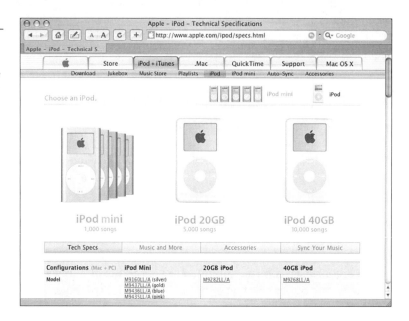

FIGURE I.2

iTunes will change the way you listen to music.

Just as with the iPod, if you have never used iTunes before, this book is perfect for you and will help you learn everything you need to know. If you have some experience, my hope is that you will learn how to get even more out of this outstanding program. Even if you have used iTunes quite a bit, you might manage to find some tidbits that will help your iTunes expertise grow.

iTunes Music Store

Using the iTunes Music Store, named as *Time* magazine's Invention of the Year for 2003, you can find, preview, and purchase music from a collection of hundreds of thousands of songs and download that music into your iTunes Music Library. Songs can be purchased individually or in albums, for $.99 per song (less when purchasing an entire album). Music you buy can be listened to, placed on a CD, and moved onto your iPod. Since its inception, the iTunes Music Store has rapidly become the most popular source of legal digital music on the Internet. After you have used it a time or two, you'll understand why.

Quick Guide to *Absolute Beginner's Guide to iPod and iTunes*

Absolute Beginner's Guide to iPod and iTunes provides all the information you need to get the most out of these amazing digital music tools. From the basics of listening to audio CDs with iTunes to the advanced customizing of music on an iPod and purchasing music online, this book equips you to use these awesome tools.

The book is organized into the following three major parts, each focusing on one of the three components of the iPod/iTunes/iTunes Music Store triumvirate:

- Part I: The iPod
- Part II: iTunes
- Part III: The iTunes Music Store

Within each part, the chapters generally start with the basics of the topic and get more advanced as you continue. Within the chapters, the information is presented in roughly the order in which you will typically perform the tasks being described.

Speaking of tasks, this book contains many step-by-step instructions—I hope your motto will be "learn by doing." You should be able to learn how to do a task fairly quickly and relatively painlessly by following the steps using your own music and your own tools. Although my writing is so utterly fascinating that you will likely want to read this book like a good novel, try to resist that urge because you will probably get better results if you actually work with the tools while you read this book.

Of course, you can read this book from start to finish in the order in which the chapters are presented. This will work fine if you have some experience with iTunes and have some music in your iTunes Library. However, because these tools are so well integrated, you can't really use the iPod or the iTunes Music Store effectively without knowing the basics of using iTunes first.

If you are totally new to these topics, I recommend that you get a jumpstart on iTunes by reading the core iTunes chapters first, which include Chapters 12, 13, 14, 15, 16, and 17. Then, you should read the core iPod chapters, which are Chapters 1, 2, 3, 4, and 5. From there, read Chapters 22 through 25 to get the scoop on working with the iTunes Music Store.

After you have finished these core "courses," you can read the rest of the chapters as they interest you. For example, when you are ready to burn your own CDs or DVDs, check out Chapter 19, "Burning Your Own CDs or DVDs." And when you want to explore the world of amazing iPod accessories, read Chapter 7, "Rocking Your World with iPod Accessories."

Going Both Ways

Because the iPod, iTunes, and the iTunes Music Store all work equally well on both Windows and Macintosh computers, this book covers these topics from both perspectives. So, you'll notice that some of the figures are screenshots taken on a Windows computer whereas others are taken on a Macintosh. Although the screens on these two computers look slightly different, they work very similarly, so seeing a screen on the Mac shouldn't cause a problem for you if you use a Windows computer, and vice versa. When there are significant differences, I explain them in the text.

Special Elements

As you read, you will see three special elements: Notes, Tips, and, only rarely, Cautions. Also, each chapter ends with a section titled "The Absolute Minimum." Explanations of each of these are provided for you here.

note

Notes look like this. They are designed to provide you with information that is related to the topic at hand but not absolutely essential to it. I hope you will find the Notes interesting, even if you don't find them useful immediately.

tip

Tips help you get something done more quickly and easily, or they tell you how to do a task that is related to what's being described at the moment. You might also find an explanation of an alternate way to get something done.

caution

If something you can do (and probably shouldn't) might end in a bad result, I warn you in a Caution. Fortunately, you won't find many of these through-out the book, but when you do see one, you might want to take a close look at it.

THE ABSOLUTE MINIMUM

Finally, each chapter ends with "The Absolute Minimum" section. The contents of this section vary a bit from chapter to chapter. Examples of this content include the following:

■ A summary of the key points of the chapter.

■ Additional tips related to the chapter's topic.

■ References to sources of additional information.

So, now that you know all you need to about this book, it's time to strike up the digital band....

PART I

The iPod

Touring the iPod

In less than three years of existence, Apple's iPod has become one of the most popular personal digital devices ever created. When initially released, the iPod's critics said it was too expensive when compared to other digital music players and that people would never spend the additional money to get the iPod's much superior functionality and style (even the critics couldn't deny the iPod's amazing attributes). As they often are, the critics were very much mistaken. People who love music love the iPod. Its combination of features and style, and because it's simply very, very cool, led it to quickly dominate sales of personal music players, a position in which it remains today.

The Apple iPod: A Lot of Hype or Really Hip?

So, what's the iPod all about?

It's about being able to take your entire music collection with you and listen to anything you want when you want to listen to it. And, using iPod's companion iTunes software, you can create and carry customized collections of your music to make getting to the specific music you want to hear even easier and more fun.

The way your music sounds on an iPod is just amazing, too. You definitely don't have to compromise music quality for portability. With the iPod, you get the best of both. If you have never heard music on an iPod before, prepare to be amazed.

That's the bottom line, but it isn't the whole story. With the iPod, you can do much more, as you will learn through the rest of this part of this book. And because of the iPod's stylish design and ease of use, you will likely want to take it with you wherever you go.

So What Is an iPod Anyway?

The iPod is a small digital device that includes a hard drive (just like the one in your computer, only smaller), an operating system, a processor and other computer components, as well as an LCD screen, controls, and other system elements needed to deliver its amazing functionality. It also includes a rechargeable lithium battery to give you plenty of listening time, a Headphones port to which you attach audio devices (including headphones, powered speakers, and so on), the iPod Remote port to enable you to use various devices (including remote controls), and the Dock port to enable you to move music from a computer onto the iPod, recharge its battery, and attach a variety of acessories.

The iPod's software enables you to manage and play digital audio files. You can also use its software to set a variety of preferences, in addition to using the iPod's other built-in tools.

Even with all this, iPods are quite small. The largest iPod is only 2.4 inches wide, 4.1 inches tall, .69 inches thick, and weighs a mere 6.2 ounces. This is roughly the size of a deck of playing cards. The smallest model, the iPod mini, comes in at a svelte

note

iPods can work with a variety of audio file formats, including AAC, MP3, Audible books, AIFF (Mac only), Apple Lossless and WAV. Because you just listen to these formats on an iPod, you don't need to know that much about them to use one. However, you will want to understand these formats when you prepare music for an iPod using iTunes. If you can't wait to learn what these formats are all about, see "Audio File Formats You Might Encounter When You Use iTunes" on page **168**.

2 inches wide, 3.6 inches tall, .5 inches thick, and a mere 3.6 ounces. This is about the size of a deck of playing cards cut in half!

All iPod Models Aren't Equal, But They Are All Cool

There have been several generations of iPods, and each new generation includes improvements to the previous generation. The current generation of iPod comes in two basic models: the iPod and the iPod mini. Previous generations of iPods look similar to the current versions, but included different controls, software, and capabilities. All of these models are definitely cool, and all perform the same basic function. However, each offers specific features and options. Let's take a quick look at the current crop of iPods and then take a brief stroll down the iPod's memory lane.

The iPod

The fourth major generation of iPods was a substantial improvement over the first three generations and quickly made the much-beloved-but-now-obsolete original iPods go the way of other extinct digital devices. Added to the previous generation's improvements of the addition of the Dock port, larger hard drives for more music storage, improved controls, better software, and more accessories were the adoption of the iPod mini's Click Wheel control and longer battery life (see Figure 1.1).

Within the iPod family are currently three major versions, the biggest difference among them being the size of the hard drive they contain. There are also minor differences in accessories between the two. Here are the current members of the iPod clan (see Figure 1.2):

note

At press time, the three versions of iPods (two models of the iPod and the iPod mini) detailed in this chapter were available. However, Apple frequently updates the iPods to increase storage space and add new features. To get the scoop on the latest iPod models right now, go to http://www.apple.com/ipod.

note

If you haven't purchased an iPod yet (what are you waiting for?), I recommend that you get the 40GB model if you can afford its additional cost. For $100 more, you get twice the storage space (which means you can take twice as much music with you) and a Dock, which you will find very handy.

FIGURE 1.1

The iPod will definitely rock your world.

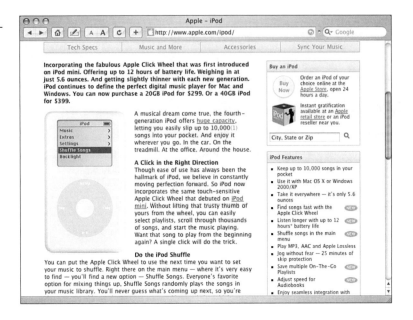

FIGURE 1.2

Pick an iPod, any iPod; you can't go wrong.

■ **20GB**—The base iPod model isn't really basic. It offers a 20GB drive and includes the same great features as its bigger sibling. The only other difference is that this model doesn't include a Dock. With its 20GB hard drive, you can fit as many as 5,000 songs on this iPod. And that's a lot of music! The current list price of this model is $299.

■ **40GB**—The top-of-the-line iPod has a 40GB hard drive, rated at 10,000 songs. Because of this, it is slightly heavier (by a mere 0.6 ounces) than the other model. The "big" iPod currently costs $399.

Small Is Beautiful: The iPod Mini

As if the iPod isn't small enough, Apple produes an even smaller iPod, known as the *iPod mini*. These smaller iPods offer similar features to their bigger cousins and include a 4GB hard drive rated at 1,000 songs. Unlike the iPod, which comes only in its elegant white and silver finish, the iPod mini comes in five colors (see Figure 1.3).

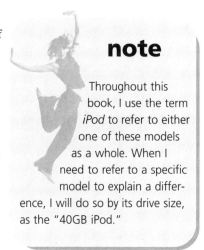

note

Throughout this book, I use the term *iPod* to refer to either one of these models as a whole. When I need to refer to a specific model to explain a difference, I will do so by its drive size, as the "40GB iPod."

FIGURE 1.3

The difference between the various iPod mini models is only skin deep.

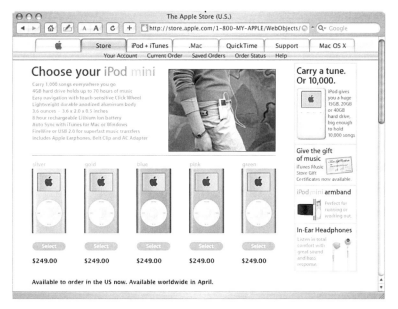

iPod: The Previous Generation

The previous generation of "full size" iPod was similar to the current models. The primary difference is that you controlled them with four buttons and a Scroll Pad instead of the more elegant Click Wheel that was introduced on the iPod mini and has been proven to be the better way to control your tunes (see Figure 1.4). The battery of these models doesn't last as long as the current editions' do; they were rated for only 8 hours of play time as opposed to the current models' rating of 12 hours. Still, this generation of iPod was a tremendous improvement over previous versions.

FIGURE 1.4

The previous generation of iPod provided four buttons and the Scroll Pad for controls.

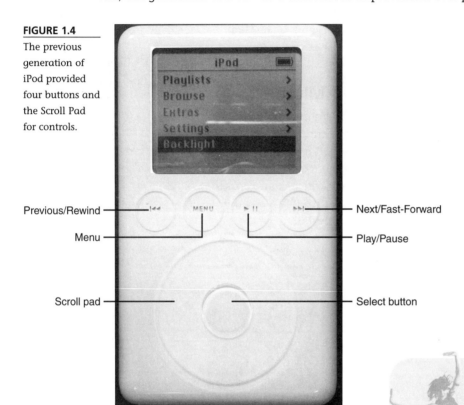

Previous/Rewind
Menu
Scroll pad
Next/Fast-Forward
Play/Pause
Select button

Because you can't buy these models anymore (at least not new ones), I won't be providing specific details on how to use them in this book. Fortunately, they work very much like the current versions do. If you have one of these models, just use its separate buttons (such as the Play/Pause button) instead of the corresponding locations on the current models' Click Wheel. There are also some minor software differences, but the vast majority of information in this book will be as useful to you as it is for someone who is using the latest and greatest iPod version.

note

If you pay close attention, you will notice that I call the current "full size" iPods the fourth generation, but I only describe three generations in this brief overview. That's because the second generation of iPod was notable only because it was the first version that was compatible with Windows computers. Also, the second generation of iPod was relatively short-lived.

The One That Started It All: The Original iPod

The first generation of iPod offered many of the same features as its successors, although it had a smaller hard drive (the first iPod included a 5GB drive) and was larger and heavier than later generations (see Figure 1.5). It was also compatible only with Macintosh computers, and its software was a bit more limited, too. Although it is no longer being produced, this is the model that started it all, and for that we owe it a debt of gratitude (if one can owe anything to a device, that is).

Because the original iPod hasn't been produced for a long time, it seems unlikely you will be using this model while you are reading this book (because the book assumes you are relatively new to the iPod world). To save some pages, I won't be covering the original iPod elsewhere in this book. Much of the information about iPods and iPod minis is also applicable to the original iPod, but there are some significant differences in its controls and software.

note

When I need to differentiate between an iPod and iPod mini, I will do so with those terms. Otherwise, *iPod* refers to both iPods and iPod minis.

note

Although the original iPod is obsolete in the sense that it is no longer in production, you might be able to find a used one for sale. If you can find a good deal on one, this can be a good way to enter the iPod market or to get a second iPod. The original iPods are still very useful; I have one myself and use it quite often.

FIGURE 1.5

The first, but not the best, iPod had a 5GB hard drive and paved the way for the later generations.

What You Can Do with an iPod

The iPod is definitely a great music player, but it is much more than that, as you will learn throughout this part of the book. For now, read about some of the great things you can do with an iPod:

- Take your entire music collection with you wherever you go.

- Play your music in many different ways, such as by album, artist, genre, song, playlist, and so on.

- Eliminate the need to carry CDs with you anywhere; using an adapter or an FM transmitter, your iPod can provide music in your home, car, or any other place you happen to be.

- View your calendar.

- Access contact information for your favorite people and companies for quick and easy reference.

- Keep track of the time and date.

- Listen to your favorite audio book.

- Have a portable hard drive for transferring information between computers or for
  backing up your files.

- Record sound.

- Store pictures from a digital camera.

The Absolute Minimum

The iPod just might be the neatest gadget ever. After you have tried one, you will likely find it to be indispensable, and you might wonder how you ever got along without it. Before we jump into configuring and using an iPod, consider the following two points:

- An iPod enables you to take all your music with you and listen to it anytime, anywhere.
- The iPod is actually a mini computer and includes a hard drive, an operating system, and other computer components.
- There are two types of iPods in production: iPods and iPod minis.
- No matter which iPod you have, you'll be amazed at all the amazing things it can do, from basic listening to being your own personal portable hard drive.
- The original iPod worked only with Macintosh computers, but soon Apple realized that there was no reason to keep Windows users out in the cold. Current iPod models work just as well for both platforms. Whether you use a Windows computer, a Mac, or both, your iPod will work great.

IN THIS CHAPTER

- Find out what cool stuff came with your iPod.

- Charge the iPod's battery.

- Install the iPod's software on your computer.

- Connect the iPod to your computer and transfer music from your computer to it.

- Use a Dock to connect an iPod to your computer.

Getting Started with an iPod

Getting started with an iPod involves the following general steps:

1. Understand what is included with the iPod.

2. Charge the iPod's battery.

3. Install the iPod's software on your computer.

4. Connect the iPod to your computer and transfer music from your computer to the iPod.

5. Disconnect the iPod from your computer.

After you have performed these steps, you will be ready to learn how to use the iPod, which you'll start doing in the next chapter.

Exploring the iPod's Box

The iPod is so cool that even its box is stylish! In this section, you'll learn about the items included in that stylish box and how and where you use them. What you get with an iPod depends on the type and model of iPod you purchased. The following list tells you what comes with each type of iPod:

- **An iPod or iPod mini**—You probably didn't need this item listed or explained, but I like to be thorough!

- **Installation CD**—This CD contains the iTunes installer you will use to install the iPod's companion software on your computer.

- **User manual**—The Getting Started booklet helps you do just that. (Because you have this book already, you might not find the booklet very useful.)

- **Power Adapter**—You use this to charge an iPod's battery.

- **FireWire to Dock port cable**—You use this cable to connect the iPod's Dock port (or the Dock port on a Dock) to a FireWire port on your computer. You can also use it to connect the FireWire port on the power adapter to the iPod's Dock port.

- **USB 2.0 to Dock port cable**—You use this cable to connect the iPod Dock port (or the Dock port on a Dock) to a USB 2 port on your computer.

- **Earbud earphones**—You use these to listen to the iPod's output.

- **Dock (some iPod models)**—Currently included with the 40GB model, the Dock is a base unit into which you can place the iPod to connect it to your

note

Unless you have an iPod and an iPod mini and you use both Windows and Macintosh computers, you won't need to read all of this chapter. That is because its sections are based on specific options, such as using an iPod mini with a Mac or using an iPod with a Windows computer. As you read through sections, skip those that don't apply to you. (Of course, should you ever need them, they will be here waiting patiently for you.)

tip

As you are handling the iPod, it will turn on if you press any control. For now, turn it off again by pressing and then holding the **Play/Pause** button down until the iPod shuts off again.

computer. The Dock eliminates the need to mess around with cables each time you connect your iPod to your computer.

■ **Belt clip (iPod mini only)**—You can insert your iPod mini into this clip and then clip the clip to a belt to carry the iPod mini with you.

note

You can purchase a Dock separately if your iPod or iPod mini if its box didn't include one.

Charging the iPod's Battery

Like all portable electronic devices, the iPod has an internal battery. Before you start using an iPod, you need to charge its battery.

To charge an iPod using the power adapter, connect the FireWire to iPod Dock port cable to the power adapter and to the iPod. Then plug the power adapter into a power outlet.

While the iPod is charging, a battery icon will appear on its display and the word "Charging" will appear at the top of the screen. According to Apple, the iPod's battery is charged to the 80% level in two hours and fully charged in four hours.

When the iPod is fully charged, the display will contain a "full" battery icon and the status message will be "Charged." Unplug the power adapter and then disconnect the cable from the power adapter and from the iPod.

Note: Some Windows computers have a four-pin FireWire port instead of a six-pin port. In this situation, you need a four-pin to six-pin adapter to be able to use the FireWire cable. However, because a four-pin FireWire port doesn't support recharging the iPod's battery, there aren't many reasons to use a four-pin FireWire connector. If your Windows computer doesn't have USB 2, but does have a FireWire port, using the FireWire port will be better than using a USB 1 port, which I don't recommend (because it is much too slow to move music files in a reasonable amount of time).

tip

If you are going to connect the iPod to a Macintosh or to a Windows computer using a six-pin FireWire cable, which comes with the iPod, you don't need to charge the iPod's battery because that is done automatically when you connect the iPod to your computer. If you use the USB cable instead, you have to charge the battery by using the power adapter.

Installing the iPod's Software (Including iTunes)

Included in the iPod's box is a software installation CD. On this CD is the iTunes application you will use to manage the music that you place on the iPod. You'll learn all about iTunes in Part II of this book, titled "iTunes." But for now, install the software by using the steps in the section that is appropriate for the type of computer you are using (Windows PC or a Mac).

note

If you'd rather, you can download and install a "fresh" copy of iTunes from the Internet. This is usually a good idea so you get the latest version. To get help doing that, see the section "Downloading and Installing iTunes on a Windows PC" on page **176**. Then come back here and complete the iPod software installation.

Installing the iPod's Software on a Windows PC

If you have installed even one application from a CD, you won't have any trouble with the iPod CD, as the following steps will confirm:

1. Insert the **Installation CD** in your computer. The disc will be mounted on your computer, the software will begin to run, and the Choose Setup Language dialog box will appear.

2. Choose the language you want to use on the drop-down list and click **OK**. Because I am linguistically challenged and can only read English, that is the language I use throughout this book. They say music is the universal language (I think it is math myself) and so iTunes can use many different languages. You can choose the language that works best for you.

   note

   If you have trouble reading the serial number, you aren't alone. The text is very small!

   After you click OK, the InstallShield Wizard window will appear, and you can watch the initial installation process. When the initial installation process is complete, the iPod **Serial Number** dialog box will appear.

3. Enter your iPod's serial number, which can be found on the back of your iPod, and click **Next**. You will see the **Select Country or Region** dialog box.

4. Read the license (sure you will, right?) and click **Yes**. The **Select Country or Region** dialog box will appear.

5. Select the country or region that is most applicable to you and click **Next**. You will see the **Registration Information** dialog box.

6. Complete your registration information. Most of it is optional; however, you do have to provide at least a name and an email address. When you are done, click **Next**. You will see the second screen in the registration process.

7. Complete the fields about where you will use the iPod and what best describes what you do, if you'd like to. These are both optional. (Speaking of which, given how easily you can carry an iPod around with you, which is the whole point, how much sense does a question about where you will use it make?)

8. If you want to receive email from Apple, click the **Yes** radio button, or click **No** if you don't want to receive email.

9. Click **Next**. You will see the **iPod configuration** screen. This screen asks you to choose whether or not you want to configure your iPod now. In order to configure your iPod, it must be connected to your computer.

10. Click **Cancel** to skip the iPod configuration step for now (you'll learn how to do this later in this chapter). The installer will do its work, and you can watch its progress in the resulting windows. When the process is complete, you will see the **iTunes for Windows** dialog box window (see Figure 2.1).

tip

If the country or region you want to choose isn't listed, check the **Show All** check box and hopefully it will be then.

note

A pet peeve of mine is forced registration like Apple requires with the iPod. One shouldn't have to register to make a product one has purchased work. Ah well, what can we do?

tip

If you have already installed a newer version of iTunes than the one shown in the InstallShield Wizard for iTunes window, you can cancel out of the iTunes installation process by clicking the Cancel button in the iTunes for Windows dialog box..

FIGURE 2.1

When you
install the iPod
software, you
can also install
iTunes.

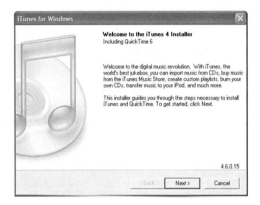

11. Read the information in the installer window and click **Next**.

12. If you have a lot of time and patience, read the license agreement; when you are done (if you are like me, you will realize it is incomprehensible and will just assume you aren't giving away your first born), click **Yes**.

13. In the resulting **Information** window, you can read information about iTunes, such as what it can do and what you need to install it. When you are done reading, click **Next**. You'll see the **iTunes for Windows Setup Type** dialog box.

14. Check the following options to make them active or uncheck them to make them inactive:

   ■ **Install desktop shortcuts**—This option places a shortcut to iTunes on your desktop. Unless you don't like desktop shortcuts for some reason, you should usually leave this option checked.

   ■ **Use iTunes as the default player for audio files**—This option causes iTunes to be used to play most audio files that you will access on the Internet, CDs, and so on. If you prefer to use another application, uncheck this check box. However, I recommend that you leave it checked; you can always change the default application to be something else after you have become comfortable with iTunes.

tip

If you choose to install iTunes from the iPod CD, you should update the application to ensure you are working with the most current version. For information about updating iTunes, see "Keeping iTunes Up to Date on a Windows PC Manually" on page **327**.

15. Click **Next**. You'll see the **Choose Destination Location** dialog box.

16. If you don't want to accept the default installation location (which is C:\Program Files\iTunes\), click the **Browse** button and choose the location you do want to use. Then click **Next**. You'll see a window advertising the iPod.

17. Click **Next**. As the installer starts to work, you will see the **Setup Status** window. This window provides you with information about the installation process.

    When the process is complete, you will see the **Installation Complete** window.

18. Click **Finish** to restart your computer and complete the installation process. When your computer restarts, iTunes will be ready for you and your iPod.

Installing the iPod's Software on a Macintosh

You can install the iPod's software on a Macintosh using the following steps:

1. Insert the **Installation CD** in your Mac. It will be mounted.

2. Using the Finder, open the **Installation CD** so you can see its folders.

3. Open the **iPod Installer** folder.

4. Open the installer package file that you see.

5. Allow the installer to check for the appropriate software by clicking **Continue**. The install window will appear (see Figure 2.2).

FIGURE 2.2
This is the initial screen of the iPod installer.

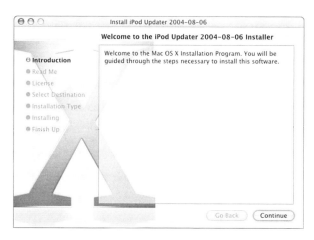

6. Click **Continue**. The installer will start and you will see the next screen in the process.

7. Read the information on each screen that appears and click **Continue** to move to the next screen.

8. When you get to the license agreement prompt, click **Agree**. You'll see the **Select a Destination** screen.

9. Choose the destination on which you want to install the iPod software. Typically, you should install the software on your active start-up drive. When you select a drive, it will be marked with a green arrow to show you the drive you have selected. In the lower part of the screen, you will see information about the drive on which you have elected to install the software.

10. Click **Continue**.

11. If prompted to do so, authenticate yourself as an administrator and click **OK**. The installer will run. When the process is complete, you will see the **installation complete** screen (see Figure 2.3).

FIGURE 2.3

When you see this screen, you are done installing the iPod software on your Mac.

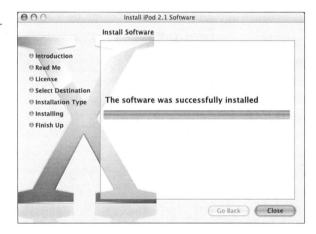

12. Click **Close**. The installer will quit. If you have connected your iPod to your Mac, the iPod Updater application will launch to enable you to update the iPod's software. You'll learn how to do that in the next section.

13. For now, quit the iPod Update by choosing **iPod Updater**, **Quit**.

You also need to have iTunes installed on your computer. Because you are using a Mac and I have assumed that you are running Mac OS X, you probably already have a copy installed on your computer. You should update the version you have installed to make sure you are using the most current version of the application. For the steps to do this, see "Keeping iTunes Up to Date on a Macintosh" on page **327**.

If you don't have a copy of iTunes installed on your Mac already, you can install it from the iPod installation CD or by downloading a copy from the Internet. For help with those tasks, see "Installing and Configuring iTunes on a Macintosh" on page **187**.

> **note**
>
> For Macs and Windows computers connecting to an iPod with a six-pin FireWire connector, connecting an iPod to the computer also charges the iPod's battery. Because of this, you should use six-pin FireWire whenever possible.

Connecting and Configuring an iPod on Your Computer

In order to load music onto an iPod, you must connect the iPod to your computer so that the music files can be moved from your iTunes Library onto the iPod.

To do this, you connect one of the cables supplied with your iPod to your computer. All iPod cables have the Dock connector on one end. You connect this to the iPod's Dock port located on the bottom of the iPod (see Figure 2.4).

> **tip**
>
> If a Dock was included with your iPod, you connect the cables to the Dock and then insert your iPod into the Dock to connect it. See "Connecting an iPod to a Computer with a Dock" on page **34**.

How you connect an iPod depends on the type of connections your computer has and the specific iPod model you have. The three types of connectors you use to connect iPods to computers are six-pin FireWire (all Macintoshes), USB 2, and four-pin FireWire (see Figure 2.5).

Bottom of an iPod mini

FIGURE 2.4

You use the Dock port on the bottom of the iPod to connect it to a computer.

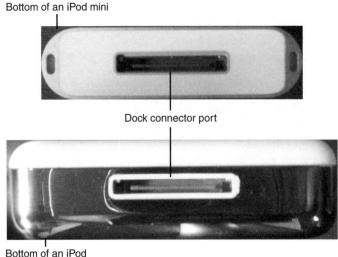

Dock connector port

Bottom of an iPod

FIGURE 2.5

These are the ports you might use to connect an iPod to your computer.

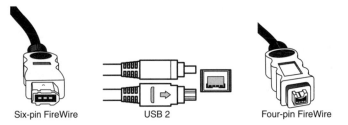

Six-pin FireWire   USB 2   Four-pin FireWire

Connecting an iPod to a Windows Computer

Connecting an iPod to a Windows computer requires that you decide on the type of connection you will be using. The following three options are possible:

- **Six-pin FireWire**—If your computer includes a six-pin FireWire port, you can use that to connect it to the iPod. This has the advantage of also charging the iPod at the same time.

- **USB 2**—If you have a computer that supports USB 2, you can use USB 2 to connect your iPod to the computer. USB 2 is slightly faster than FireWire, but your iPod won't also charge its battery when it is connected to your computer in this way.

> # caution
> When you connect an iPod to a computer using USB 2, it is not charging and so uses battery power. You can run the battery down if you use your iPod while it is connected to your computer.

If you want to be able to charge your iPod and connect it to your computer with USB 2 at the same time, you will need to purchase the iPod Dock Connector to FireWire and USB 2.0 cable. This cable is actually two cables linked to a single iPod Dock port connector. You can connect the USB 2 cable to your computer and the FireWire connector to the iPod's power adapter. This enables you to charge the iPod while it is also connected to your computer. You can purchase the iPod Dock Connector to FireWire and USB 2.0 Cable at the Apple Store (http://store.apple.com/).

■ **Four-pin FireWire**—If your computer includes a four-pin FireWire connector, you can use that to connect the iPod by using an optional six-pin to four-pin adapter. This method is not as desirable as using six-pin FireWire because it doesn't charge the iPod while it is connected to your computer, and it is slightly slower than USB 2. You should use this option only if one of the others isn't available to you.

note

As soon as you connect an iPod to your computer, the iTunes application will open and will begin transferring music in your iTunes Library onto your iPod. Of course, if you don't have any music in your iTunes Library because you haven't added any to it yet, this won't do very much. You will need to build an iTunes Library before you can transfer any music onto your iPod. To get help with this, jump over to Part II of this book and read Chapters 11–16. After you have created an iTunes Library, you can transfer its music to your iPod.

Assessing Your Windows Computer for an iPod

The first step to deciding which connection type to use is to determine which types are supported by your computer. There are a couple of ways you can do this.

Look at your computer to see which ports it includes. If it has at least one six-pin FireWire port available, you don't need to do anything else because this is the method you should use. Because a six-pin FireWire connection also charges the iPod when it is connected to your computer, this is the best option. If your computer doesn't support six-pin FireWire, consider adding a FireWire PCI card. These are relatively inexpensive at around $40 and require only a few minutes to install.

caution

You can't use a four-pin FireWire cable with an iPod mini even if you get an adapter for it. With a mini, you can only use six-pin FireWire or USB 2.

If you don't see a six-pin FireWire connector, locate the USB ports on your computer. Unfortunately, you can't tell by observation whether a USB port supports USB 2 or USB 1 because the ports are identical in appearance. Check the documentation that came with your computer to determine if it supports USB 2. If you can't find that information, contact your computer's manufacturer. If your computer does support USB 2, you are in good shape.

If your computer doesn't have a six-pin FireWire connector and doesn't support USB 2, look for a four-pin FireWire port. If it has one, you might be able to use a six-pin to four-pin FireWire adapter to connect your iPod to your computer.

If your computer doesn't have any FireWire ports and does not support USB 2, you'll have to add a PCI FireWire or USB 2 card to your computer before you can connect an iPod to it.

To use an iPod with a Windows computer, you must also be running Windows 2000 with Service Pack 4 or Windows XP Home or Professional.

Using Six-Pin FireWire to Connect an iPod to a Windows Computer

If your computer has a six-pin FireWire port, use the FireWire cable included with your iPod. Connect the Dock connector end to the Dock port on the iPod and the FireWire end to the FireWire port on your computer. The iPod will immediately be mounted on your computer. Skip to the section titled "Configuring an iPod on Your Computer" on page **31**.

Using USB 2 to Connect an iPod to a Windows Computer

If your computer supports USB 2, use the USB 2 cable or the accessory FireWire/USB 2 cable you purchased to connect your iPod to the computer. Use a USB 2 port that is on the computer itself rather than one that is on a keyboard, monitor, or other peripheral.

To use the USB 2 cable included with the iPod, plug the Dock connector end into the Dock port on the iPod and the USB 2 end into the USB port on your computer. The iPod will immediately be mounted on your computer. Skip to the section titled "Configuring an iPod on Your Computer" on page **31**. Make sure you insert the Dock connector end of the cable into the iPod's Dock connector port so that the icon on the connector is facing toward the front face of the iPod. If you attempt to force the connector in upside down, you can damage your iPod.

caution

Because the iPod will charge when it is connected to your Mac, you need to use a powered port, which is one located on the Mac itself. If you use a port on a FireWire hub or other FireWire device, it might or might not be powered.

To use the iPod Dock Connector to FireWire and
USB 2.0 cable, connect the Dock connector end to
the Dock port on the iPod (this cable is not supported on a iPod mini). Then, connect the USB 2
cable to a USB port on your computer. Connect the
FireWire end to the iPod power adapter and then
plug the power adapter into a power outlet. The
iPod will immediately be mounted on your computer. Skip to the section titled "Configuring an
iPod on Your Computer" on page **31**.

Using Four-Pin FireWire to Connect an iPod to a Windows Computer

To use four-pin FireWire, you will need to have a
four-pin to six-pin FireWire adapter. Connect this
adapter to the FireWire end of the iPod's FireWire
cable. Next, connect the Dock end to the Dock connector port on the iPod. Then, plug the four-pin end
of the adapter into your computer. The iPod will immediately be mounted on your
computer. Move on to the section titled "Configuring an iPod on Your Computer" on
page **31**.

> **note**
>
> I don't really rec-
> ommend using
> four-pin FireWire. It
> doesn't perform as
> well as USB 2 and
> doesn't charge the iPod
> battery like six-pin
> FireWire. You can purchase a
> FireWire or USB 2 PCI card for
> just a few dollars more than the
> adapter you need to use four-
> pin FireWire, so you won't save
> much money by using it.

Connecting an iPod to a Macintosh Computer

All Macintoshes produced in the past several years have at least one six-pin FireWire
port. You can use the FireWire cable included with your iPod to connect it to your
Mac. Connect the Dock connector end of the cable to Dock port on the iPod. Then
plug the FireWire end of the cable into a FireWire port on your Mac.

Many Macs also support USB 2, but because the iPod will charge when you use a
six-pin FireWire cable to connect it to your Mac, you should use FireWire instead of
USB 2. However, if you don't have an available FireWire port, you can use the USB 2
cable included with the iPod or the iPod Dock Connector to FireWire and USB 2.0
cable to connect an iPod to your Mac. See the section titled "Using USB 2 to Connect
an iPod to a Windows Computer" on page **30** for information about using USB 2 to
connect an iPod to your computer.

Configuring an iPod on Your Computer

The first time you connect an iPod to your computer, the iPod will turn on and
immediately be mounted on your computer, iTunes will open, and the iPod Setup
Assistant will open (see Figure 2.6). Type a name for your iPod in the text box. You

can use any name you'd like; this will be the name of your iPod when it is shown in the iTunes Source List. Check the **Automatically update my iPod** check box if it isn't checked already. Then click **Finish** (Windows) or **Done** (Mac). iTunes will update the iPod and will transfer all the music in your iTunes Library onto the iPod—if it can.

FIGURE 2.6

The trusty iPod Setup Assistant is ready to do its work.

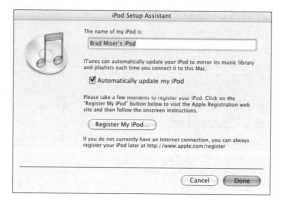

While music is being transferred, the iPod icon on the iTunes Source List will flash red (see Figure 2.7). You'll also see information about the transfer in the iTunes Information area at the top of the iTunes window.

FIGURE 2.7

If this book were printed in color, you would see that the iPod icon in the iTunes Source List is flashing red to show that music in the selected playlist is being moved onto the iPod.

If all the music in your iTunes Library will fit on the iPod, the process will complete without any further action from you. When this process is complete, you will hear a "whoosh" sound and you'll see the "iPod update is complete" message in the information area at the top of the iTunes window. The "OK to disconnect" message will also be displayed on the iPod's screen. When you see these messages, you can disconnect your iPod from your computer. Squeeze the buttons on each side of the Dock connector end of the cable and remove the cable from the iPod; the iPod will be ready to use. You can leave the cable plugged into your computer if you want to.

If there is more music in your iTunes Library than can fit on the iPod, you will see a message telling you that the iPod doesn't have enough room for all your music (see Figure 2.8). In this case, iTunes will create a playlist of music that will fit on the iPod and then transfer this music to your iPod. This is fine for now; in later chapters, you'll learn how to choose which music is transferred onto your iPod. Click **OK** to close the message window.

iTunes will move the playlist it created (whose name will be the name of your iPod plus the word "Selection") onto your iPod. When this process is complete, you will hear a "whoosh" sound and you'll see the "iPod update is complete" message in the information area at the top of the iTunes window. The "OK to disconnect" message will also be displayed on the iPod's screen. When you see these messages, you can disconnect your iPod from your computer. Squeeze the buttons on each side of the Dock connector end of the cable and remove the cable from the iPod; the iPod will be ready to use. You can leave the cable plugged into your computer if you want to.

FIGURE 2.8

Because I had more music than can be stored on an iPod mini, iTunes lets me know about it.

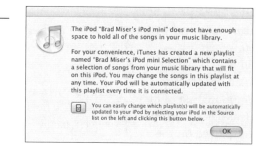

The iPod "Brad Miser's iPod mini" does not have enough space to hold all of the songs in your music library.

For your convenience, iTunes has created a new playlist named "Brad Miser's iPod mini Selection" which contains a selection of songs from your music library that will fit on this iPod. You may change the songs in this playlist at any time. Your iPod will be automatically updated with this playlist every time it is connected.

You can easily change which playlist(s) will be automatically updated to your iPod by selecting your iPod in the Source list on the left and clicking this button below.

OK

Connecting an iPod to a Computer with a Dock

If your iPod came with a Dock, you can connect the Dock to your computer instead of the iPod itself. When you want to transfer music to the iPod, you simply set it into the Dock. Using a Dock means that you don't need to mess around with cables (see Figure 2.9).

FIGURE 2.9

An iPod Dock eliminates the need to mess around with cables every time you connect your iPod to your computer.

To use a Dock, connect the Dock connector end of the cable you use to connect the iPod to your computer into the Dock port on the Dock instead of the port on the iPod. To connect the iPod to the computer, simply set it into the Dock. When the Dock can communicate with the iPod, you'll hear a tone. Other than that, using an iPod in a Dock is just like using one connected to a computer by a cable. When you connect the Dock connector end of the cable into the Dock connector port on the Dock, make sure the icon on the cable faces up. If you try to insert the cable in upside down, you can damage the connector.

When you want to disconnect your iPod from the computer, lift it out of the Dock. (You might have to place one hand on the Dock to keep it from lifting up when you lift the iPod out.) Before you pull an iPod out of a Dock, make sure the "OK to disconnect" message appears on the iPod's screen.

The Absolute Minimum

Fortunately, a lot of the material in this chapter is only useful the first time you use your iPod. After all, installing software and connecting cables isn't all that thrilling. But it is necessary to do the thrilling stuff that starts in the next chapter. Before we leave this topic, consider the following points:

- You can install more than one iPod on the same computer. For example, you might be fortunate enough to have an iPod and an iPod mini. If you have more than one iPod, use a different name for each so you can keep them straight. You can even connect them to your computer at the same time if you have enough ports and cables available to do so.

- If your iPod didn't come with a Dock, you can purchase one separately. I strongly recommend that you do so because a Dock makes connecting and disconnecting an iPod much easier. You'll learn more about Docks in Chapter 7.

- The Dock includes a Line Out port. You can use this to connect the Dock to speakers or other audio device to play the iPod's music on that device. You'll learn more about this in Chapter 8, "Using an iPod with a Home Stereo or Car Stereo."

IN THIS CHAPTER

- Connect an iPod to headphones or speakers so you can hear its music.

- Turn an iPod on and learn about its controls.

- Tour the iPod's menus and screens.

- Light up your iPod's world with the Backlight.

- Turn an iPod off.

Using an iPod

The iPod is a well-designed device that is easy to control—once you understand its controls and how they work. Because the iPod is likely quite different from other devices you have used, it can take a little time to get totally comfortable controlling one. That's where this chapter comes in. Whether you have an iPod or an iPod mini, you'll learn about the iPod's controls and how to use them. You'll also come to know (and love) the iPod's menu structure and the major screens with which you will deal. You'll get into the details of using all these controls and screens in subsequent chapters.

Getting Ready to Play

In order to hear the music that is stored on your iPod, you must attach a sound output device to it. The most common one you might think of is the earbud headphones that were included in the package.

To use these, you connect the mini-jack on the earbud cable to the Headphones port located on the top of the iPod (see Figure 3.1). When you do so, you'll hear any sound coming from the iPod through the earbuds.

FIGURE 3.1

The top of an iPod is where you plug in headphones, speakers, or other audio output devices.

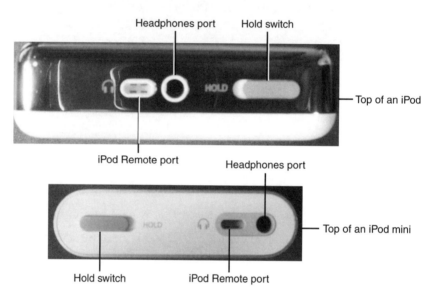

Headphones port   Hold switch

Top of an iPod

iPod Remote port

Headphones port

Top of an iPod mini

Hold switch   iPod Remote port

Although you are likely to use earbuds or other headphones with an iPod, those are certainly not the only audio output devices through which you can play an iPod's music. Following are some other devices you might want to use:

■ **Powered speakers**—You can connect a set of powered speakers to the Headphones port to play your iPod's music on those speakers. For example, you can use any set of computer speakers to create a mini stereo system.

If you connect a set of unamplified speakers, you aren't likely to hear very much if anything. The iPod doesn't put out enough power to drive a set of unpowered speakers.

note

On the top of the iPod, you'll also see the iPod Remote port in which you connect a remote control (you'll learn about these in later chapters). And, you'll also see the Hold switch, which you'll learn about later in this chapter.

- **FM Transmitter**—You can connect an FM transmitter to the Headphones port to broadcast your iPod's output over FM (some transmitters connect to the Dock port). You can then tune into your iPod's music on an FM tuner, such as the one in your car or home stereo system.

- **Home or Car Stereo**—You can use various cables and connectors to connect the Headphones port to an input port on a home stereo receiver, a car stereo, or boom box to play your iPod's music over one of these devices. You'll learn how to do this in Chapter 8, "Using an iPod with a Home Stereo or Car Stereo."

Controlling an iPod

While the iPod is slightly larger than the iPod mini, the controls on each are the same. Figure 3.2 shows the face of an iPod while Figure 3.3 shows an iPod mini. As you can see, these devices are quite similar. The main controls on an iPod are all located on the Click Wheel (see Figure 3.2).

FIGURE 3.2

The controls on the iPod will become second nature to you after you use them a few times.

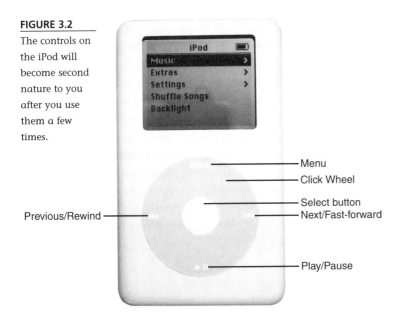

iPod

Music >
Extras >
Settings >
Shuffle Songs
Backlight

Menu
Click Wheel
Select button
Next/Fast-forward
Previous/Rewind
Play/Pause

Turning an iPod On

To turn an iPod mini on, press the **Click Wheel** in any location or press the **Select button**. You'll see the Apple logo on the iPod's screen, and after the iPod starts up, you'll see the main menu.

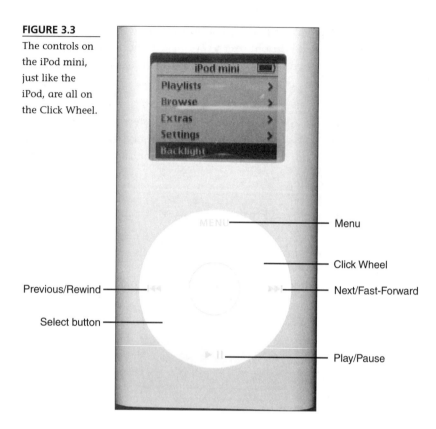

The controls on the iPod mini, just like the iPod, are all on the Click Wheel.

Menu

Click Wheel

Previous/Rewind

Next/Fast-Forward

Select button

Play/Pause

Choosing an iPod's Language

The first time you turn an iPod mini on, you'll immediately move to the Language selection screen that you use to choose the language in which your iPod will display information. To choose a language, slide a finger or thumb clockwise on the **Click Wheel** to move down the language list or counterclockwise to move up the list. When the language you want to use is highlighted, press the **Select button** to choose it. You will then move to the main menu. You only have to do this the first time you turn an iPod on or after you reset it.

Making Selections on an iPod

The previous paragraph about selecting a language gives you a specific example of how you control an iPod mini. Now, let's give you the general concept of how you move around your iPod mini to make it follow your commands.

The iPod is based on menus on which you make choices. To make a choice on a menu, you slide a finger or thumb clockwise on the **Click Wheel** to move down the current menu or counterclockwise to move up on the current menu. As you move up or down, a different command on the menu will be highlighted. When the command you want to use is highlighted, press the **Select button** to choose it. If the command is for another menu, that menu will appear. You can then move up and down that menu to choose another command. If the menu provides a list of songs, albums, or other categories, you can use the same process to select and play an item, such as a song.

To move back to a previous menu, you press the **Menu button**, which is located on the top edge of the Click Wheel.

You'll learn the specific menus and screens you will use later in this chapter. For now, just understand how to move up and down the iPod mini's menu structure.

Using the iPod's Click Wheel

The iPod's Click Wheel is kind of cool because it contains both the wheel that you use to move up and down the menus and the various buttons you use to control the iPod itself. These buttons are located at each 90-degree point around the **Click Wheel**. To use a button, you simply press down on its icon on the wheel. The button will click and the action it represents will happen.

Because there isn't a clear delineation between locations on the wheel, you don't have to be precise when you press a button. Press down close to the button's icon on the wheel and you will likely get the expected action.

Changing Volume

When a song is playing, you control the iPod's volume by sliding a finger or thumb on the **Click Wheel** clockwise to increase the volume or counterclockwise to decrease it.

Looking at the iPod's Menus and Screens

Now that you have an idea of how to move around your iPod, let's get a good understanding of its menus and screens by moving among them using the following steps:

1. Slide your finger or thumb clockwise on the **Click Wheel** to move down a menu or counterclockwise to move up a menu. As you move your digit, different menu options will be highlighted on the screen to show that they are selected.

2. When you want to use a menu command, highlight it and press the **Select button**. That command will be active and the screen will change to reflect what you have done. For example, if you selected another menu, that menu

will appear on the screen. If you select a song, the Now Playing screen will appear and that song will start to play.

3. To move back to a previous screen, press the **Menu button**. You'll move back to the screen you were on before the current one. Each time you press the Menu button, you'll move back one screen until you get back to the Main menu.

> **tip**
>
> You can change the contents of various menus, as you will learn later in this part of the book. The menus I describe here are the iPod's and iPod mini's default menus.

The Main Menu

The iPod's Main menu provides the major (dare I say main?) commands available to you (see Figure 3.4).

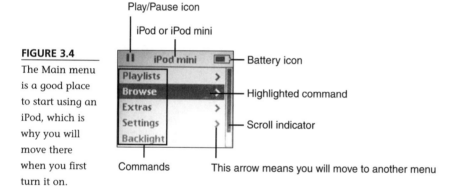

Play/Pause icon

iPod or iPod mini

FIGURE 3.4

The Main menu is a good place to start using an iPod, which is why you will move there when you first turn it on.

Battery icon

Highlighted command

Scroll indicator

Commands

This arrow means you will move to another menu

The specific commands you see on an iPod are slightly different from those on an iPod mini (or a earlier generation iPod), but once you have seen one Main menu, you will quickly understand any of the Main menus you see. On the iPod, the Main menu commands are the following:

- Music
- Extras
- Settings
- Shuffle Songs
- Backlight
- Now Playing (appears when a song is selected and playing, even if it is paused)

All these commands take you to their respective menus, except for the Backlight and Now Playing commands. The Backlight command turns the iPod's Backlight on (more on this later). The Now Playing command, which appears only when you have selected and are playing music, takes you to the Now Playing screen (more on this later, too).

When a menu choice leads to another menu, a right-facing arrow will appear along the right edge of the screen for that choice. If you don't see an arrow for a command, that command will cause an action to happen instead.

When there are more options on a menu than can be listed on the screen, you will see the Scroll bar; the dark part of the bar represents how much of the menu you are seeing on the screen out of the total menu, which is represented by the full bar. (Remember that to scroll up and down a menu, you slide your finger or thumb around the Click Wheel.)

> **note**
>
> That clicking sound you hear is the iPod's way of providing additional feedback to you each time you move to a different menu option. Oh, by the way, the technical term for this feature is the Clicker.

The Music Menu and Screens

The Music command takes you to the Music menu. This menu enables you to browse the music stored on your iPod by Playlists, Artists, Albums, Songs, Genres, Composers, or Audiobooks. When you select one of these options, you will move to a menu that lists each category within the category you selected. For example, when you browse by Artists, you'll see a list of all the artists with which music on your iPod is associated. You'll get the scoop on browsing in Chapter 4, "Listening to Music on an iPod."

> **note**
>
> There is one playlist on the iPod that you won't find in iTunes because it wasn't created there. That is the On-the-Go playlist. You can create this playlist from music that is stored on the iPod. You'll learn how to use this in Chapter 4.

For now, consider the Playlists command that takes you to the Playlists menu, which lists the playlists that are stored on your iPod. (If you haven't read Part II of this book, titled "iTunes," playlists are collections of music that you create in iTunes.) On the Playlists menu, you will see each playlist you have created in iTunes. Because each playlist represents a "menu" of the songs in that playlist, when you select it, you will see the songs menu that lists each song in the playlist. You'll learn how to work with the Playlists menu and screens in detail in Chapter 4.

The Extras Menu and Screens

The Extras command takes you to the Extras menu. On this menu, you will find various options that are related only because they are on the same menu. These commands enable you to access the iPod's non-music features, such as the Clock, Calendar, and so on. You'll learn about these extras in Chapter 9, "Using the iPod's Calendar, Contact Manager, and Other Non-Music Tools."

The Settings Menu and Screens

The Settings command is like the Preferences command in most computer programs. It enables you to configure various aspects of your iPod, such as the contrast of the screen, the Clicker settings, and so on. You'll use this command to configure the Backlight, as you'll learn later in this chapter, and we'll get into it in detail in Chapter 6, "Configuring an iPod to Suit Your Preferences."

> **note**
>
> On an iPod mini's Main menu, the Music command doesn't appear. Instead, you'll see the Playlists and Browse commands. The Playlists command does the same thing as the Playlists command on the Music menu. The Browse command shows you a similar set of menus that you can use to browse your music by Artists, Albums, and so on, just like you can using the Music menu.

The Shuffle Songs Command

The Shuffle Songs command, located on the Main menu of an iPod, not an iPod mini, causes all of the songs on your iPod to play in random order. (You can configure shuffle playback more precisely on iPods and iPod minis using the Shuffle command on the Settings menu. You'll learn how to do this later.)

The Backlight Command

This option turns the iPod's Backlight on if it is off or off if it is on. See the section titled "Using the iPod's Backlight" below to learn more about the iPod's Backlight.

The Now Playing Menu

The Now Playing command appears on the Main menu only when you have selected and played music (it continues to appear when you pause music). When you choose this command, you move to the Now Playing screen, which shows you the song that is currently playing (see Figure 3.5). This is an important screen because you can control various aspects of how music is playing from this screen, such as the volume level. You'll explore the Now Playing screen in more detail in Chapter 4.

FIGURE 3.5
The Now
Playing screen
shows you the
music currently
playing on an
iPod.

caution

The Backlight uses quite a bit of power. To maximize the play time you get between recharges, you should use the Backlight only when you really need it or you should set the automatic settings to have it on only briefly.

Using the iPod's Backlight

The Backlight lights up the iPod's or iPod mini's screen so you can see it in dark conditions. You can turn the Backlight on or off manually and you can configure it to turn on each time you press a control and then turn off automatically after a specific period of time.

Turning the Backlight On

To turn the Backlight on, move to the **Main menu**, select **Backlight**, and click the **Select button**. The Backlight will come on and your iPod's world will be a lot brighter.

After a set amount of time passes, the Backlight will turn off automatically. (The amount of time will be the default until you set a backlight off time, as you will learn how to do in the next section.)

Configuring the Backlight

If you don't want to have to manually turn the Backlight on, you can set the iPod to turn it on briefly each time you press a button. This is very useful because you can always see what you are doing no matter what lighting conditions you are in. You can also have the backlight on at all times, but I don't recommend that option because of the drain on the iPod's battery.

note

To enable me to write and you to read fewer words, I've used some shorthand to indicate iPod menu selections. For example, when you see "choose **Main menu, Settings**," this means to move to the iPod's Main menu and then to the Settings menu by highlighting the Settings command and pressing the Select button. When you see "Choose **Backlight Timer**," that means to highlight the Backlight Timer command and click the Select button.

You can configure your iPod's Backlight settings by performing the following steps:

1. Choose **Main menu**, **Settings**. You'll see the Settings screen.

2. Choose **Backlight Timer**. You'll see the Backlight Timer screen (see Figure 3.6).

3. If you want the backlight to come on each time you press a control, choose the amount of time you want it to remain on. Your options are 2, 5, 10, and 20 seconds.

4. If you want the backlight to come on only when you choose the Backlight command on the Main menu, choose **Off**.

5. If you want the backlight on all of the time, choose **Always On**.

6. Press **Menu** twice to move back to the Main menu.

tip

For battery conservation, I don't recommend the 10- or 20-second settings. Try the 2- or 5-second setting because it provides a decent length of illumination time, but won't be quite so hard on your battery.

FIGURE 3.6

You use the Backlight Timer menu to configure your iPod's Backlight.

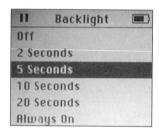

Putting an iPod on Hold

In Figure 3.1, you can see the Hold switch. This switch disables all the controls on an iPod so that you don't inadvertently press a button, such as if you carry your iPod in your pocket.

To disable the iPod's controls, slide the **Hold switch** to the left on an iPod or to the right on an iPod mini (these directions assume you are looking at the iPod's face with its top pointing up). When you do so, the area underneath the switch that was exposed when you slid it will be orange to indicate that the iPod is in the Hold mode. You'll also see the Lock icon on the iPod's screen (see Figure 3.7).

To reenable the iPod's controls, slide the **Hold switch** to the right on an iPod or to the left on an iPod mini (these directions assume you are looking at the iPod's face with its top pointing up). The orange area of the Hold switch and the Lock icon on the iPod screen will disappear and you can again control your iPod.

tip

If your iPod isn't responding to your attempts to control it, check the Hold switch to make sure it isn't active. It is amazing how easy it is to forget that you put your iPod in Hold mode and then wonder why you can't control it.

Lock icon

FIGURE 3.7

When you see the Lock icon, the Hold switch is active and you can't use any of the iPod's controls.

► 🔒 Now Playing

3 of 1834

She Loves You

The Beatles

1

1:01   -1:29

Turning an iPod Off

To turn an iPod off, press and hold the **Play/Pause button** for a second or two. The iPod screen will turn off. You can turn the iPod off from any screen, whether or not music is playing.

note

If you aren't playing music, iPods will turn themselves off after a period of inactivity in order to conserve their battery.

The Absolute Minimum

iPods and iPod minis are great devices that do all sorts of cool things. Like any other piece of technology, iPod controls can require a bit of getting used to before using one becomes second nature to you. Fortunately, as you have seen in this chapter, the iPod's design does make sense, and after you gain an understanding of how the menus and screens are laid out, you won't have any trouble learning to use them in detail, which is where we are headed next. For now, review the following list to see where you've been:

- To hear music on your iPod, you need to attach an output device to it, such as headphones or powered speakers.

- You use the iPod's Click Wheel to control it. Move your finger or thumb around the wheel to highlight a command on a menu and press the Select button to activate it. Press the wheel near any of the icons located at the top, each side, and bottom to perform that action, such as using the Next button to move to the next song.

- iPods have a menu structure that enables you to access its various screens and commands; in this chapter, you saw an overview of these.

- You won't always be using an iPod in bright conditions; its Backlight helps you see the screen better.

- You use the Hold switch to prevent unintentionally activating commands.

- To turn an iPod off, press and hold the Play button down until its screen turns off.

In this chapter

- Pick some music, any music.
- Control your music like a pro.
- Create and listen to an On-The-Go playlist.
- Check your battery.
- Make your iPod obey you from a distance.

Listening to Music on an iPod

In this chapter, you'll learn how to listen to and control your iPod tunes. Like any other device on which you listen to music, listening to music on an iPod is a two-step process. You first select the music to which you want to listen. Then you play and control that music.

As you rock on, jazz up, classical out, etc., you'll also find some other tasks useful, such as creating and using an On-The-Go playlist, rating your tunes, and monitoring your battery.

Selecting Music to Which You Want to Listen

The iPod is cool, but it isn't psychic. You need to tell it what music you want to listen to. There are two primary ways you do this: You can use playlists or you can browse all the music stored on the iPod.

Selecting Music with Playlists

When you transfer music from your iTunes Library to an iPod, the playlists you have created and that are shown in the iTunes Source List come over, too. You can select music to listen to by choosing a playlist using the following steps:

1. If you are using an iPod, choose **Main menu, Music, Playlists**. If you are using an iPod mini, choose **Main menu, Playlists**. You'll move to the Playlists menu (see Figure 4.1).

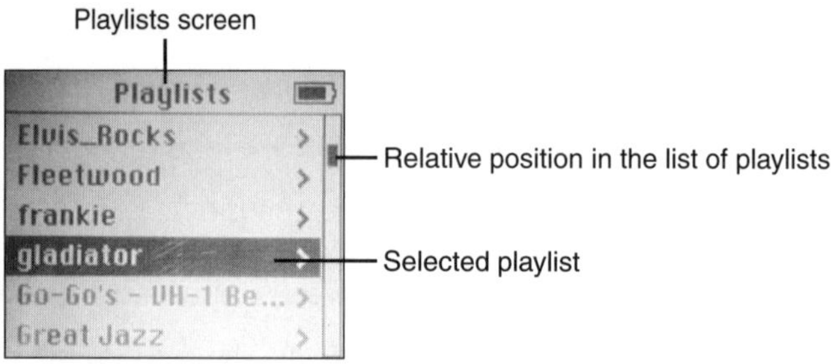

> **note**
>
> In order to play music on an iPod, you must have some stored on it. You do this by loading music into your iTunes Library and then transferring that music to the iPod. For help with the first part, see Chapters 11 through 16. For help with the second part, see Chapter 2, "Getting Started with an iPod."

FIGURE 4.1

Almost all the playlists you see on an iPod's Playlists menu should look familiar to you because they are the same playlists that appear in your iTunes Library.

Playlists screen

Relative position in the list of playlists

Selected playlist

2. Highlight the playlist you want to listen to and press the **Select button**. The songs in that playlist will be shown (see Figure 4.2).

> **tip**
>
> Remember that you can scroll up or down any menu, including the Playlists menu, by using the Scroll pad or Click Wheel.

3. If you want to play the entire playlist, press the **Play/Pause button**. If you want to start with a specific song, highlight it and press the **Select button**. The Now Playing screen will appear, and the first song in the playlist or the one you highlighted will begin playing (see Figure 4.3).

4. Use the techniques you'll learn throughout this chapter to control the tunes.

> **tip**
>
> If you want to play the entire playlist and don't want to see the songs it includes, you can just select the playlist and press the Play/Pause button (in other words, step 3 is optional). The Now Playing screen will appear, and the first song in the playlist will begin to play.

Playlist title

FIGURE 4.2

This playlist is called "gladiator" because it contains the *Gladiator* soundtrack. Here, you see the list of songs in the playlist.

FIGURE 4.3

One of the songs from the selected playlist is now playing.

Browsing Your iPod's Music

Choosing music with playlists is great, and you might often find that method to be the one you end up using most because it gets you to specific music quickly. However, some music stored on your iPod might not be in a playlist, you might want to listen to all the music by a specific artist, and so on. In these cases, you can browse the music stored on your iPod to choose the music to which you want to listen. You can browse your music by the following categories:

- Artists
- Albums
- Songs
- Genres
- Composers

To browse your iPod's music, do the following steps:

1. If you are using an iPod, choose **Main menu**, **Music**. You'll see the Music menu that contains the Playlists option along with the other categories you can browse. If you are using an iPod mini, choose **Main menu**, **Browse**. You'll see the Browse menu, which contains the categories listed previously (see Figure 4.4).

2. Highlight the category by which you want to browse your music, such as Artists to browse by artist, and press the **Select button**. You will see the menu that shows you all the music that is associated with the category you selected in step 1. For example, if you choose Artists, you will see all the artists whose music is stored on your iPod (see Figure 4.5).

> **note**
>
> If you are wondering how this information gets associated with your music, don't wonder any longer. It all comes from your iTunes Library. See Chapter 15, "Labeling, Categorizing, and Configuring Your Music," to learn how your music gets categorized.

FIGURE 4.4

The Browse menu enables you to browse your music by various categories.

Browse menu

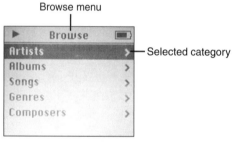

Selected category

FIGURE 4.5

When you browse by a category, such as Artists, you will see all the music on your iPod that is associated with that category.

> **note**
>
> In Figure 4.4, you see an iPod mini screen. You can tell that because the menu is called Browse. If you were using an iPod, this would be the Music menu that looks very similar and works in the same way. (The primary difference is that the Playlists option appears on the Music menu while it appears on the Main menu on an iPod mini.)

3. Browse the resulting list of music that appears until you find a category in which you are interested; then press the **Select button**. You will see the list of contents of the category you selected. For example, when I was browsing by artist and chose B.B. King, the list of my B.B. King music was displayed (see Figure 4.6).

tip

If you choose the All option on any of the category screens, all your music for that category will be shown on the next screen.

FIGURE 4.6

This screen shows all the music on this iPod by B.B. King.

4. To move down to the next level of detail, select an item on the current list and click the **Select button**. The resulting screen will show you the contents of what you selected. For example, I selected the B.B. King album called "Spotlight on Lucille" and saw that album's contents (see Figure 4.7).

tip

You can start playing music at any time by making a selection and pressing the Play/Pause button. The entire contents of what you select will begin to play. For example, if you select the name of an artist on the Artists list, all the music by that artist will start playing, beginning with the first song on the first album. You don't have to drill down to lower levels of detail as these steps show you how to do.

FIGURE 4.7

Here, I am looking at the contents of a specific album by B.B. King.

5. To play everything shown on the screen, starting at the top, press the **Play/Pause button**. To start with a specific song, select it and press the **Play/Pause button**. The Now Playing screen will appear, and the first song or the song you selected will start to play (see Figure 4.8).

I drilled down to a specific album and pressed the Play/Pause button to hear it.

Although the previous steps used the Artists category as an example, you can browse and select music in any of the other categories in just the same way.

Controlling Your Music

OK, so now you have selected music and started to play it. What's next? Learn to control it of course.

Playing the Basic Way

Here are the basic controls you can use:

- **Play/Pause**—When music is paused, pressing this button causes it to play again. When music is playing, pressing this button causes the music to pause.

- **Previous/Rewind**—If you press this button once quickly, you will jump back to the start of the song. If you press this button twice quickly, you will jump back to the start of the previous song. If you press and hold this button down, the music will rewind; release the button when you get to the point at which you want it to start playing again.

- **Next/Fast-forward**—Press this button once and you will jump to the start of the next song. Press this button down and hold it, and you will fast-forward the song; release the button when you get to the point in the song where you want to be.

note

After you have selected and started to play music using these steps, you can use the techniques you'll learn throughout this chapter to control the tunes.

note

No, an iPod doesn't have a Stop button. But, thanks for asking.

- **Click Wheel**—When the Now Playing screen is shown, drag a digit clockwise to increase the volume or counterclockwise to decrease the volume. When you start to drag on the Click Wheel, the Volume bar will appear on the screen to visually indicate the current volume level; the shaded part of the bar represents the current volume level (see Figure 4.9). As you change the volume, the shaded area will expand or contract, depending on whether you increase or decrease the volume. A second or two after you release the Click Wheel, the Volume bar will disappear.

> **tip**
>
> As you control your music, you can use the information at the bottom of the Now Playing screen to see where you are. You'll learn all about this screen shortly.
>
> You can rewind or fast-forward music whether it is playing or not.

FIGURE 4.9
When you drag on the Click Wheel, the Volume bar appears, and you can drag on the Wheel to change the volume level.

Volume bar

Current volume level

You can only change the volume using the Click Wheel when the Now Playing screen is shown. That is why the Now Playing option is listed on the Main menu. You can quickly jump to this screen to change the volume when you need to. (If you aren't at the Now Playing screen, dragging on the Click Wheel moves up or down the current screen.)

Playing the iPod Way

The basics of listening to music are cool. Now let's take a look at some of the cool iPod playback features that aren't so obvious.

You can move around menus while music is playing just like you can when it isn't. As you choose other menus, the music will continue to play until you pause it or choose different music and play that instead.

> **tip**
>
> Remember that you move "up" the menu structure by pressing the Menu button.

The Now Playing screen provides lots of information about the music that is currently playing or paused (see Figure 4.10).

Number of song out of total selected

FIGURE 4.10

The Now Playing screen is packed with features, some of which might not be obvious to you.

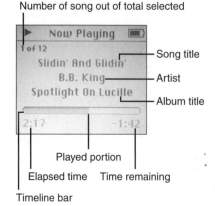

- Song title
- Artist
- Album title

Played portion

Elapsed time   Time remaining

Timeline bar

At the top of the screen, you see information about the number of the current song out of the total you selected. For example, if you are playing the first song in a playlist containing 50 songs, this will be 1 of 50. This information helps you know where you are in the selected source.

In the center of the screen, you will see information about the song currently selected, including song title, artist, and album. If any of this information is too long to be shown on one line, it will begin scrolling across the screen a second or two after a song starts playing.

> **tip**
>
> If you selected All in any category and then played it, the display will tell you how many songs are stored on your iPod.

At the bottom of the screen, you will see the Timeline bar. In the normal mode, this gives you a visual indication of the song's length and how much of the song you have played so far (represented by the shaded part of the bar). Under the left edge of the bar, you will see the amount of time the current song has been playing. At the right end of the bar, you will see the time remaining to play (this is a negative number and counts down to zero as the song plays).

If you click the **Select button** one time, the Timeline bar changes to indicate that you can now rewind or fast-forward using the Click Wheel (see Figure 4.11). When the Timeline bar is in this mode, you can drag on the **Click Wheel** clockwise to fast-forward or counterclockwise to rewind the music. As you drag, the Current Location marker moves to its new location and the time information is updated. When you release the Click Wheel, the Timeline bar will return to its normal mode in a second or so.

If you click the **Select button** twice, the Timeline bar is replaced by the Rating display. If the song currently playing has been rated, you will see the number of stars for that song (see Figure 4.12). If

> **note**
>
> Sometimes when song information is too long to fit onto one line, it's cut off and ellipses are used to indicate that there is more text. Frankly, I wasn't able to determine why some song information scrolls and some doesn't.

the song hasn't been rated, you see five dots instead (see Figure 4.13). You can rate the current song by dragging the **Click Wheel** clockwise to give the song more stars or counterclockwise to reduce the number of stars. A second or so after you stop touching the Click Wheel, the Timeline bar will return to its normal mode.

FIGURE 4.11

When the Timeline bar looks like this, you can rewind or fast-forward using the Click Wheel.

Current Location marker

FIGURE 4.12

You can rate your music in iTunes and display the rating on your iPod.

The neat thing about this is that the next time you connect your iPod to your computer, the rating information you set on the iPod is carried over to that music in your iTunes Library. So, you need to rate a song in only one place.

Creating and Using an iPod On-The-Go Playlist

Working with playlists that you create in iTunes is very useful, but you can also create a single playlist on the iPod and listen to that playlist as much as you'd like. This enables you to create a playlist when you are away from your computer in order to listen to a specific collection of music.

Creating the On-The-Go Playlist

To create and add a song to your On-The-Go playlist, view a list—such as the list of songs on an album—on which the song is listed. Highlight the song you want to add and hold the Select button down until the highlighting on the song flashes. Continue adding songs using the same process until you have selected a group of songs.

If you highlight an album, artist, or other category and hold the Select button down until your selection flashes, the entire contents of the selected category will be added to the On-The-Go playlist. This makes it easy to add multiple songs to the playlist quickly and easily.

note

You can rate your music in iTunes. For more information on why and how you do this, see Chapter 15 for details.

tip

When you are viewing a playlist, including the On-The-Go playlist, that contains the song that is currently playing, it is marked with a speaker icon.

When the On-The-Go playlist is empty and you select it, you will see an informational message about how to add songs to it. This can be handy if you forget and you don't have this book with you (which I know is unlikely to ever happen).

Viewing and Playing the On-The-Go Playlist

To see the contents of your On-The-Go playlist, move to the Playlists screen and scroll to the bottom of the Playlists menu. Highlight the On-The-Go playlist and press the Select button. You will see the contents of the On-The-Go playlist that you have created. You can play this playlist just like any other playlist on your iPod.

To see the contents of your On-The-Go playlist, choose **Main menu**, **Playlists**, **On-The-Go**. You will see the contents of the On-The-Go playlist that you have created. You can play this playlist just like any other playlist on your iPod.

Saving an On-The-Go Playlist

If you create an On-The-Go playlist that you want to keep permanently, open the On-The-Go screen. Scroll down until you see the Save Playlist command. Highlight Save Playlist and press the Select button. Then, choose Save Playlist again on the resulting Save screen.

When you do this, the playlist will be renamed "New Playlist X," where X is a sequential number that represents each playlist you have saved. The current On-The-Go playlist will be cleared as soon as you save it. So, you can create another playlist without changing the previous one.

Using this technique, you can create and save as many playlists as you'd like.

When you connect your iPod to your computer, the current On-The-Go playlist and any On-The-Go playlists you have saved will be transferred into iTunes and will be available on the iTunes Source List. You can change them in iTunes, such as renaming them, changing the songs they contain, and so on. The next time you update your iPod, the changes you make to these playlists in iTunes will be reflected on your iPod.

caution

After you create an On-The-Go playlist, you should play at least one song it contains. If you don't, it is possible you will lose the contents of the playlist if it isn't played within 36 hours.

tip

As long as you play at least one song on the On-The-Go playlist, you don't need to save it. It will remain on your iPod until you clear it. You really only need to save an On-The-Go playlist if you want to create a new one without getting rid of the current one.

Clearing the On-The-Go Playlist

If you want to clear the On-The-Go playlist without saving it, open the On-The-Go playlist screen and choose Clear Playlist, and then Clear Playlist on the Clear screen (no, that isn't a mistake, you choose this command twice, but each is on a different screen). All the songs that were in the playlist will be removed, and it will become empty again. (The songs that were in that playlist are not removed from your iPod; the playlist is just cleared of those songs.)

Monitoring an iPod's Battery

Even though the iPod's battery lasts a long time, it will eventually run out of juice and your music can come to a crashing halt. To prevent this, keep an eye on your iPod's Battery icon (see Figure 4.14). As your battery drains, the shaded part of the battery will decrease to indicate how much power you have left. When 1/4 or less is shaded, you should think about recharging your iPod. (For more information about the iPod's battery, see Chapter 11, "Maintaining an iPod and Solving Problems.")

Battery icon

FIGURE 4.14
Is this iPod mini's battery half full or half empty? You make the call.

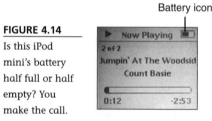

Adding and Using Apple's iPod Remote

Some iPod models include Apple's iPod Remote. This is a clever gadget that you plug into the iPod's Headphones port and Remote port and then plug your headphones or speakers into it. When you do this, you can use the controls on the remote to control your iPod (see Figure 4.15). This is particularly useful when you are carrying your iPod in a belt case or in another way such that its controls aren't easily accessible. Because the remote is on a wire, you can place it in an accessible location using its clip, such as on your clothing.

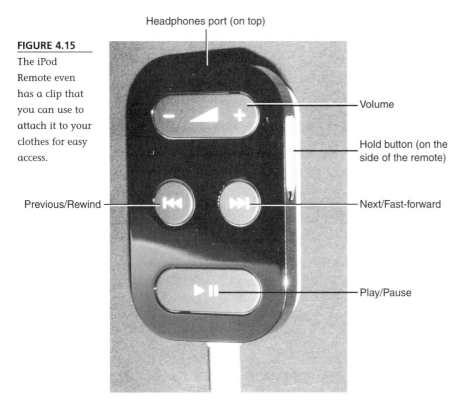

Headphones port (on top)

FIGURE 4.15

The iPod Remote even has a clip that you can use to attach it to your clothes for easy access.

Volume

Hold button (on the side of the remote)

Previous/Rewind

Next/Fast-forward

Play/Pause

The controls on the remote work just like those on the iPod itself. One exception to this is that you can use the Volume control on the remote to change the volume regardless of what screen is currently being displayed. The other is that you don't have a Scroll pad or Click Wheel on the remote, so you will choose your music using the iPod's controls and then control its playback using the remote.

note

If you do carry your iPod in a case or other way, I strongly recommend that you get a remote to make controlling the iPod much easier.

The Absolute Minimum

Now you know just about everything you need to listen to music on your iPod. It isn't that difficult because the iPod's controls are very well designed. Not to get controlling on you, but here are few more control points for your consideration:

- The first step to listening to music is to choose the music you want to listen to. You do this by choosing playlists or browsing your iPod's music.

- After you have selected music, you can use the pretty-obvious playback controls to control it. You also learned some useful but not so obvious ways to control it, too.

- After you have used it for a bit, you'll find that you can easily control an iPod or iPod mini with a single thumb. Often, the best way to hold an iPod is to set it in your palm and use your thumb to control it. It doesn't take long until you can navigate like a pro.

- When you use the Click Wheel to move around the iPod's screens or to control music, don't think you have to drag on it slowly or in small increments. You can move quite rapidly by dragging your finger or thumb quickly. You can move even faster by moving your digit in complete circles.

- You can use the On-The-Go playlist to create a playlist on the iPod.

- As you play your music, keep an eye on your iPod's battery so you don't run out of power.

- Apple's iPod Remote is really cool, and if you have it, use it. However, other kinds of remotes are available as well. For more information on the Apple iPod Remote and other remotes, see Chapter 7, "Rocking Your World with iPod Accessories."

- Get an overview of how to build your iTunes music Library.

- Determine how much iPod space you need and how much you have.

- Understand and configure your iPod update options.

- Update specific songs and playlists on your iPod automatically.

- Update your iPod's music manually.

- Play an iPod's music on a computer other than the one you use to build the iPod's music library.

5

Building an iPod's Music Library

The first time you connected your iPod to your computer, all the music in your iTunes Library was transferred to your iPod automatically—that is, all the music that would *fit* within the iPod's disk space limitations. If your iPod has enough disk space to hold all your iTunes music, then everything is just fine. However, as you build your iTunes Library, there may come a day when this isn't true anymore and you can't just let everything run on automatic to keep your iPod's music library current. That's where this chapter comes in. Here, you'll learn how to take control over the music stored on your iPod, especially if your iPod's disk isn't large enough to hold your entire iTunes music.

Creating an iTunes Music Library

As your learned back in Chapter 2, "Getting Started with an iPod," and will read in each of the following two chapters, you manage the music that you store on your iPod within the iTunes application. The iTunes Library and the playlists you create within iTunes are the sources of music that you listen to with an iPod. The two general steps to creating these music sources are to build your iTunes Library and to create iTunes playlists.

Building an iTunes Music Library

You can get music for your iTunes Library from three main sources: your audio CDs, the iTunes Music Store, and the Internet. Although the specific steps you use to add music from these various sources to your Library are a bit different, the end result is the same. Your iTunes Library will contain all the music in your collection.

I don't provide the details of building and managing an iTunes Library here because Part II of this book is dedicated to iTunes and provides all the information you need to use this excellent application. The chapters that specifically focus on building your Library are Chapter 14, "Building, Browsing, Searching, and Playing Your iTunes Music Library," and Chapter 15, "Labeling, Categorizing, and Configuring Your Music," but you'll also want to read Chapters 11 through 13 to install and learn to use iTunes.

Creating iTunes Playlists

From the earlier chapters in this part of the book, you learned that the playlists stored within iTunes are transferred to your iPod so that you can listen to them. You create and manage these playlists within iTunes. Chapter 16, "Creating, Configuring, and Using Playlists," provides an in-depth look at playlists and gives you all the information you need to create and manage your playlists.

> **note**
>
> Throughout this chapter, I assume that you have a good working knowledge of iTunes, hopefully from reading Part II, "iTunes." If you haven't read Part II of this book yet, you need to at least read Chapter 11, "Touring iTunes," and Chapter 12, "Getting Started with iTunes," so you understand the very basics of the application. However, the process of managing your iPod's music library will be much better if you have read Chapters 11 through 16 before reading through the rest of this chapter.

> **note**
>
> Remember that there is one special playlist, called the *On-The-Go playlist*, that you can create on the iPod. You can save these playlists on your iPod and then transfer them to your iTunes Music Library when you update your iPod.

Assessing the Size of Your iTunes Library and How Much Disk Space Your iPod Has

In order to determine how you are going to manage the music on your iPod, you need to understand how large your music collection is and how much storage space is available on your iPod. This information will determine the way in which you build and maintain your iPod music library.

Determining the Size of Your iTunes Library

You can determine how much storage space you need in order to move your entire music collection in just a few steps. Open **iTunes**. Choose **Library** in the Source List. With the Browser open, select **All** in the Genre or Artist column. The iTunes window will show all the music you have placed in your Library. Look at the **Source Information** area at the bottom of the iTunes window (see Figure 5.1). Here, you will see the number of songs, the total playing time, and the disk space required to store all the music in your Library. The number you should be most interested in is the disk space required because that is what you use to determine if all your music can fit onto your iPod's disk.

FIGURE 5.1

At this point in time, my Library required 10.06GB of disk space.

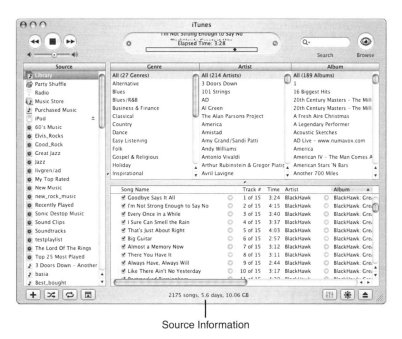

Source Information

Determining How Much Storage Space You Have on an iPod

You have two ways to determine how large the disk is in your iPod.

One is to refer to the documentation that came with your iPod, or perhaps you can simply remember the size of iPod you purchased. At press time, the possibilities for new devices were about 4GB for an iPod mini and 15GB, 20GB, or 40GB for an iPod. (Older models of the iPod can have 15GB or 30GB disks.) This method is easy and provides a pretty good estimate of the room on your iPod's disk.

If you can't remember or want to determine the iPod's available disk space more accurately, you can get this information directly from the iPod itself. To do this, choose **Main menu**, **Settings**, **About**. On the resulting About menu, you'll see the capacity of your iPod's disk (see Figure 5.2).

FIGURE 5.2
This iPod mini has a disk capacity of 3.7GB.

About	
BRAD'S IPOD	
Songs	508
Capacity	3.7 GB
Available	1.5 GB
Version	1.0

The capacity shown on the About menu is the amount of storage space available for your music. Some space is required to store the files needed for the iPod to function. This is the reason that the capacity you see will always be slightly less than the rated size of the iPod's disk.

Understanding and Configuring iPod Synchronization Options

After you know how much space you need to store all your music (the size of your iTunes Library) and how much space is available on your iPod (its disk capacity), you can choose how you want to build and manage your iPod's music library.

Understanding Your Synchronization Options

Three basic options are available for managing the library of music on your iPod:

- **Automatically Update All Songs and Playlists**—When you use this method, the entire process is automatic; iTunes makes sure your iPod's music library is an exact copy of your iTunes Library each time you connect your iPod to your computer.

- **Automatically Update Selected Playlists Only**—When you use this method, iTunes still manages the update process for you, but it updates only the specific playlists you select.

- **Manually Manage Songs and Playlists**—When you use this method, you manually move songs and playlists onto your iPod.

note

If you don't want iTunes to open automatically when you connect an iPod to your computer (why you might not want this to happen, I don't know), open the iPod Preferences dialog box and uncheck the "Open iTunes when attached" check box.

When you first connected your iPod to your computer, an automatic method was used to move songs onto your iPod. However, if there were more songs in your iTunes Library than could be stored on your iPod, some slight of hand was done by iTunes so that you wouldn't have to get into the details of this process before listening to music on your iPod. In that case, iTunes created a playlist containing a selection of your music that would fit on your iPod, and iTunes moved that music to your iPod so you can listen to it.

After the first time, you need to choose the synchronization method you want to use. Finding the right method for you is a matter of preference, but I can provide some general guidelines for you.

If all the music in your iTunes Library will fit onto your iPod (the space required for your iTunes Library is less than your iPod's disk capacity), I recommend you use the Automatically Update All Songs and Playlists option. This option is the easiest because it requires literally no work on your part. Each time you connect your iPod to your computer, the update process is performed automatically, and you will have your complete music collection available on your iPod.

note

Even if you have enough space on your iPod for all your iTunes music, you can still choose one of the other update options if they suit your preferences better.

If the size of your iTunes Library is larger than the disk capacity of your iPod, managing the music library on your iPod is slightly more difficult.

If you take full advantage of iTunes playlists to create collections of music to which you listen, using the Automatically Update Selected Playlists Only option is a good choice. After you choose the playlists you want to be updated, iTunes handles the process of keeping them up to date for you so you don't have to think about it each time you connect your iPod to your computer. Of course, you need to make sure you create and can select playlists that contain the music you want to be able to listen to on your iPod. This can require some effort, but because playlists are so useful, you will likely do that work anyway so you can listen to them on your computer.

Finally, if you don't use a lot of playlists or you simply want to choose the specific music you want to place on your iPod, you can use the manual method to do so.

After you have determined how you want to manage your iPod's music library, you need to configure iTunes to implement your decision.

caution

If you use the same iPod with more than one computer, you need to be careful before selecting one of the automatic methods. When you use an automatic method, iTunes will copy its Library onto the iPod. When it does this, it will also remove any songs on the iPod that aren't in its Library so that the music on the iPod is an exact copy of the music in the iTunes Library. If you use the iPod on more than one computer, you should not use the Automatically Update All Songs and Playlists method if you have different music in the iTunes Library on each computer. Fortunately, iTunes warns you about this when you connect the iPod to a different computer than the one from which it was last updated.

Understanding How iTunes Updates Playlists on the iPod

When iTunes updates a playlist on your iPod, it takes a "snapshot" of that playlist and places it on the iPod. If you change the playlist in some way, the next time you update your iPod, the previous "snapshot" is replaced by the new playlist.

For example, suppose you have a smart playlist that is dynamic and plays the 50 songs you have played most. As you listen to songs in iTunes, the contents of that playlist change to reflect the songs you have listened to. When that playlist is moved to the iPod, it contains the songs as they were in the playlist when you performed the update. The playlist on the iPod will remain unchanged until you perform the next update. At that time, if the contents of the playlist have changed, the revised playlist will replace the one currently stored on the iPod.

The same principle applies when you make changes to a playlist manually, too. For example, if you sort a playlist to change the order in which songs play, that order will be reflected in the playlist when you update it onto your iPod. If you change the order of the songs in the playlist again in iTunes, the next time you update the iPod, the songs will play in the new order on the iPod.

When iTunes moves a playlist from its Library onto an iPod, it moves only the songs in that playlist onto the iPod. This can sometimes be confusing. For example, if you purchase an album by a specific artist and then include only some of the songs on that album in a playlist that gets moved to an iPod, only those songs by that artist in the playlist get moved onto the iPod. As an example, this can be confusing the first time you browse your iPod by artist and can't figure out why a song you know you have by that artist is not on your iPod.

Configuring iTunes to Automatically Update All Songs and Playlists

Choosing the "fully automatic" method is automatic in itself in that this is the default option. However, should you ever need to choose this option, you can do so with the following steps:

1. Connect your **iPod** to your **computer** (remember Chapter 2!). iTunes will open automatically and the iPod will appear on the Source List.

2. Select the iPod on the Source List and click the **iPod Options** button (see Figure 5.3). You'll see the iPod Preferences dialog box.

3. Click the **Automatically update all songs and playlists** radio button (see Figure 5.4).

> **tip**
>
> By default, when iTunes performs an update, it moves all the songs from each affected source onto the iPod. If you don't want specific songs to be moved onto an iPod, open the iPod Preferences dialog box and check the "Only update checked songs" check box. If a song's Selected check box is not checked, it won't be included in the music moved onto an iPod during an update.

> **caution**
>
> Whichever update method you choose, make sure that the "OK to disconnect" message is showing on your iPod's screen before you disconnect it from your computer. It is also safe to disconnect your iPod when the large battery charging icon or battery charged icon appears on the iPod's screen.

Selected iPod

FIGURE 5.3

To choose an
update method,
select the iPod
and click the
iPod Options
button.

Selected iPod

FIGURE 5.4

The iPod
Preferences dia-
log box enables
you to configure
the update
process for your
iPod.

4. Click **OK**. The dialog box will close,
   and the automatic update will be performed. The next time you connect
   your iPod to your computer, iTunes will
   attempt to update its library automatically. As long as there is enough space
   on your iPod, you won't need to do
   anything else.

caution

If your iTunes Library is
too large for your iPod's
disk space, you will have
to use one of the other
methods to update it or
live with the "Selection"
playlist that iTunes creates for
you. (More on this later in this
chapter.)

Every time you connect your iPod to your computer, the update will be performed. You will see the update information in the Information area of the iTunes window, and the iPod icon will flash red. When the process is complete, you will see the "iPod update is complete" message in the Information area, and the "OK to disconnect" message will be displayed on the iPod's screen. Then, it is safe to disconnect your iPod from your computer.

If you use the "fully automatic" method when your iPod doesn't have enough space to store all your iTunes Library, iTunes creates a special playlist called *nameofyouripod* Selection, where *nameofyouripod* is the name you gave your iPod when you configured it. This playlist contains a selection of music from your iTunes Library that will fit on your iPod. If you don't change the update option, iTunes will update this playlist (and only this playlist) each time you connect your iPod to your computer. (It actually changes the update mode to "Automatically update selected playlists only" and chooses the *nameofyouripod* Selection playlist on the playlists list in the iPod Preferences dialog box.) You can use this playlist just like the others in your iTunes Source List, such as adding songs to it, removing songs from it, changing their order, and so on.

caution

If you disconnect your iPod during the update process, you can damage its data.

Configuring iTunes to Automatically Update Selected Playlists

To have iTunes automatically update selected playlists only, use the following steps:

1. In iTunes, create the **playlists** you want to place on your iPod.

2. Connect your **iPod** to your **computer**. It will appear on the Source List and an update determined by the current update option (such as fully automatic) will be performed.

3. Select the **iPod** for which you want to set an update option and click the **iPod Options** button. The iPod Preferences dialog box will appear.

note

When you change the update method, you will see a warning prompt telling you that the current music on the iPod will be replaced by the new update method. This should be what you expect, so just click OK to clear the prompt.

4. Click the **Automatically update selected playlists only** radio button (see Figure 5.5). Just below this button, you will see a list of all the playlists configured in your iTunes Library. Next to each is a check box. If that check box is checked, that playlist will be updated automatically. If that check box is not checked, that playlist will be ignored.

FIGURE 5.5

You can choose the playlists that are updated automatically by checking their check boxes.

5. Click **OK**. The dialog box will close and the playlists you selected will be updated on your iPod. The next time you connect your iPod to your computer, the playlists you selected will be updated automatically.

Configuring iTunes So You Manually Manage Songs and Playlists

When you choose this option, you manually place songs and playlists on your iPod. To choose this option, do the following steps:

1. Connect your **iPod** to your **computer**. It will appear on the Source List and an update determined by the current update option (such as fully automatic) will be performed.

2. Select the **iPod** for which you want to set an update option and click the **iPod Options** button. The iPod Preferences dialog box will appear.

note

If you use the Automatically update selected playlists only option, smart playlists are even more useful because their content can be dynamic (see Chapter 16). For example, you can create a playlist that automatically contains all the new music in your iTunes Library. If you choose to have this playlist updated automatically, each time you connect your iPod to your computer, that playlist will be updated, so your newest music will always be placed on your iPod.

3. Click the **Manually manage songs and playlists** radio button. You will see a prompt explaining that with this option, you must manually unmount the iPod before disconnecting it; read the information and click **OK** to close the prompt. (I'll explain what this means in a later section.)

4. Click **OK**. The dialog box will close. An expansion triangle will appear next to the iPod on the Source List, and all the playlists stored on it will be shown under its icon. You can then manually add or remove songs or playlists (the steps to do this appear in a later section).

Updating Specific Songs and Playlists Automatically

If you chose the Automatically update selected playlists only option, the playlists you selected are updated on your iPod each time you connect it to your computer. To change the contents of your iPod's music library, change the contents of the playlists that you have selected to update. When you connect the iPod to your computer, those playlists will be updated. For example, for playlists, you can add songs, remove songs, and so on. The next time you connect your iPod to your computer, the changes you made will be reflected on the iPod's version of that playlist.

note

Smart playlists can change over time automatically. These playlists will automatically change on your iPod each time you connect it to your computer. This is great way to keep the music on your iPod fresh.

Every time you connect your iPod to your computer, the update will be performed. You will see the update information in the Information area of the iTunes window, and the iPod icon will flash red. When the process is complete, you will see the "iPod update is complete" message in the Information area, and the "OK to disconnect" message will be displayed on the iPod's screen. Then, it is safe to disconnect your iPod from your computer.

Manually Updating an iPod

If you choose the manual option, you must manually move songs and playlists onto the iPod. To do this, use the following steps:

1. Connect your **iPod** to your **computer**.

2. Select the iPod you want to update. If it isn't expanded already, click the **Expansion triangle** next to the iPod on the Source List. In the iTunes Content pane, you will see all the songs in the iPod's music library. Under the iPod's icon on the Source List, you will see the playlists it contains (see Figure 5.6).

Songs on the selected iPod

iPod's Expansion triangle

FIGURE 5.6

When you con-figure an iPod for manual updating, you can expand it on the Source List to see the playlists it contains.

	Song Name	Track #	Time	Artist	Album
	I Walk The Line	1 of 16	2:43	Johnny Cash	16 Biggest Hits
	I Still Miss Someone	2 of 16	2:36	Johnny Cash	16 Biggest Hits
	The Legend Of John Henry's Hammer	3 of 16	8:26	Johnny Cash	16 Biggest Hits
	Don't Take Your Guns To Town	4 of 16	3:02	Johnny Cash	16 Biggest Hits
	In The Jailhouse Now	5 of 16	2:22	Johnny Cash	16 Biggest Hits
	Ring Of Fire	6 of 16	2:36	Johnny Cash	16 Biggest Hits
	Understand Your Man	7 of 16	2:43	Johnny Cash	16 Biggest Hits
	The Ballad Of Ira Hayes	8 of 16	4:08	Johnny Cash	16 Biggest Hits
	Folsom Prison Blues	9 of 16	2:45	Johnny Cash	16 Biggest Hits
	Daddy Sang Bass	10 of 16	2:23	Johnny Cash	16 Biggest Hits
	A Boy Named Sue	11 of 16	3:44	Johnny Cash	16 Biggest Hits
	Sunday Morning Coming Down	12 of 16	4:09	Johnny Cash	16 Biggest Hits
	Flesh And Blood	13 of 16	2:37	Johnny Cash	16 Biggest Hits
	Man In Black	14 of 16	2:52	Johnny Cash	16 Biggest Hits
	One Piece At A Time	15 of 16	4:02	Johnny Cash	16 Biggest Hits
	(Ghost) Riders In The Sky	16 of 16	3:43	Johnny Cash	16 Biggest Hits
	Johnny B. Goode--MP3	4 of 21	2:43	Chuck Berry	20th Century M
	Johnny B. Goode	7 of 11	2:41	Chuck Berry	20th Century M
	Metamorphosis	1 of 19	4:54	Phil Keaggy	Acoustic Sketch
	Rivulets	2 of 19	3:00	Phil Keaggy	Acoustic Sketch
	Nellie's Tune	3 of 19	3:26	Phil Keaggy	Acoustic Sketch
	Passing Thought	4 of 19	1:32	Phil Keaggy	Acoustic Sketch
	The Marionette	5 of 19	3:51	Phil Keaggy	Acoustic Sketch
	Del's Bells	6 of 19	1:33	Phil Keaggy	Acoustic Sketch

Source: Library, Party Shuffle, Radio, Music Store, Purchased Music, iPod mini, Good_Rock, Great Jazz, livgren/ad, The Lord Of The Ring, 3 Doors Down - Anot, christian_rock, fire_up_tunes, gladiator, Johnny Cash, Johnny Cash - Americ, Kerry Livgren AD - Ti, Los Lonely Boys - Los, Lynyrd Skynyrd, Lynyrd Skynyrd All Ti, mellow_instrumental, Mike Cleason, Motown 1's, Neil Young, One More From the R

Used: 3.71 GB   Free: 81.1 MB

732 songs, 2.1 days, 3.67 GB

3. To add a **playlist** to the iPod, drag it onto the Source List and drop it on the **iPod icon** (see Figure 5.7). When you are over the iPod, the plus sign will appear next to the pointer to show you that you can release the mouse button. When you do so, the playlist and the songs it contains will be moved onto the iPod.

note

As songs are moved onto the iPod, you will see information about the process in the iTunes Information area at the top of the iTunes window.

FIGURE 5.7

When you drag a playlist into an iPod, it and the songs it contains will be moved into the iPod's library.

4. To remove a playlist from the iPod, select it by clicking it in the list of playlists under the iPod and pressing the **Delete** key. You will see a prompt asking you to confirm that you want to delete the playlist.

5. Click **OK**. The playlist will be deleted from the iPod.

6. To add songs to the iPod, select the **source** containing those songs, such as the Library. The contents of that source will be shown in the Content pane. Drag the **songs** you want to add from the Content pane and drop them on the iPod's icon. The songs you selected will be copied into the iPod's music library.

note

When you remove a playlist from an iPod, you only remove the playlist, not the songs it contains. You can still play those songs by browsing for them.

7. To remove **songs** from the iPod, select the iPod on the Source List, select **the songs you want to delete** in the Content pane, and press the **Delete** key. These songs will be deleted from the iPod. They will also be deleted from any playlists on the iPod containing them.

8. When you are done updating the **iPod**, unmount it by selecting **its icon** and clicking one of the **Eject** buttons (see Figure 5.8). After the iPod has been successfully unmounted, it will disappear from the Source List and you will see the "OK to disconnect" message on its screen.

tip

If you don't want to be bothered by the confirmation prompts, check the Do not ask me again check box.

FIGURE 5.8

Before you disconnect an iPod that you have manually updated, you must eject it.

Eject buttons

9. Disconnect your **iPod** from your **computer**.

You must eject an iPod that you manually update before disconnecting it because iTunes doesn't know when it should shut down any processes it is using that are related to the iPod. Because it is, in effect, a hard disk, the iPod must not be in use when you disconnect it; otherwise, its data can be damaged. When the update process is handled by iTunes automatically, it "ejects" the iPod for you. When you do the update manually, you need to tell iTunes that you are done so that it can prepare the iPod to be disconnected safely.

> **caution**
>
> Don't disconnect your iPod from your computer unless the "OK to disconnect" message is displayed on its screen. If you do so, you can damage its data. It is also safe to disconnect your iPod when the large battery charging icon or battery charged icon appears on the iPod's screen.

Playing an iPod's Music on a Different Computer

One of the cool, but not so obvious, things you can do with an iPod is use it to play its music on a computer that is different than the one you use to build the iPod's music library. For example, suppose your home computer contains your music library, but you would like to be able to play your iPod music through your laptop or on your work computer. To play an iPod's music on a computer that is different than the one you use to configure the iPod's music library, perform the following steps:

1. Connect the iPod to the computer on which you want to play its music. You'll see a prompt explaining that the iPod is linked to a different iTunes music library and asking if you want to replace the iPod's music with the library on the current computer (see Figure 5.9).

> **caution**
>
> If you click Yes in the warning prompt, all of the music on the iPod will be replaced by the contents of the current iTunes Music Library.

FIGURE 5.9

You'll see this prompt when you connect an iPod to a computer that you don't use to update its music library.

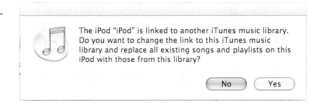

The iPod "iPod" is linked to another iTunes music library. Do you want to change the link to this iTunes music library and replace all existing songs and playlists on this iPod with those from this library?

No   Yes

2. Click No. The iPod will be mounted on the computer and will be shown in the iTunes Source List.

3. Select the iPod and click the iPod Preferences button.

4. Choose the Manually Manage Songs and Playlists option, click OK in the warning prompt, and click OK to close the iPod Preferences dialog box. You'll return to the iTunes window and the iPod will be available as a source on the Source List.

5. Expand the iPod to see the music it contains.

6. Select and play music on the iPod just like you do other sources, such as CDs and playlists.

The next time you reconnect the iPod to the computer you use to manage its music library, you will need to reselect the update option, such as automatic updating, because that preference is stored on the iPod. (Assuming you don't use the manual option, of course.) When you do this, the iPod will be updated according to your preference. The next time you want to play its music on a different computer, you'll need to change the update preference back to manual again.

caution

You can't share the same iPod on a Windows computer and a Mac. An iPod has to be formatted specifically to work with each operating system. If you connect an iPod to a computer with a different operating system, you'll have to reformat the iPod's drive before your can use it (which means all of its music will be erased).

note

Some of the commands available on the Main Menu menu are useful only if you have accessories. For example, the Voice Memos command is useful if you have a microphone accessory, but the Photo Import command is meaningful if you have an external card reader. These devices are covered later in this part of the book.

The Absolute Minimum

Managing the music on your iPod is essential if you are to be able to listen to the music you want to when the mood strikes you. Fortunately, maintaining your iPod's music library isn't all that hard. As you build and maintain that library, keep the following points in mind:

- You use the iTunes application to create the music library on your iPod.

- You can determine the amount of used and free space on the iPod's hard disk in a number of ways, including by using the iPod's About command.

- There are three ways to synchronize the music in your iTunes Library and on your iPod.

- When you use the "fully automatic" option, the synchronization is done for you automatically, and your iPod will be updated with your current iTunes Library each time you connect the iPod to your computer.

- You can also choose to have only specific playlists updated automatically.

- You can manage the music on your iPod manually as well.

- If you configure an iPod to be manually updated, you can play its music on the computer to which it is connected. This is a great way to play an iPod's music with a computer other than the one you use to build an iPod's music library.

- If you have more than one iPod, such as an iPod and an iPod mini, you can choose different update options for each. For example, you might want to use the "Automatically update selected playlists only" option for the iPod mini and the "fully automatic" option for the iPod.

Configuring an iPod to Suit Your Preferences

Back in Chapter 3, "Connecting an iPod to Your Computer," you learned how to configure an iPod's Backlight using the Settings menu. As you no doubt noticed, there are more options available on the Settings menu than just the Backlight. In this chapter, you'll learn about many of these settings that you can use to customize an iPod to suit your personal preferences.

Configuring Music Playback

Several of the iPod's settings relate to the way in which music plays. These include Shuffle, Repeat, and Sound Check.

Shuffling Music with Shuffle Settings

You can use the iPod's Shuffle feature to have songs play in a random order. To shuffle music, use the following steps:

1. Choose **Main menu**, **Settings**. You'll see the Settings menu.

2. Highlight the **Shuffle** command (see Figure 6.1).

FIGURE 6.1

You can use the Shuffle setting to have an iPod play your music in a random order.

3. If you want the songs within a selected browse category or playlist to play in a random order, press the **Select** button once. The Shuffle setting will become Songs. This causes the iPod to shuffle the songs within a music source when you play it.

4. If you want the iPod to select random albums when you select a browse category or playlist, press the **Select button** twice. The Shuffle setting will become Albums. This causes the iPod to select an album randomly, play all the songs on the album, choose another album randomly, and repeat this pattern until you turn Shuffle off again.

> **note**
>
> The Shuffle Settings feature works on any source of music you select, including playlists or any of the Browse categories, such as Artists, Albums, Genre, and so on. When you use the Songs mode, all the songs will be selected and play in a random fashion.

5. Select the **music** you want to play in a randomized fashion and play **it**. On the Now Playing screen, you'll see the Shuffle indicator to remind you that you are in Shuffle mode (see Figure 6.2).

FIGURE 6.2

The Shuffle indi-
cator reminds
you that you are
playing in the
Shuffle mode.

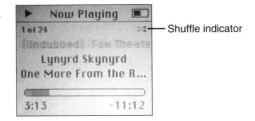

— Shuffle indicator

6. To disable the Shuffle feature, press the **Select button** until you see Off next to the Shuffle setting. Your music will again play in a linear fashion.

Shuffling Music with the Shuffle Songs Command

On an iPod's Main menu (this command doesn't appear on an iPod mini's Main menu), you'll see the Shuffle Songs command. If you choose this command, all the songs on the iPod will play in random order. You can't choose a specific group of songs to play, such as a playlist, this command plays all the songs in the iPod's music library.

Repeating Music

The Repeat feature enables you to repeat an individual song as many times as you'd like or to repeat all the songs in a selected music source as many times as you can stand.

To repeat the same song ad infinitum, choose **Main menu**, **Settings**. Highlight **Repeat** and press the **Select** button once so that One is displayed next to the Repeat setting. Select the **song** you want to hear and play it. It will play and then play again until you pause the iPod or choose a different song. While the song plays, the Repeat One indicator will appear on the Now Playing screen (see Figure 6.3).

note

Like the Shuffle Settings feature, the Repeat feature works with any music source you select, including playlists or any of the Browse categories.

FIGURE 6.3

You can make
the same song
play over and
over until you
just can't take it
anymore.

— Repeat One indicator

If you want to repeat all the songs within a selected music source, choose **Main menu**, **Settings**. Highlight **Repeat** and press the **Select button** twice so that All is displayed next to the Repeat setting. Select the **music source** (such as a playlist) you want to hear and play **it**. It will play and then repeat until you pause the iPod or choose a different music source. While the music source plays, the Repeat All indicator will appear on the Now Playing screen (see Figure 6.4).

FIGURE 6.4

You can use the Repeat All mode to repeat all the songs in a selected music source, such as a playlist.

Repeat All indicator

To turn Repeat off, choose **Main menu**, **Settings**. Highlight **Repeat** and press the **Select button** until Off is displayed next to the Repeat setting. Music will again play one time through and then stop.

Using Sound Check

iTunes' Sound Check feature causes songs to play back at the same relative volume level—if you have ever been jolted out of your chair because of one song's volume level being much higher than the next one, you know why this is a good thing. Using the iPod's Sound Check setting, you can cause the iPod to use the volume levels set by iTunes when Sound Check is on.

To use **Sound Check**, make sure it is on in iTunes. Then, connect **your iPod** to **your computer** so the iPod's music will be updated, or you can perform a manual update if that is how you have configured iTunes for your iPod. After the update is complete, on the iPod choose **Main menu**, **Settings**. On the Settings menu, highlight **Sound Check** and press the **Select button**. The Sound Check setting will become On to show you that it is in use. When you play music back, it will play at the same relative volume level.

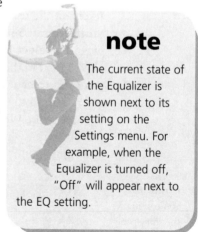

note

The current state of the Equalizer is shown next to its setting on the Settings menu. For example, when the Equalizer is turned off, "Off" will appear next to the EQ setting.

To return the volume level to the "normal" state, choose **Main menu**, **Settings**. Highlight **Sound Check** and press the **Select button** so that Off appears as the Sound Check setting.

Using the iPod's Equalizer

The iPod also has a built-in Equalizer that you can use to improve (*improve* being a relative term, of course) the music to which you listen. The iPod includes a number of presets designed to enhance specific kinds of music and other audio sources. To use the iPod Equalizer, do the following steps:

1. Choose **Main menu**, **Settings**.

2. Highlight the **EQ** setting and press the **Select button**. You'll see the EQ menu (see Figure 6.5). On this menu, you will see all the presets that are available to you. The list is pretty long, so you will need to scroll down to see all your options. The presets include those designed for specific styles of music, such as Acoustic, Classical, Jazz, and so on, as well as for situations in which you might be using your iPod to play music, such as on Small Speakers.

note

If you have created your own presets on the iTunes Equalizer, they won't be available on your iPod. The iPod includes a set of presets, and those are all that you can use. Fortunately, the list of presets is quite large, so this isn't much of a limitation.

FIGURE 6.5

Choose an Equalizer preset on the EQ menu to activate it.

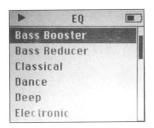

tip

If you want to see a visual representation of the effect of the Equalizer preset you are using, view the Equalizer in iTunes with the same preset selected. See Chapter 17, "Equalizing Your Music," to learn how to do this.

3. Highlight the **preset** you want to use and press the **Select button**. You'll return to the Settings menu, and the preset you selected will be shown next to the Equalizer setting (see Figure 6.6). When you play music, the Equalizer will adjust the volume levels of various frequencies to enhance certain frequencies and to reduce the levels of others.

Setting Up Your Main Menu Preferences

You can configure the commands on the iPod's Main menu to customize it to suit your preferences. For example, suppose you frequently browse your music by artist. You can add the Browse by Artist command to the Main menu so that you don't have to drill down through the Music or Browse menu to get to this category. To configure your Main menu, do the following steps:

1. Choose **Main menu**, **Settings**. The Settings menu will appear.

2. Highlight **Main Menu** and press the **Select button**. You'll see the Main Menu menu (see Figure 6.7). On this menu, each command is listed along with its current Main menu state. If "On" is listed next to a command, it appears on the Main menu. If "Off" is listed to a command, it doesn't appear on the Main menu.

FIGURE 6.7

You can add items to the Main menu by turning them on or remove them by turning them off.

3. To add a **command** to the Main menu, highlight it and press the **Select button** so that "On" is listed next to that command. That command will then appear on the Main menu.

4. To remove a **command** from the Main menu, highlight it and press the **Select** button so that "Off" is listed next to that command. That command will not appear on the Main menu.

tip

To return the Main menu to its default commands, choose **Main menu, Settings, Main Menu, Reset Main Menu**. Select **Reset** again to confirm the command. The iPod's Main menu will be just like it was when you first powered it up.

5. Repeats step 3 or 4 for each command until you have set all the commands you want on the Main menu to "On" and all those you don't want to appear on the Main menu to "Off." When you view the Main menu, your command preferences will be in effect (see Figure 6.8).

FIGURE 6.8

Using the Main menu settings, I customized the Main menu on this iPod (notice that I can use the Artists command on the Main menu to more quickly browse this iPod's music by artist).

Setting the Screen's Contrast

You can adjust the contrast of the iPod's screen so that you find it easier to read. To do this, choose **Main menu**, **Settings**, **Contrast**. You'll see the Contrast menu, which consists of the Contrast slider (see Figure 6.9). Drag the **Scroll pad** or **Click Wheel** clockwise to increase the contrast (which makes the text and background darker) or counterclockwise to decrease the contrast, making the text lighter. As you drag, the shaded part of the Contrast bar indicates the current relative contrast level. When you think you have a setting that suits you, move to other menus to see if the setting is correct for your eyes and viewing conditions. Otherwise, continue to adjust it until it is correct.

tip

You can reset an iPod's contrast to the default setting by pressing and holding the **Menu** button for about 4 seconds.

FIGURE 6.9

Increasing the contrast of the iPod's screen can make it easier to read.

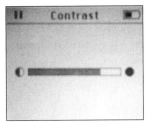

Setting the Sleep Timer

You can configure your iPod to turn itself off automatically after a specific period of time passes. To do this, use the following steps:

1. Choose **Main menu**, **Extras**, **Clock**, **Sleep Timer**. You'll see the Sleep menu, which consists of a list of sleep time periods, from Off (meaning that the Sleep Timer is turned off) to 120 Minutes (meaning that the iPod will shut off in 2 hours).

2. Choose the **Sleep Timer setting** you want by highlighting **it** and pressing the **Select button**.

When you have the sleep timer on and view the Now Playing screen, the current amount of time until the iPod sleeps is shown at the top of the screen (see Figure 6.10). When the counter gets to zero, the iPod will turn itself off. This happens regardless of whether you happen to be listening to music at the time or not. So, if your iPod suddenly shuts off and you don't first see a "battery low" warning, this is likely the reason.

FIGURE 6.10

This iPod will turn itself off in 29 minutes.

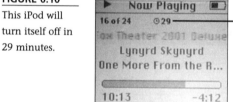

Time remaining until the iPod sleeps

Configuring the Clicker

As you select various menu options, your iPod "clicks" to give you audible feedback. You can configure how the clicker works using the Clicker setting options. The options you have depend on whether you are using an iPod or an iPod mini.

If you have an iPod, you choose to have the Clicker play through the iPod's Speaker, which means you hear the Clicker whether any output device is attached to the iPod or not; Headphones, which causes the Clicker sound to play only through a connected output device (such as earbuds); Both, which causes the Clicker sound to play through the speaker and through an output device; or Off, which turns the clicking sound off. To set one of these options, choose **Main menu**, **Settings**. Highlight the **Clicker** command and press the Select button until the setting you want appears next to the Clicker preference.

If you have an iPod mini, you can only turn the Clicker on or off. You can turn it off by choosing **Main menu**, **Settings**. Then highlight the **Clicker** option and press the **Select button** so that its setting becomes Off. Your iPod mini will start running in silent mode. To make your iPod mini click again, highlight the Clicker option and press the **Select button** so that its setting becomes On. Your iPod mini will happily click away as you move around its menus.

Working with the iPod's Language

When you first turned your iPod on, you selected the language in which you wanted it to communicate with you. In most cases, you will never need to change that initial setting. However, you can if you do need to for some reason.

To choose a different language, choose **Main menu**, **Settings**, **Language**. You'll see the Language menu (see Figure 6.11). Highlight the **language** you want your iPod to use and press the **Select button**. The menus will change and use the language you selected.

FIGURE 6.11

If I were multi-lingual, one of these settings might be useful, but since I am language limited, they aren't.

Returning an iPod to That Factory-Fresh Feeling

On occasion, all your work configuring your iPod might not be what you intended. Fortunately, you can return the iPod settings to their default values with a single menu command.

To do this, choose **Main menu**, **Settings**, **Reset All Settings**. You'll see the Reset All menu.

tip

If you accidentally select a language that you can't read, you can use the information in the next section to reset the language even if you can't read the iPod's menus.

tip

If you have set your iPod to use a language that you can't read, you can reset it by choosing the Settings command, which is the fourth command on the Main menu (by default), and then choosing the last command on the Settings menu (which is the Reset All Settings command). On the resulting menu, choose the second command and press the **Select** button to reset the iPod. Of course, if you have customized the Main menu, the Settings command might or might not be the fourth one down. When you customize the Main menu, it is a good idea to remember where that command is, just in case.

Highlight **Reset** and press the **Select** button. Your iPod's menus and all other settings will be returned to their default condition.

The Absolute Minimum

In this chapter, you've explored many of the options on the Settings menu and you've learned quite a number of ways to make your iPod suit your personal preferences. Check out the following list to review what you have learned and to pick up a few more pointers:

- Use the Shuffle, Repeat, Sound Check, and Equalizer to configure how music plays on your iPod.
- You can determine which commands appear on the Main menu by using the Main menu settings.
- Use the Contrast setting to set the contrast of the iPod's screen.
- Use the Sleep Timer to have your iPod go to sleep automatically.
- If you don't like the clicking sound that the iPod makes when you press a button, you can turn it off.
- Your iPod is multilingual; use the Language settings to determine which language your iPod uses.
- You can restore your iPod to its factory settings with the Reset All Settings command.
- The About command on the Settings menu provides important information about your iPod, including its name, disk capacity, available space, the software version installed on it, its model, and serial number.
- The Audiobooks setting enables you to set the speed at which audiobooks play back. You can make audiobooks play more quickly by choosing Faster or more slowly by choosing Slower. Audiobooks will then play according to your preference. This can be useful if a book you are listening to plays too slowly; use the Faster setting to speed things up. Or if a book plays too quickly, you can slow it down a bit. (This setting does not affect music.)
- The Date & Time settings enable you to configure and work with your iPod's clock. You'll learn about those settings in Chapter 9, "Using the iPod's Calendar, Contact Manager, and Other Non-Music Tools."
- You use the Contacts setting to choose how contacts on your iPod are displayed. You'll learn about that in Chapter 9, too.
- The Legal setting takes you to the oh-so-useful Legal screen, which contains lots of legalese that you can read should you have absolutely nothing else to do.

Toys for Your iPod

Owning an iPod is only the start of a love affair with your music. Although the iPod alone is a great product, there is a plethora of Apple and third-party accessories that take your iPod to the next level.

Over the following pages, you take a look at the most popular add-ons for your iPod, including headphones, carrying cases, batteries, adapters, media readers, and much more. If you thought you were done spending money once you got the iPod, you were happily wrong!

Headphones

The first thing you will notice as a new iPod owner is that the white headphones that Apple Computer ships with your iPod leave a lot to be desired. Upgrading your headphones is the single most popular upgrade iPod owners make. All the following headphones work with all iPod and iPod Mini units.

Apple Headphones

Besides the headphones Apple bundles with the iPod, they also sell an in-ear headphone. These headphones fit completely in your ear (hence the name) and offer a noticeable improvement in sound quality over the stock iPod headphones.

They come with three different sized caps, to ensure a fit with all the different ear sizes out there.

There are much better sounding in-ear headphones out there, but none come close to the price range of these.

Price: $39.00

www.apple.com/ipod/accessories.html

> **tip**
>
> Not all headphones sound the same to everyone. Your best bet is to actually try the headphones before you buy them.
>
> Even headphones that look alike don't feel alike. Comfort is very important in your choice of headphones. Try them on before you buy them! Remember, they will be sitting on your head for long periods of time, so you want something that fits and feels well.

Shure—www.shure.com

Shure makes a number of different headphones that you can enjoy with your iPod. They range in price and performance, and are all in-ear. The different models include the following.

E2 Sound Isolating Earphones

These are similar to the Apple In-Ear headphones. They perform well, and have a richer overall sound than stock Apple headphones.

Price: $99.00

E3 Sound Isolating Earphones with Extended Frequency Response

The only real difference between the E2 and E3 is better sound quality and price.

Price: $179.00

E5 Sound Isolating Earphones

The granddaddy of the Shure line of headphones, the E5 sports dual micro speakers per headphone. They sound terrific, look great, and cost as much as your iPod!

Price: $499.00

Learn more about the Shure line of headphones at www.shure.com.

Bose—www.bose.com

Known for years as one of the premium home speaker makers in the world, Bose is also known for their superior headphone audio quality. As an iPod owner, you obviously love music, and want to have it reproduced in the best sounding headphones you can afford. Bose has two different headphones that you might be interested in, depending on your budget.

QuietComfort 2 Noise Cancellation Headphones

One of the problems you will encounter when trying to listen to your headphones is background noise. For those who try to enjoy your portable music on an airline or in a noisy room, you will appreciate the Noise Cancellation technology Bose has built in to the QuietComfort 2s.

In essence, these headphones cancel out any external background noise, such as an airliner's engines, loud air conditioning, and any other general "white noise" sound that can interfere with your listening enjoyment.

Combine the ability to cancel out the background noise with the superior sound quality of the QuietComfort 2 headphones, and you are in for a music lover's treat! These headphones are not earbuds or inner ear, but are more conventional looking, over-the-ear headphones. And for most people, they are much more comfortable to wear for extended periods than the inner ear or earbud variety (although obviously not a wise choice for joggers).

Price: $299.00

TriPort Headphones

Not as expensive as the previous QuietComfort 2s, and with no noise reduction technology, you will still be pleased at the tonal quality of the TriPort headphones. They, too, are over-the-ear headphones, so they are not ideal for joggers or more active iPod users. However, if you do not listen to your iPod while on the move or in an excessively loud environment, you will enjoy these headphones.

Price: $149.00

Sennheiser—www.sennheiserusa.com

Most of you reading this have probably never heard of the Sennheiser brand, but they are quickly making a big name for themselves in the world of audio. Not only are they making headphones for your iPod and computer, as well as for your home entertainment system, they are also making cutting-edge amplifiers for your iPod. But more on that later.

PCX250

I personally reviewed these headphones back in September of 2003, and they became the headphones I use more than any other. With noise reduction technology, similar to the above-mentioned Bose, the PCX250 does an admiral job of both quieting loud background sounds and reproducing music much better than the standard Apple earbud headphones. These are over-the-ear headphones, rather than the inner or earbud types. They are very comfortable, but you need two AA batteries for the noise reduction to work.

Price: $199.99

Sony—www.sony.com

Known for their top-quality products and brand recognition, Sony headphones will probably be the easiest to find in stores in your area. They make a wide range of headphones that will work great with your iPod. Here are some good choices if you are looking at Sony headphones.

MDR-EX71SL

These earbud type headphones are very similar to the earbuds that ship with the iPod, with two advantages. First, they sound much better, which is the reason you want to upgrade. Second, these earbuds are much more comfortable than the Apple earbuds.

Price: $49.99

MDR-V300

These over-the-ear headphones sound wonderful, and are very comfortable as well. Surprisingly, these are also very lightweight for their size, and perform well in office settings. They are not easy to transport, however, but more than make up for it with their folding design. These are nice headphones—you would not be disappointed.

Price: $49.99

MDR-G72LP

Although these are over-the-ear, they actually wrap around the back of your head, rather than the top. The MDR-G72LP sport a nonslip design, so that they do not fall off as easily as other behind-the-head designed headphones. The biggest drawback with these, however, is their not-so-superior sound quality. Only slightly better, if at all, than the iPod stock headphones.

Price: $39.99

Koss—www.koss.com

It is impossible to think about headphones without thinking about Koss. They have been making headphones since the 1950s. Koss has been at the forefront of headphone design and innovation for years, and continue to lead the industry in sales, service, and quality products.

UR29

These over-the-ear headphones are both comfortable and affordable, and more importantly, are very decent sounding. You can get much better headphones for twice the money, but they do sound better than the stock Apple earbuds.

Price: $25.99

SportaPro Traditional Collapsible Headphones

An earbud headphone is of a different flavor, in that they fit in your ear differently than most others. Don't let the differences sway you away from taking a closer look at the SportaPros, though, as they sound very good. They also have a volume control switch on the cord, though some people have reported problems with some iPod models. This is a nice headphone buy.

Price: $29.99

QZ-2000 Technology Noise Reduction

Another in the popular noise reduction category, the QZ-2000 sound fantastic, which, for the price, you would expect. These over-the-ear headphones are a bit bulky, and the twisted bulky cord is more "1970s" than any other headphone listed here. For the price, these are very nice headphones.

Price: $199.99

Portable Speakers

Because the iPod and iPod Mini use an industry-standard headphone jack, you are not limited to only using headphones to listen to your music. The iPod can act as a portable music player, as well. Although the iPod is great for personal use, sharing your music with family and friends or co-workers, can be even more enjoyable.

Because the iPod does not generate enough power through the headphone jacks, you need a powered speaker system or amplifier to get the most sound out of your iPod.

tip

Remember that price does not always equal quality! If you prefer one set of speakers over another, don't let the cheaper price deter you.

If you plan to play your speakers outdoors, be certain to buy speakers that won't get ruined if it rains! Many speakers are waterproof, so do your homework before deciding which speakers fit your needs the best.

inMotion Portable iPod Speakers

The word "portable" in the name means you can use these inMotion speakers anywhere, without the need to plug into a power outlet. They work with four AA batteries, which can last up to 24 hours on continuous play. The inMotion speakers are small, weighing it at only 8 ounces, so you can take it with you easily. Even better, it has its own amplifier built-in, delivering 2 watts of power in each speaker.

The inMotion Portable iPod speakers are for use with the third generation iPod only, including the iPod Mini with adapter sold separately. The inMotion speakers act as a dock, and your iPod plugs into it via the dock adapter.

Price: $149.00

www.alteclansing.com

Ezison Personal Speakers for iPod

These are small, battery-powered speakers similar to the inMotion speakers, but these work with any full-size iPod. Simply set the iPod in the cradle, plug them in via the headphone jack, and enjoy.

Price: $199.99

www.welovemacs.com

Sony SRS-T55 Folding Travel Speaker

These folding speakers work perfectly with any generation iPod, as they draw their sound from the headphone jack. They weigh about one pound, produce 2 watts of power, and fold up into a purse or bag.

Price: $49.99

www.sony.com

iPod Carry Speaker Tote Bag Groove Bag Triplet and Tote

Think of this as a purse, but with built-in speakers and a slot for your iPod. This is an amazingly clever Gucci-like handbag, with nice-sounding speakers. Although obviously not for the male iPod owner, this speaker bag has been featured on TechTV (G4TV), Fox News, Style.com, and even Wired. 0.5 watts produces little in the way of real power, but this speaker bag is more about style than practicality—a neat item.

Price: $139.00

www.drbott.com

iPal Portable Speaker with Tuner

The iPal supports all iPods, as it uses the headphone jack to get the music from the iPod to its speakers. Unlike the previous speakers, the iPal is also an AM/FM radio using Automatic Frequency Control (AFC), which is one of the best ways to keep a radio station in tune. Because it is also a radio, the iPal has a telescoping antenna. Even better, the iPal has a rechargeable NiMH battery, which recharges in as little as three hours, and lasts longer than the charge in your iPod!

The iPal is an attractive, great-sounding external speaker for your iPod.

Price: $129.99

www.tivoliaudio.com

iPod in Your Car

Unless you own a 2002 or later BMW, and purchase the BMW iPod adapter for your car, you need to take a look at a few different ways and products to get your iPod to play in your car. Sure, you can always listen to headphones while driving, but safety issues aside, how much fun is that? You want to listen to your music over all those speakers in your car, and here are the different ways to do it!

tip

Don't keep your iPod in your car in plain sight unattended. iPods are very popular, and one car window is a small price to pay for a determined thief who wants your iPod!

Sony CPA-9C Car Cassette Adapter

If you have a cassette player in your car, one of the easiest ways to get your iPod music to play over your automobile speakers is a handy cassette adapter. These have been around since the portable CD player was big. From the headphone jack of your iPod (or CD player), you plug in the cable, which connects at the other end to a cassette tape. It is not, actually, a cassette tape, but it acts as a go-between for your iPod and the tape player head in your cassette deck. The Sony CPA-9C is a very nice model. You can find cheaper models from other companies, but I have found the Sony model to be a little superior in reliability.

Price: $19.99

www.sony.com

The Belkin TuneCast II Mobile FM Transmitter

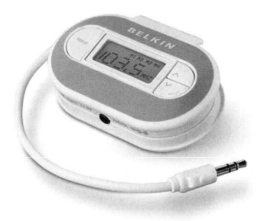

The name is a dead giveaway for what this does. It broadcasts your music via FM radio wave, which you then dial in on your radio. This works in a car, home stereo, or even portable radio. The sound quality varies, depending on your stereo, antenna type, and distance from the antenna. I have found that antennas on the rear of a car have a harder time picking up the signal than do antennas in the front.

The Belkin TuneCast II Mobile FM transmitter broadcasts on any FM frequency, can memorize up to four channels, and runs for up to four hours on two AAA batteries. The unit plugs into your headphone jack on your iPod, rather than a dock. One drawback is that the Belkin unit does not directly attach to your iPod. It works with any iPod model.

Price: $39.95

www.belkin.com

tip

Rechargeable batteries with a car adapter are a good way to keep your FM transmitter ready to go when you want it. Nothing is as sad as looking forward to listening to your iPod in your car and having dead batteries.

Griffin iTrip

The Griffin iTrip for the new iPod plugs into the top of your iPod directly, sitting atop the unit while broadcasting the signal on any FM radio frequency, just like the Belkin unit. The latest iTrip for iPod works with the third generation iPod only, and plugs not only into your headphone jack, but the FireWire port as well. In this way, the iTrip does not use batteries, it uses the iPod itself as a power source. What's more, it autopowers off after 60 seconds of silence, just as your iPod does.

The Griffin iTrip for third generation iPods is very stylish, blending in very well with the iPod design and aesthetics. Griffin also makes an iTrip for the iPod Mini, as well as the first two generation of iPods.

Price: $35.00

www.griffintechnology.com

Monster iCarPlay Wireless

Another FM transmitter, the Monster iCarPlay Wireless plugs into your iPod headphone jack, but pulls its power from your automobile's cigarette lighter. Even better, the Monster iCarPlay Wireless also charges your iPod as it goes, filling up the iPod rapidly then turning into a trickle charge as to optimize performance.

The Monster iCarPlay Wireless only works with dock connector iPods (meaning the third generation iPod and the iPod Mini). Like other FM transmitters, you simply select which frequency you want to broadcast your iPod on, tune in your radio, and your iPod is playing over your car stereo.

Price: $69.95

www.monstercable.com

Auto Chargers

Although it is easy to play your iPod through your car audio system, you might simply want a way to charge your iPod in your car. Here are three products that do just that.

XtremeMac Car Charger for New iPods and FireWire Car Charger for Original iPods

They might look different, and plug into each of their respected iPods differently, but the XtremeMac car chargers do the same thing, charge your iPod from your cigarette lighter plug. The all-white design matches your iPod well, unless you have a colorful iPod Mini.

Price: $19.95

www.xtrememac.com

Griffin PowerPod Auto Charger

Similar to the XtremeMac model, the PowerPod comes with a four-foot extension, so you can pretty much charge your iPod anywhere in the front of the vehicle. It works with all iPod models, and recharges your battery even when it is in use.

Price: $24.99

www.griffintechnology.com

Belkin iPod Auto Kit

The Belkin unit only works with newer, dock connector iPods (and iPod Mini) but gives the added feature of also being able to power the Belkin TuneCast II FM transmitter. It also features an illuminated indicator so you can tell at a glance if it is connected properly to your cigarette lighter.

Price: $49.99

www.belkin.com

iPod Automobile Mounting Kits

Although you can easily set your iPod in your lap while driving, it really is not a good idea. Nor is it a good idea to set your iPod on your dashboard; one sharp turn and your iPod might crash to the floor, or even fly out the window if you have a window down, which was the fate of my first portable CD player over a decade ago. Ouch!

The best solution is to securely mount your iPod in your car, and the following sections list a number of units that allow you to do that.

tip

Be certain you do not mount your iPod in a spot that will be in direct sunlight for extended periods of time. Prolonged exposure to sunlight is not good for your iPod.

Belkin TuneDok Car Holder

If you have a cup holder in your car, truck, or minivan, this is an inexpensive solution for holding your iPod securely. The TuneDok simply fits into your cup holder, and the iPod attaches to the Air Grip mount. It sports a ratcheting neck so that you can position your iPod to fit your reach more easily. There are two different models—one for the regular iPod and one for the iPod Mini.

Price: $29.99

www.belkin.com

DLO TransPod FM (New iPods and iPod Mini Only)

This is an all-in-one type of unit. Not only does the DLO TransPod act as a mounting system and battery charger, it is also an FM transmitter. The unit allows for easy mounting of your third generation iPod, or the iPod Mini, in your car, while transmitting the music to your car stereo system. It also sports a very nice LCD display so that you can easily view which FM station the iPod is playing on. This is a nice unit, well worth a look.

Price: $99.99

www.netalog.com

Voice Recorders

Do you regularly attend meetings, conduct interviews, or simply have a need to record conversations? If so, you could go out and buy a cheap mini cassette deck or a digital voice recorder. But if you already have an iPod, why bother? All you need is one of these two voice recorders.

The big benefit to using your iPod as a voice recorder is the massive amount of storage space. The ability to store said recordings on your computer, even using iTunes to catalog and sort them, is another huge benefit. Smaller digital voice recorders usually support less than 100MB, have poor audio quality, and can be quite expensive. Traditional cassette tapes are hard to manage and catalog; you cannot store the recordings on your computer, and must use cheap and easily damaged tapes. The iPod is the perfect voice recorder, and you already have one. (Note: The iPod Mini does not support any voice recordings, only the third generation iPod with dock connector does.)

Belkin Voice Recorder for iPod

With the Belkin Voice Recorder, you simply attach the unit to the top of your iPod, and you are all set to record (after the Belkin software has been installed on your iPod, of course). You can then use it to record and play back your voice recording via the built-in speakers of your iPod's headphones. What's more, the Belkin Voice Recorder can also double as an alarm clock!

Price: $59.99

www.belkin.com

Griffin Technology iTalk

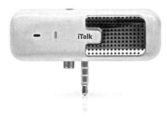

The iTalk, like the Belkin unit, plugs into the top of your iPod, and can be used to record sounds directly to your iPod. The iTalk records up to 100 feet away, and even supports the use of external microphones. It also has a 2-watt speaker built in, so that you can listen to your recordings without the need of a headphone.

Price: $39.99

www.griffintechnology.com

Belkin Universal Microphone Adapter

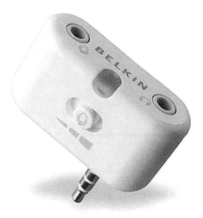

Perhaps you already own a monoaudio microphone, and don't need all the features of the previous units. In that case, all you really need to get sound into your iPod is a Microphone Adapter, and Belkin iPod Microphone Adapter fits the bill. It allows a mono audio microphone with a 3.5mm plug to work with all iPods that have a dock connector (third generation iPods).

Price: $39.99

www.belkin.com

Media Readers

As great as digital cameras are, they have one big problem: After the media card is full, you cannot take any more pictures until you empty the card again. If you are carrying your iPod anyway, with its huge amount of storage capacity, why not turn your iPod into a portable hard drive for your digital photos?

tip

Photo files take much more room on your iPod's hard drive than sound files do if you are using a high megapixel camera. If you plan to use your iPod to store photos, be certain to delete them from your iPod after you transfer them to your computer.

Belkin iPod Media Reader

This is a great unit, which acts as a digital media reader for most flavors of digital camera media cards. The iPod Media Reader allows you to take the media card out of your camera and transfer those files directly to your iPod. No more taking your expensive laptop out with you to hold your photos! Nor do you need to buy more than one digital media card for your camera.

Supported digital media card formats include CompactFlash (Type 1 and 2), SmartMedia, Secure Digital (SD), Memory Stick, or MultiMediaCard (MMC).

Price: $109.00

www.belkin.com

Apple World Travel Adapter Kit

If you plan to go on a long overseas trip and want to take your iPod with you, how do you plan on recharging your iPod while away? The solution is simple: Apple will happily sell you the World Travel Adapter Kit, which allows you to plug your iBook, PowerBook G4, or iPod into outlets in North America, Japan, China, United Kingdom, Continental Europe, Korea, Australia, and Hong Kong. It works with the white power adapter that shipped with your iPod, and supports all iPods and the iPod Mini.

Cost: $39.00

www.apple.com

> **tip**
>
> The Apple World Adapter Kit also works with any Macintosh with the white brick power adapter!

iPod Stands

In today's age of electronic gizmos, our work desks tend to get cluttered fairly quickly. My digital camera with its dock is over there. Next to that is my iSight video camera that I use to videoconference. Then there is the spot for my Canon Digital Camcorder for when I need to import video to my computer. Of course, you cannot forget the place my high-tech speakers go. Oh, and the media card reader for the various digital cameras I review. And on and on it goes. Every few months, it seems, some new gizmo pops up that somehow finds a place on my desk. Does this sound like you?

The iPod is not an inexpensive toy—just the opposite, in fact. When you are not using your iPod, you can't simply lay it on its back on your desk. How cool would that be? So, unless you have an iPod Dock, you need to buy a stand for your iPod. Prices vary, of course, and some stands look better with your computer desk layout than others. You can go for a more traditional looking stand, high-tech, brushed metal, clear plastic, colored plastic, and many other cool stands. They all perform the same function, so look at price and design when making your choice.

> **tip**
>
> If you move your iPod from your computer desk to, for example, your home audio cabinet, consider buying more than one stand, so that you don't have to move the stand from place to place. And if you dust as infrequently as I do, moving the stand gives away how much dust is actually on your furniture!

Habitat

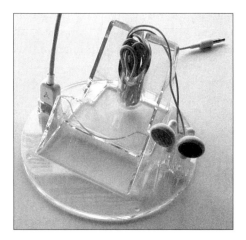

The Habitat is a clear plastic stand from Bubble Design. Unlike some other stands, the Habitat, besides holding your iPod, also has a place for your earbud headphones and FireWire (or USB 2.0) wires. It is very attractive, and helps with clutter. Your iPod fits into a slot standing up at a 60-degree angle or so. One drawback, however, is that because the iPod fits in a slot, this is not an ideal solution for iPod Mini users, nor iPod users who use a protective carrying case.

Price: $24.99

www.BubbleDesign.com

ModPod

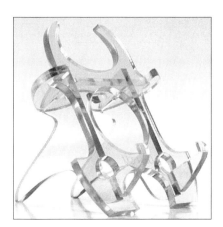

Another plastic stand, this one comes in a variety of colors besides clear. The ModPod allows easy access to the front of your iPod and to the cables, and has clips on the back of the stand to help control wire clutter. Like the Habitat, you cannot use the ModPod if your iPod is in a protective case. It works with all models of iPod, including the iPod Mini, though it will not hold the thinner Mini as securely.

Price: $14.95

www.MacSkinz.com

PodHolder

The PodHolder was one of the first iPod stands on the market. It is a simple "L" design with rubber bumpers to both protect your iPod from scratches, and keep it from sliding around. A clear piece of plastic, the PodHolder almost disappears when an iPod is sitting in its cradle. The simple, but effective, design makes the PodHolder a nice unit.

Price: $9.95

www.PodShop.com

PodBoard

A very unique product, the PodBoard works with all iPods, except the iPod Mini. This flat piece of stainless steel has leather straps on the back, and displays your iPod on a flat panel. Think of it as a picture frame for your iPod. The iPod fits into the PodBoard almost flush, and you can also download "skins" for it. A skin is nothing more than a picture, but it gives the PodBoard the option of looking like a piece of art on your desktop. There is also a plastic wire clip on the rear of the PodBoard to help hide and organize your FireWire and headphone wires. This is a very unique product!

Price: $37.00

www.alscher.ch/podboard.html

iPod Cases

One of the great things about the iPod is how sexy and sleek it is. The brushed metal look is great, but it has one major problem—scratches. Apple does not like to voice the problem, but if you use an iPod without a protective case for very long, the chances of scratching your iPod are very great. Thankfully, iPod cases are the number one accessories iPod users buy, and many vendors have hundreds of different cases from which you can choose. No matter what model iPod you own, you can find the perfect case for your needs. The following sections discuss just a tiny fraction of the available iPod cases.

tip

Even if you don't take your iPod with you often, you still need to think about buying a case to protect it from scratches.

Sheldon iPod Case

These come in a variety of colors and styles, such as Metallic Blue, Miami Geo, Pink Polish, Silver Bullet, and Checkerboard.

Price: $24.95

www.ebags.com

Speck iPod Skins

This is not so much a case as a new skin for your iPod. These protective rubber cases fit very snug, and can even give your iPod some of that iPod Mini color you want so badly! They also work with the iPod Dock, so that you don't have to remove your iPod from its skin simply to plug it in to the Dock.

Price: $19.95

www.speckproducts.com

Speck iStyle

The Speck iStyle is a leather case that sports a very nice snap-over lid, as well as a plastic shield to cover the iPod's screen. It ships with a swivel belt clip.

Price: $34.95

www.speckproducts.com

Belkin Leather Flip Case

This attractive case can flip open for quick access to the front of your iPod.

Price: $29.99

www.belkin.com

MARWARE Sportsuit Convertible Case

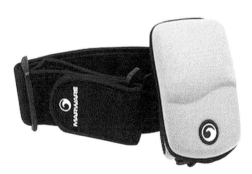

This iPod Mini case, made from 2mm neoprene outer construction, is great for those Mini owners who take their iPod with them to work out. It features an interchangeable clip so that you can wear it as an armband or on your belt. You can also connect your iPod Mini to your computer without taking it out of the case. It comes in a variety of colors to match your iPod Mini.

Price: $34.95

www.marware.com

MARWARE SportSuit Safari

Without the picture, you probably would not believe this one. Yes, an iPod Mini case looks (and feels!) like fur! Made from neoprene and faux fur, you can get these little fuzzy cases in Panther (black), Polar Bear (white), Flamingo (pink), Giraffe (brown and white), Leopard (brown, black, and white), and Zebra (black and white). What, no Smurf Blue?

Price: $19.95

MARWARE 3G SportSuit Convertible

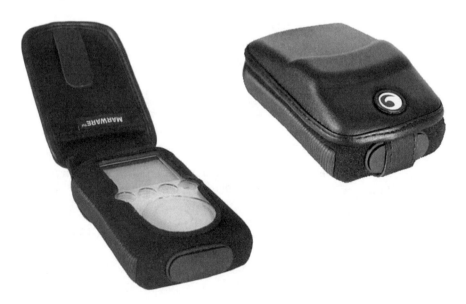

The SportSuit Convertible is a great-looking case made from rugged neoprene. It can quickly flip open to reveal a snug and protected iPod. You can even connect your iPod to your computer without removing it from the case. And most importantly, of course, it comes in a variety of colors, including Blue, Graphite, Red, and Yellow.

Price: $39.95

www.marware.com

PodSleevz/Mini Sleevz

Most iPod and Mini cases either flip, fold, or leave a cutout so that you can get to the controls. After all, you have to physically run your finger over the controls to operate it. Not so with the PodSleevz—for both iPod and the Mini! This superthin (less than 1mm in thickness) is a soft, yet very tough fabric that fits your iPod like a formfitting glove! They also come in a variety of colors.

Price: $19.95 ($17.95 Mini)

www.radtech.us

Gucci iPod Case

If you are a fashion maven, you know all about Gucci. This iPod case is not about protection, but fashion. And the price reflects that!

Price: $199.99

www.gucci.com

TimBuk2 iPod Case

If simplicity is more to your liking, take a look at the TimBuk2 iPod case. It attaches to a belt or a shoulder strap. Elastic side panels mean your iPod fits nice and snug. The Velcro top keeps it secure. It also comes in 12 colors!

Price: $20.00

www.timbuk2.com

Anetagenova iPod Case

Cutting-edge fashion for the iPod is found with the Anetagenova iPod case. The Anetagenova line of iPod cases come in a variety of different styles and colors. Not cheap, but still not Gucci priced, these iPod cases are certain to get attention!

Price: $79.00–$129.00

www.anetagenova.com

PodPaqnappa

Made from fine nappa leather, this iPod case is as beautiful as it is sturdy. It features a removable (via sturdy metal clips) front flap.

Price: $39.95

www.booqbags.com

Burton Shield iPod Jacket

You are probably wondering how a winter skiing jacket made it into a book about iPods and iTunes, right? Well, this is the first (and, as far as I know, only) jacket that has iPod control on the arm! The iPod is stored in the specially designed EVA molded chest pocket for protection against the elements and the stray tree branch. Burton makes both a men's and women's version. Yes, they are pricy, but this is not only a high-quality Burton ski jacket, it is also technically an iPod case as well!

Price: $379.95 (Men) $359.95 (Women)

CD-ROM Contents

On the accompanying CD-ROM disc, you will find programs for the Mac and PC that enhance your iPod and iTunes experience. Some programs are free for you to use and enjoy, whereas you have to pay for other programs should you choose to keep them. The disc contains three different categories of software, which are discussed in the following sections.

Freeware

This is software made by either a company or an individual who has decided not to charge for their work. Freeware is, as the name implies, free! If you do decide to keep and use any freeware program, it is customary to at least send an email to the creator thanking them for their generosity. This shows your appreciation, and a nice email is a sure way to keep them either updating the program, or creating other worthwhile programs.

Shareware

This is software that is usually free to use for a set amount of time, after which you agree to pay the price should you choose to continue using it. Shareware is not quite commercial software, but neither is it freeware. It falls somewhere in the middle. A shareware author is usually creating software in his spare time, and allows users to download and freely use it to get a taste of how it works before committing their money.

Commercial Software

These are the big boys of the software industry. More often than not, you have to pay for these programs before using them. However, some companies freely give away their programs for one reason or another. A prime example is the Apple Computers, Inc. program iTunes. iTunes is free to download and use. Apple does not charge a dime for iTunes, for either Mac or PC users. However, iTunes is still not free-ware in the pure definition of the word, but rather commercial software that is given away. In this case, Apple gives away iTunes to boost iPod sales, as well as an incentive to use the program to purchase downloadable music from the iTunes Music Store.

XPlay for Windows is another commercial program found on the CD-ROM. This program, unlike iTunes, is not free, though they do allow you to use it in Demo mode, free of charge. In this case, XPlay uses a shareware form of distribution.

If you find software you enjoy on the CD-ROM, please take a moment to follow the licensing agreement of the program in question.

Macintosh iPod Software

These are the programs for Macintosh computers found on the accompanying CD-ROM.

PodWorks   One of the antitheft options Apple uses to prevent iPod users from simply plugging their iPod into another Mac and copying all his music files over, is its one-way transfer. In other words, you can only copy songs to the iPod, not from it. But what happens when your Mac dies, and you lose all your music files? You might still have them on the iPod, but that does you no good. The answer is a third-party utility titled "PodWorks" from developer Sci-Fi Hi-Fi. It copies all the file metadata from the ID3 (Identification Tag Studio3) stored on every song on the iPod. It then copies that data back to the "clean" version of iTunes on another Macintosh.

Price: $8.00

www.scifihifi.com/podworks/

tip

Read the licencing agreement before installing any software to be certain you are not installing any spyware programs as well!

Always run virus detection software on a PC before and after installing anything downloaded from the Internet.

As with any software found on a CD-ROM, you might want to check to see if there are updated versions of the software online before installing.

BiblePod   Want to read chapters from the King James Version of the bible on your iPod? BiblePod for Mac and Windows lets you do just that. BiblePod is a free program that uses the English KJV XML Bible markup language project.

biblepod.kainjow.com/

Price: Free!

Pod2Go   Pod2Go is a great application that "Takes an ordinary iPod and makes it extraordinary." Using Pod2Go, you can sync news, weather information, movie listings, horoscopes, stock quotes, driving directions, and more. What's more, the software autoupdates itself, helps you publish a listing of your music to a web page, and gives you the ability to quickly and easily manage your iPod's notes. Pod2Go is a really great program, full of features you did not even know you wanted until now!

Price: Free, but donations are welcome.

www.kainjow.com/pod2go/

PodMail   Want to transfer your email to your iPod for later viewing? PodMail is an open-source program that does just that, though you cannot use it to reply to your emails. But if you have a lot of email you would rather read later, this is a great way to take it with you.

Price: Free!

www.podmail.org/

Ejector   The Ejector is a great utility that adds an iPod icon to your Mac OS X menu bar, through which you can eject any removable disk, including an iPod, CD, DVD, or any other hardware device that shows up on your desktop.

Price: Free!

www.jeb.com.fr

iPod Launcher   The power of AppleScript is used in iPod Launcher. When you plug your iPod into your Mac via the FireWire cable, iPod Launcher launches applications for you. For instance, if you manually fire up your iSync application after connecting the iPod, iPod Launcher can automate that for you.

Price: $4.95

www.zapptek.com/

iPod It   If you use Entourage, Mail, Stickies, Address Book, or iCal, you can use iPod It to transfer your PIM (Personal Information Manager) data over to the iPod. This is a great way to carry all your contact information from those applications without having to purchase a separate Personal Digital Assistant (PDA). You can also transfer all your mail messages and events from iCal, download weather and news headlines, and much more. The iPod It is also from ZappTek software.

Price: $14.95

www.zapptek.com/ipod-it/

iSpeak It   A very underutilized feature in Mac OS X is the computer's ability to speak any text onscreen. With iSpeak It, you can take any document, be it a web page, email message, or PDF (Adobe's Portable Document File format) file, and save the spoken words to iTunes. From there, it is a simple matter of loading it onto your iPod, and you now have a vocal recording of said work anywhere you go. This is yet another great application from ZappTek Software.

Price: $12.95

www.zapptek.com/

iPodRip The ability to move your music from your iPod to your computer is smart. Apple does not let you do it. IPodRip does, and supports iTunes song information, including ratings and play count. It can also recover songs and playlists. It provides print, HTML, and XML support, as well as an iTunes style browser. This is a nice piece of software from The Little Appfactory.

Price: $10.00

www.thelittleappfactory.com

Ollie's iPod Extractor A simple and direct way of moving your music files from your iPod to your Macintosh, Ollie's iPod Extractor supports an easy-to-use interface, and the cost is just right!

Price: Free!

www.isophonic.net/applications/

iPod Organizer You can use this program to store phone numbers, email addresses, flight numbers, and appointment times. The program, from proVUE Development, does not install any special or third-party software on your iPod. Instead, iPod Organizer exports the information that you input into the Mac-based software as MP3 files, allowing you to quickly find and use the information on your iPod. This is a great utility, and has received favorable comments from everyone who has reviewed it on the Mac web.

Price: $19.99

www.provue.com/ipodorganizer.html

iPod.iTunes Using a tabbed interface for the software, iPod.iTunes does a good job of syncing the music files from your iPod to iTunes. Intelligent enough not to copy duplicates, iPod.iTunes copies the music files back from the iPod to iTunes that are missing. If, for instance, you accidentally deleted your music files from iTunes, iPod.iTunes saves your bacon! iPod.iTunes also works with not just MP3 files, but also with your protected (iTunes store purchased) .ACC files, audible tracks, and even playlists! This is a great software title to add to your iPod software collection.

Price: 29.90 Euros (use PayPal for currency conversion)

www.crispsofties.com

iPod Decloak iPod Decloak is another program that allows you to view the hidden files (MP3, ACC, and so on) on your iPod. Very similar to many other programs, it works well.

Price: $2.00

www.ipoddecloak.com/

iPod Access   The iPod Access is a tool for moving songs from your Mac to your iPod by artist/album or composer/album. Featuring an easy-to-use interface, iPod Access does a minimum task, which iTunes (free from Apple) does much more easily. Still, the program is worth taking a look at if you are having program problems with iTunes.

Price: $10.00

www.ipodaccess.com/index.html

iPod Play List Cloner   iPod Play List Cloner copies playlists from your iPod to your Mac, in a folder of your choice. Using scripts, it can then add an identical playlist to iTunes (version 3 or later), saving you the time to rebuild your playlists by hand in case you lose your iTunes playlists. This is a handy utility that could potentially save you a lot of time!

Price: Free!

homepage.mac.com/beweis/

Toggle iPod Battery Status   A nifty utility that allows you to change the battery life icon on your iPod from the battery icon to a number between 1 and 500, which represents how much voltage is remaining in your battery. This is a great little application, well worth the small fee.

Price: $2.00

homepage.mac.com/rulerk/

Rip to iPod   This nifty AppleScript only does one thing, but it does it well. It rips (copies) files seemingly directly from a CD to your iPod. In reality, it copies the files to iTunes first, then copies said files to your iPod, and finally deletes the songs from your iTunes.

Price: Free!

www.malcolmadams.com/itunes/index.php

FileMaker to iPod   If you need your vCard information in a FileMaker database, this utility allows you to transfer your contacts to your iPod. Imagine using FileMaker's powerful searching capabilities or sorting options to only copy the needed contacts to your iPod.

Price: Free!

www.bossbizapps.com/

OmniOutliner Export to iPod   For OmniOutliner users, these two AppleScipts let you export your outlines to either iPods Notes or Contacts menu.

Price: Free!

www.omnigroup.com/

Slurp   Slurp is a nice working iPod management tool that maintains a database of all the music files on your iPod. From there, you can perform search and sorts, export the data as text files, copy your music from your iPod to your hard drive, or even burn a CD directly from your iPod to your CD-RW/SuperDrive. The only drawback to Slurp is that the developer, Ambroise Confetti, has halted development on it, releasing only this working beta version.

Price: Free!

www.cellulo.info/slurp/

PodQuest   It is not always feasible to take your computer with you on a trip, but with an iPod and PodQuest, you can take both MapQuest and MapBlast driving instructions on the road. PodQuest adds a menu bar that allows you to download said directions to your iPod. The utility works well, and adds more usefulness to iPod users who are on the road often.

Price: $9.95

www.mibasoft.dk/

Lyripod   What are you missing from your iPod while listening to your music? The lyrics to your music, of course! Lyripod is a simple utility that searches the Internet (lyrics.astraweb.com) for the song you choose, and downloads it to your iPod in the Lyrics folder under Extras. This is still early in the software development stage, and does not work 100% of the time. But, it can't harm your iPod, and is worth giving a try.

Price: Free!

Windows PC iPod Software

These are the programs for Windows-based computers found on the accompanying CD-ROM.

XPlay   XPlay is a commercial software program that gives you much more flexibility with your iPod than ever before. With XPlay, you can drag and drop MP3, M4A, Audible (.aa) the popular WAVE (.wav) or AIFF (.aif, the digital format CDs use) to your iPod without the need to use Apple's iTunes software. Created long before Apple made iTunes for Windows, XPlay is also the only way for those with an older Windows OS, such as Windows 98 or Me, to be compatible with the iPod. Included on the CD-ROM is a 15-day trial demo of the software, courtesy of the Mediafour Corporation.

Price: $29.95

www.mediafour.com/products/xplay/

GoogleGet   GoogleGet is a handy utility for downloading the latest news from Google News to your iPod. This is a handy feature, and shows the power of the iPod. As of this writing, GoogleGet is a free application.

Price: Free!

www.mesmerized.org/teki/extra/googleget/index.html

Weather For Me   Windows users should not feel left out, as Weather For Me downloads a 10-day forecast onto your iPod. This is a great utility if you are planning to take your iPod on vacation, and want a weather forecast for your destination. It includes foreign zip code support, auto updater, and more.

Price: Free!

www.staylazy.net/software/

Feed My Pod   Feed My Pod is a very neat software title that takes content from the iPodLounge website (a great website for all iPod owners) and puts it on your iPod. Simply put, Feed My Pod takes all the news and downloads it to your iPod, allowing you to read it at your own leisure offline.

Price: Free!

www.staylazy.net/feedmypod/

Apple iPod Plug-in for MusicMatch Jukebox   This allows you to transfer music from the MusicMatch Jukebox software to the iPod, much like Apple's own iTunes. If you are a MusicMatch user, this is the software you will want as an iPod user.

Price: Free from Apple Computer, Inc.

docs.info.apple.com/article.html?artnum=120313

PocketMac iPod Edition   If you are a Microsoft Outlook user, and store your contact information in that application, you can now use PocketMac iPod Edition to transfer Contacts, Calendar, Tasks, Notes, and even email to your iPod.

Price: $23.41

Please visit www.pocketmac.net/products/pmipodwin/demo.html to download a demo today!

Anapod Explorer   Anapod Explorer is the first and only iPod software that allows full Windows Explorer integration with the iPod as a device in My Computer. It allows a web page interface to your iPod through its built-in web server. This gives you a powerful search and reporting capability using a Structured Query Language (SQL) database. It does not yet work with the iPod Mini.

Price: $25.00

www.redchairsoftware.com

k-pod   This allows you to download all your email from your inbox to your iPod, making a new folder titled "Mail" in your "Notes" screen on the iPod. It is very simple to use!

Price: Free!

k-deep.com/k-pod.htm

euPOD VolumeBoost   When Apple shipped the iPod to Europe, for some reason they put a restriction on how loud the volume will go. The developer of euPOD VolumeBoost wanted to crank up his music, so he wrote this small program to solve the problem. It works with all iPods, but does not work to the same extent with U.S. iPods as it does with European iPods.

Price: Free!

www.espen.se

WinniePod Updater   If you have a first or second generation Macintosh-compatible iPod, and want to use it with your PC without losing all the music files, this is the application for you.

Price: Free!

www.the-midfield.com/ipod.aspx

CopyPod   This is a small program that allows you to save your iPod music to your computer. This is a nice tool if you have to send your iPod in for repair.

Price: $8.00

copypod.ouvaton.org

iPodLibrary   Ever want to read your e-Books on your iPod? iPodLibrary lets you do just that. You can import all major e-Book formats, including .LIT, .PDF, .HTML, and .TXT. It also allows you to save your last position in each book. Unfortunately, it only works with the third generation iPods.

Price: Free!

www25.brinkster.com/carmagt/ipodlibrary

MyPodPlayer   With MyPodPlayer, you can play all the music on your iPod on your computer. Simply connect the iPod, and MyPodPlayer reads all your music, allowing you to listen on your computer. You can view the music very similar to iTunes, by artist, genre, album, playlist, and so on. MyPodPlayer also allows you to copy songs from your iPod to your PC.

Price: Free!

www.ipodsoft.com/mypodplayer.aspx

iStoryCreator   Want to create your own Text Adventure games for your iPod? That is what iStoryCreator does. Do you remember the "Choose your own ending" books in which you had to turn to a certain page in the book, depending on what you wanted the character to do? This is the same premise that iStoryCreator uses to create Text Adventure games. It can be hours of fun creating and sharing your adventures with people online! To install the iStoryCreator to your computer, you must first have the ".NET Framework" installed. You can get this here:

download.microsoft.com/download/a/a/c/aac39226-8825-44ce-90e3-bf8203e74006/dotnetfx.exe

Price: Free!

www.ipodsoft.com/iCreator.aspx

In addition to iStoryCreator, 28 iStories are included for your enjoyment. Please note: The iStories found on the CD-ROM are to be viewed at your own discretion, and have not been edited by this book's publisher.

Macintosh iTunes Software

The following is software that works with the iTunes software for Macintosh computers.

NiceCast   Imagine being able to use your Macintosh as a broadcasting radio station over the Internet. Imagine no more, as NiceCast does exactly that. NiceCast broadcasts music either across the world or across you house, directly from iTunes.

With iTunes and NiceCast, you can set up a playlist for DJ-like broadcasts. All anyone else needs to listen to your music is a streaming MP3 player, the address you are broadcasting from, and you are now your own radio station.

NiceCast is a very simple-to-use application, with a level of control not found in other, similar applications. You can set the compression level so that those with slower Internet connections are also able to listen.

You will find a fully functional demo of NiceCast on the included CD-ROM. If you enjoy it, please be certain to visit NiceCast online and purchase a copy!

Price: $40.00

www.rogueamoeba.com/nicecast

RockStar   RockStar is a single- or multiperson music game that uses your very own iTunes library in a very new and innovative way. Do you remember the old game show "Name That Tune"? The concept is similar here. RockStar plays clips of your own iTunes music library, and gives you five multiple-choice answers.

The game gives you the choice of game play. You can either guess song title, artist, album, or a mixed bag of all three. During game play, you are presented with five choices, and the goal is to correctly answer in the shortest amount of time possible. During game play, a counter quickly counts down, so that when you make a correct selection, you are awarded the time left on the counter.

Multiplayer games, or "Party Games" as they are called, are a great deal of fun as well. Here, you can have up to five teams, and you rotate teams every five songs. The highest-scoring team wins. As the title suggests, this is a fun party game.

Price: $9.00

freshsqueeze.com/products/rockstar

Name That iTune! Very similar to RockStar, it is a game that starts playing random music from your iTunes software. Your skill at answering the questions correctly, in a given time frame, reflects a good score. The questions range from naming the artists or song title. You are presented with four choices, and the longer it takes you to answer correctly, the lower your points. Not quite as much fun or polished as RockStar, but the price is better.

Price: Free!

homepage.mac.com/jonn8/as/

RadioLover With RadioLover, you can record Internet-streaming audio as separate tracks, including iTunes Radio Tuner stations, and then save them as MP3 files for later listening. It can also record multiple streams at once, and even has a scheduling feature to record when you are away.

This is great software, and a free demo is included on the CD-ROM!

Price: $15.00

www.bitcartel.com

iTunes Publisher Do you have a desire to publish your iTunes song list on a website? Or, do you want a printout of all your music file names? Perhaps you have a database, which you use to store all your song information. If so, iTunes Publisher is the software you have been looking for. With it, you can export in the following formats: HTML, Tabbed Text, QuickTime Streaming Server, M3U, and the general playlist formats in other audio applications, such as WinAMP.

Price: $5.00

www.trancesoftware.com

iTunes Timer This is a fun little AppleScript studio application that calculates the total time iTunes has been playing. It can calculate on playlist, or even your entire iTunes library.

Price: Free!

webpages.charter.net/remsoftware/index.html

iTunes Library Manager With iTunes Library Manager, you are able to make backup copies of your iTunes library and preferences. Why do you need this? If you have given your music ratings, and you lose all the preferences to iTunes (a bad crash, new version of iTunes, and so on), you have to manually go back in and change them again. Also, if you imported music in which you had to manually name the songs, album, artist, and so on, you must reenter all that information again if you changed computers. With iTunes Library Manager, this is no longer a problem.

Price: $5.00

www.malcolmadams.com/itunes/index.php

iTunes Alarm   Do you want to use your iTunes as an alarm clock? iTunes Alarm does just that by specifying a time for iTunes to play, at what volume, and even what song. This makes a great alarm clock. Simply put your Mac next to your bed, and you can wake up to the sweet sound of music or any other audio file in your iTunes library.

Price: Free!

www.johnnarun.com

iTunesCool   As you know from reading this book, you can import album artwork into iTunes. This is a tool for doing just that, without the need to copy and paste yourself. You can select multiple songs to update the artwork, as well. iTunesCool also can export artwork, delete artwork, and export iTunes library to HTML. This is a handy time-saver.

Price: $6.00

www.sandme.info

iEatBrainz   iEatBrainz is a handy, though not foolproof, method of correcting missing information tags from your MP3s. If, for some reason, a song is listed correctly, but the artist is not, this program attempts to repair it for you by using the MusicBrainz.org database.

Price: Free

homepage.mac.com/jbtule/software.html

Synergy   This is a very small application that puts three button controls on your menu bar, Previous Track, Next Track, and Play/Pause, that control iTunes. This way, whenever you need or want to either replay a song, skip to the next one, or just stop the music for a moment, you no longer have to either visit the Dock or bring iTunes to the forefront.

What's more, it also displays in various ways what is playing in iTunes. It can display floating transparent windows that show the song, album, artist, ratings, and even album art—which are all customizable! You can even set Hot Keys for systemwide control of iTunes. Even better, Synergy actually downloads album art for you. The price is cheap for everything this program does.

Price: 5 Euros

wincent.com

Track Manager   Track Manager exposes the ability to rate the playing track or copy it to other playlists without having to bring iTunes to the front and dig through the full-sized window. For convenience, most of the fundamental features of the mini iTunes window (track name, play, and volume controls) are reproduced.

Price: $10.00

www.sentientfood.com

iTunesRating   iTunesRating is a simple utility that displays the rating of the song currently playing on iTunes. It also lets you change or edit the rating with a simple click.

Price: Free!

homepage.mac.com/mhandley/

iTunesBrushKiller   Some people really dislike the brushed metal look of iTunes. Enter iTunesBrushKiller. This application keeps the metallic look, but does away with the brushed metal look.

Price: Free!

sveinbjorn.vefsyn.is/software

iTunes Screensaver Add-ons   As you know, iTunes sports a great visualizer. Sort of a screensaver, people love to watch the visualizer in action. But you don't have to be limited to the cool effects that ship free with iTunes! Many other third-party visualization animations are available for iTunes. Here are a few we have included on the CD-ROM.

Fountain Music   This animation has particles exploding to the beat of the music. You can control gravity, particle size, edges, and more—very neat!

Price: Free!

www.binaryminded.com

WhiteCap   One of the oldest, and coolest visualization plug-ins for iTunes (and other MP3 players), WhiteCap produces more than 190 effects. Truly stunning to watch, you get hours of enjoyment watching the engaging displays. It can also respond to line-in audio sources.

Price: Free!

soundspectrum.com

G-Force   G-Force features fast, antialiased effects, millions of possible effect combinations, savable and scriptable effects, video file export capabilities, and unparalleled expandability. G-Force is designed to entertain you on its own, but it can be customized and extended in many ways.

Price: $10.00

soundspectrum.com

vTunes   vTunes is a simple OpenGL iTunes visual plug-in.

Price: Free!

lorenb.com/

LED Spectrum Analyser   This visualizer displays a hi-fi style electronic display.

Price: Free!

www.maczoop.com

Using an iPod with a Home Stereo or Car Stereo

Louis L'Amour once wrote "Nobody got anywhere in the world by simply being content" and that holds true for iPod users. Why should you be content to simply listen to your iPod wearing a pair of headphones?

Do you remember how long it took you to transfer all your CDs to your computer? Too long I am sure. In fact, if your CD collection is even half the size mine is, it was a multiple day process. Feed a CD in, wait for the computer to rip each song as an MP3, eject the CD, and insert another…Lather, rinse, and repeat ad nauseam. But now that is done, so you can put aside those CDs and treat them as simple storage devices that hold your music on the off chance you will need to rerip them again someday.

"Wait, wait!" I hear you cry, "We still listen to our CDs in the car, and on our home entertainment system (where the good speakers are!)" To that, I say, "Why?"

Why are you content to lug around CDs in your car, or flip them in and out of your home CD player? Why not simply use your iPod, which holds all your music, and put those CDs in their proper place? (Storage.)

Your iPod is your entire CD collection, as well as any music you purchased online from the iTunes Music Store, and all it needs to play nice with either your car stereo or home entertainment system are a few accessories. Then, you have the convenience of having all your music with you wherever you're at.

This chapter looks at different methods of how to get your iPod to work in your car or truck stereo, as well as in your home audio system. From wired to wireless technology, there are many different ways to get the iPod to work with your other audio equipment.

On the Go! iPod in Your Car

The iPod and iPod Mini are more than storage for your music: It is all ready to accompany you in your car, and with a little planning, you don't even have to touch it.

As with any other distraction a driver has to deal with while on the road, you need to minimize how much you need to touch your iPod. Although no solution listed here is completely hands free, many will help you manage your iPod better while in your vehicle.

You need either one of two things to get your iPod to work in your car; a wireless FM transmitter or an audio-in jack in your car stereo. They both have their own merits, and the following sections look at the two apporaches.

tip

Driving and operating your iPod do not go hand in hand, so as a good driving tip, avoid actually manipulating your iPod while driving. If you have to change songs or playlist, please do us other drivers the courtesy and park first.

On the Go! FM Wireless Transmitter

This is an external device that plugs into either your iPod dock connector or headphone jack. In essence, the unit broadcasts the music playing on your iPod on an FM radio frequency, and you simply tune your radio to that frequency to listen. As an example, suppose you are using an FM transmitter that broadcasts on 88.7MHz. To listen to your music, you would set your car stereo to 88.7.

Some FM transmitters allow you to set the radio frequency manually. This is great, as there is the possibility that a radio station could be broadcasting on the frequency that your FM transmitter uses. Bad news, though, because your car stereo locks onto the most powerful signal, meaning you either do not hear the music from your iPod, or you get "bleed" from both sources. Bleed means you hear both signals, causing you a massive headache! Ever try listening to two songs at once? It is not fun.

FIGURE 8.1

A typical example of an FM wireless transmitter.

With your FM transmitter, your iPod is in essence a very tiny radio station, and you are the DJ. The range of the transmission is not great, so you do not have to worry about other cars and trucks picking up your music. Nothing would be more embarrassing than the guy in the SUV behind you knowing you keep playing the same song over and over again!

Be aware also that not all FM transmitters perform the same in every way. Back when Belkin first released its TuneCast Mobile FM transmitter, it worked great in my wife's Ford Taurus, but was worthless in my Pontiac Grand Prix. Why? Well, I don't think the fault was with the TuneCast itself, but rather the antennas or radios in the cars. My wife's Ford's original radio was able to pick up many more stations, and in better clarity, than the aftermarket radio in my Pontiac. Perhaps the difference was in the antenna, though on both vehicles they are located on the rear fender. Either way, keep in mind that an FM transmitter does not work the same on all vehicles, so be certain that you are able to return the unit if it does not work in your car.

Another potential downfall to an FM transmitter is that the sound quality, at best, has about the same clarity as a local FM radio station. This is not CD-quality sound, and some audio aficionados want the highest possible sound quality—but you will not get that here.

On the plus side, some FM transmitters actually charge your iPod's battery while in use! Try that with a pair of headphones. This is great if your car trip is long, and the battery in your iPod only lasts four to six hours before needing a charge.

Another benefit is you can transfer the FM transmitter from one vehicle to another with little, if any, trouble. I own a truck in addition to my Pontiac for when I need to move something large. The stereo in the truck is horrible—no CD player! And only two tiny in-dash speakers. But with an FM transmitter and my iPod, I can at least listen to what I want when I want. It made driving the old truck less of a pain.

On the Go! Direct Connection

Not everyone either wants or can use an FM transmitter. Perhaps, like in my own car, the FM transmitter doesn't work correctly. Or, you want a better quality sound. Either way, directly connecting your iPod to your car is the second choice for taking your iPod with you! In either of the direct connect models, wires are the key. Yes, I know you hate wires. Everyone hates wires. Wires have invaded our lives like never before. But wires are the only way to directly connect your iPod to your car stereo if you are not doing so wirelessly.

The Cassette Adapter

The first option is to use a cassette player adapter (see Figure 8.2). These faux cassette tapes slide into your car cassette deck with a wire trailing out. At the end of this wire is a mini-jack plug, which you plug into the headphone jack of your iPod.

FIGURE 8.2

Using a cassette adapter enables you to play your iPod through your stereo.

These have been around since the portable CD player was first introduced, and can be found everywhere. In fact, I even found one at a local gas station for under five dollars! I don't know how well it worked, but to simply find one so cheap in a gas station of all places should tell you how prevalent these are.

They work fine, though don't expect the highest quality audio if you go this route. It is, by far, the cheapest way to get your iPod to work in your car if you have a cassette player. Most quality units run less than $20, so you have very little invested in it if you don't like the sound quality or the wires.

The Adapter Cable Method

To directly connect your iPod to the input jacks on your car stereo, you need an adapter plug that converts the mini headphone jack to a two-prong RCA jack (see Figure 8.3). This allows your iPod to play through the AUX setting on your car stereo. This setup gives you the best sound quality—with no loss of fidelity than if you plugged a pair of speakers into your iPod.

FIGURE 8.3

Adapter cables provide a high-quality connection between your iPod and your stereo.

This only works if your car stereo supports RCA input cables, which many factory stereos do not. If you have an aftermarket car stereo, you should have RCA inputs. Consult an expert if you are uncertain.

Because it is usually necessary to take apart your entire dashboard to get to the back of your car stereo, it is best to have a professional install the cable for you. Be certain to tell him where you

tip

If you are unsure if your aftermarket car stereo has input jacks, take it into a local car stereo shop and they will tell you.

note

Computers and iPods have ports— FireWire port, USB port, and so on. Audio components, such as a CD player, have jacks. What's the difference? A jack is usually one-way communication; a port is two-way communication.

tip

If you use the headphone jack to connect your iPod to your home or car audio system, remember that the volume control can be adjusted from both the audio amplifier and the iPod.

want the iPod side plug to be, with as much slack in the cable as you need to reach wherever your iPod will be located while in the car.

If you have a boom car, and we all know what those are, chances are you also have an amplifier or crossover in your car as well. Some amplifiers also sport RCA input jacks, so you could connect your iPod directly to your amplifier, thus bypassing your in-dash stereo all together. If your amplifier is in your trunk, you need a very long cable to reach the iPod. The longer a cable, the better the chance of a decrease in sound quality, so keep that in mind.

The price of a mini plug jack to an RCA jack is less than $20 for most brands. Monster Cable (www.monstercable.com) has a higher-quality product called Monster Cable for iPod, which will run you around $30, but they are 24k gold plated. Yes, gold! Does it sound better? Depends on who you ask, but I like the fact that my iPod is so cool that someone makes gold-plated cables for it!

iPod in Your Home

Connecting an iPod to your home theater system is very simple. On the back of almost any home theater amplifier are RCA input jacks. These are red and white, which are color-coded for left- and right-side inputs. If you are connecting a CD player, for instance, you connect it to your RCA jacks named "CD Player In" or a similar naming convention.

No "iPod In" jack exists on the back of your amplifier, however, so you need to use either an AUX IN jack, or any free RCA input. It does not matter if the jack is for tape or CD, they only refer to what setting you need to make on your amplifier to listen to the music or sound input coming through that jack.

The same cable you use to directly connect your iPod to your car stereo, the mini plug jack to RCA jack (such as the Monster Cable for iPod) can also be used to connect your iPod to your home audio system.

Plugging the mini jack into your iPod, and the RCA jack to your home amplifier, are the only steps involved. All you need to do to start enjoying your iPod's music library on your home theater is to set the amplifier to the input setting the iPod is using, such as AUX 1 or CD, adjust your volume, and you are ready to go!

You can also use an FM transmitter to send your iPod's music to your home receiver, but I have found that it is both cheaper to directly connect the iPod with a cable, and the sound quality is much better with a wire, as well. However, if you do decide to go the FM transmitter route, any FM transmitter works as long as it does not require you to plug it into a DC outlet, such as your car's cigarette lighter.

IN THIS CHAPTER

- Use your iPod like it is a $2 watch.

- Keep your appointments by placing calendar events on your iPod's calendar.

- Take your contact information with you wherever you go.

- Store text gems on your iPod so you can read them at your leisure.

Using the iPod's Calendar, Contact Manager, and Other Non-Music Tools

The iPod is all about music, but it also can do a number of other useful things that might not be obvious to you. These "other things" include providing an alarm clock, displaying a calendar, showing contact information, displaying text notes, and even playing games. Although none of these features alone would make the iPod great, they are nice extras, which is, I suppose, why they are located on the Extras menu.

Keeping Track of Time with the iPod Clock

You can use your iPod to keep track of time and as a basic, but perfectly functional, alarm clock. This is handy when you travel because you don't need to carry a separate clock with you. Or, if you are like me and don't wear a watch, an iPod can help you keep track of time.

Configuring the Time on an iPod

Before you use the iPod as a clock, you need to configure its time and date. Use the following steps to do this:

1. Choose **Main menu**, **Extras**, **Clock**, **Date & Time**. You'll see the Date & Time menu (see Figure 9.1).

FIGURE 9.1

You use the iPod's Date & Time menu to configure your iPod's clock.

2. Choose **Set Time Zone**. You'll see the Time Zone menu.

3. Scroll on the list of time zones until you see the time zone you are in.

4. Highlight your time zone and press the **Select button**. The iPod's time zone will be set to the one you selected, and you will return to the Date & Time menu.

5. Choose **Set Date & Time**. You'll see the Date & Time menu again, except that this time it will be in the set date and time mode (see Figure 9.2). The hour will be highlighted.

FIGURE 9.2

You use this screen to set the time and date on your iPod.

6. Use the **Click Wheel** to increase or decrease the hour until the correct hour is displayed.

7. Press the **Fast-forward button** so that the minute display is highlighted.

8. Use the **Click Wheel** to increase or decrease the hour until the correct minute is displayed.

9. Press the **Fast-forward button** so that the AM/PM indicator display is highlighted.

10. Use the **Click Wheel** to change AM/PM setting if necessary.

11. Continue using the **Fast-forward button** and **Click Wheel** to set the correct date, month, and year.

> **tip**
>
> You can press the Select button instead of the Fast-forward button to set the current value and move to the next field.

12. Press the **Select button**. The date and time you selected will be set, and you will return to the Date & Time menu.

13. Highlight the **Time** setting. The default value is to use a 12-hour clock.

14. To use a 24-hour clock, press the **Select button**. The Time setting will become 24-hour, and a 24-hour clock will be used.

15. To display the time in the menu title area, highlight **Time in Title** and press the **Select button**. The Time in Title setting will become On, and the time will be displayed in the title bar—instead of the menu title (see Figure 9.3).

FIGURE 9.3

Placing the time in the title bar makes using an iPod as a clock much more convenient.

16. Press the **Menu button** to return to the Clock menu.

Displaying the Time on an iPod

There are a couple of ways to display the time and date on an iPod:

- Choose **Main menu**, **Extras**, **Clock**. You'll see the Clock display (see Figure 9.4). In the title area, you'll see the current date. Just below the title, you'll see the current time.

- If you turn the Time in Title setting to On (as described in step 15 in the previous list of steps), the time will be displayed in the title area of every screen a second or two after you move to a new screen. When you first move to a screen, you will see the title, but after that small amount of time passes, the title will be replaced by the current time.

tip

For faster access to the Clock display, add the Clock command to the Main menu. See "Setting Up Your Main Menu Preferences" on page **86**.

FIGURE 9.4
Who says an iPod can't do everything that a $2 watch can do?

Setting and Controlling an Alarm

You can also use the iPod's alarm clock to wake you up or remind you of an important time. To set an alarm, perform the following steps:

1. Choose **Main menu**, **Extras**, **Clock**, **Alarm Clock**. You'll see the Alarm Clock screen (see Figure 9.5). By default, the alarm is turned off, which is indicated by the Off setting.

note

The Sleep Timer feature of the iPod clock is explained in "Setting the Sleep Timer" on page 88.

FIGURE 9.5
You use this screen to set your iPod's alarm.

2. Highlight **Alarm** and press the **Select button**. The Alarm setting will become On, and the alarm will be active. The time at which the alarm is currently set to go off is shown next to the Time option on the Alarm Clock menu.

3. Highlight **Time** and press the **Select button**. You'll see the set alarm time screen.

tip

Even though you set the alarm by the minute, you can get to any time quickly by rapidly dragging around the Scroll pad or Click Wheel in full circles.

4. Use the **Scroll pad** or **Click Wheel** to choose the
   time you want the alarm to sound. Drag clockwise
   to increase the time or counterclockwise to
   decrease it.

5. When the correct alarm time is set, press the **Select
   button**. You'll return to the Alarm Clock menu.

6. Highlight **Sound**. By default, the alarm sound setting will be Beep, which you can hear even if you
   don't have earphones or speakers connected to the
   iPod. If you choose a different sound, you have to
   have speakers or headphones attached to the iPod to
   hear the alarm.

note

You can't set the iPod's alarm for more than 24 hours from the current time, which is just like a typical bedside clock.

7. If you want to have a playlist start playing instead, press the **Select button**.
   You'll see a list of playlists on your iPod.

8. Highlight the playlist you want to use as the alarm sound and press the
   Select button. You'll return to the Alarm Clock menu, and the name of the
   selected list will be shown as the Sound setting.

9. Press the **Menu button**. You'll return to the Clock display. A bell icon will
   appear on the right side of the time to indicate that the alarm is set.

When the appointed time comes along, your iPod will turn on and play the beep
sound or the selected playlist. Unless you are an incredibly light sleeper, don't expect
the Beep sound to wake you up. It isn't very loud, and it doesn't play very long.
You'll have better luck if you connect your iPod to speakers and use a playlist
instead.

Planning Your Days with the iPod Calendar

You can use an iPod to display a calendar, and you can add events on a calendar
application, such as Outlook or iCal, to the iPod calendar so that you can view those
events. The iPod's calendar isn't designed as a replacement for a PDA or other full-
featured calendar. Its purpose is only to enable you to view your calendar. For example, you can't add or delete events from the iPod calendar without using a computer.

Setting Up Your iPod Calendar

To start using your calendar, you need to add information to it. Because of space
limitations, I have included coverage of the most popular calendar applications on
each platform. You can use similar steps to add calendar information from other
applications to an iPod. The iPod's Calendar feature is quite limited, but even so, it
can be useful.

Moving Calendar Information from Outlook to an iPod (Windows)

To move calendar events from Outlook to your iPod, perform the following steps:

1. Open your Outlook calendar.

2. Select an event you want to move to your iPod calendar.

3. Choose **File**, **Save As**.

4. In the resulting Save As dialog box, move to the folder in which you want to store the events, choose **iCalendar Format** or **vCalendar Format** on the **Save as type** drop-down list, and click **Save**. The event will be exported from Outlook in the format you selected.

5. Repeat steps 2 through 4 until you have saved all the events you want to move onto your iPod. Unfortunately, repeating events are not moved. You have to move each event individually.

6. Connect your iPod to your computer. For this process to work, your iPod must be configured so it can be used as a hard disk. See Chapter 10, "Taking the iPod Further," for details.

7. Open the folder in which you saved the events you exported in step 4.

8. Open the **My Computer** folder in another window and then open the **iPod** so that you see the folders it contains (see Figure 9.6).

FIGURE 9.6

To add calendar events to your iPod, place them in the Calendars folder.

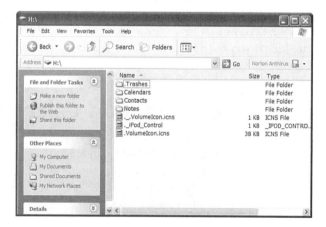

9. Drag the calendar events from the folder you opened in step 7 and place them in the **Calendars** folder on the iPod. When you do this, the events will be added to your iPod's calendar.

Moving Calendar Information to an iPod Using iSync and iCal (Mac)

Synchronizing your iCal calendar on your iPod is very straightforward, and you can even configure this to happen each time you connect your iPod to your Mac. Follow these steps:

1. Connect your iPod to your Mac and open the **iSync** application.

2. If you have never used iSync to synchronize your iPod before, choose **Devices**, **Add Device**.

3. Click the **Scan button**. You will see the iPod at the top of the iSync window.

4. Double-click the **iPod's icon**, and the iSync options dialog box will appear (see Figure 9.7).

FIGURE 9.7

You can configure iSync to automatically move all your iCal events and Address Book contacts to your iPod.

5. Check the **Turn on *ipodname* synchronization** check box, where *ipodname* is the name of your iPod.

6. Check the **Automatically synchronize when iPod is connected** check box.

7. Check the **Contacts** check box and choose the specific contacts you want to move to your iPod on the **Synchronize** menu. For example, to have all your contacts synchronized, choose **All contacts**. If you want only a specific group of contacts to be moved, select that group instead.

8. Check the **Calendars** check box and choose the calendars you want to be moved to your iPod. Choose all your calendars by clicking the **All** radio button or choose specific calendars by clicking the **Selected** radio button and then checking the check box next to each calendar you want to place on your iPod.

9. Click the **Sync Now** button. The information you selected will be moved onto your iPod.

You only need to do these steps the first time you synch your iPod with iCal and your Address Book. If you configure automatic synchronization, this information will be updated each time you connect your iPod to your Mac.

Viewing Your iPod Calendar

To view your iPod calendar, do the following steps:

1. Choose **Main menu**, **Extras**, **Calendar**. You'll see the Calendar menu (see Figure 9.8).

FIGURE 9.8

Choose a calendar to view it.

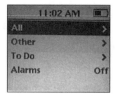

2. Highlight the calendar you want to view and press the **Select button**. If you want to see all the calendar events, choose **All**. You'll see the Calendar display (see Figure 9.9). The current date is highlighted. Dates with one or more events scheduled are marked with a black box.

Date with event

FIGURE 9.9

Dates with an event are marked with a black box in the lower-right corner of the date box.

3. To get details for an event, use the **Click Wheel** to move to the date in which you are interested. As you move away from the current date, its box will take on a lighter shade and the currently selected date will be highlighted in the darker shade.

4. When the date in which you are interested is highlighted, press the **Select button**. The events for that date will be listed.

5. To see the detailed information for an event, highlight it and press the **Select button**. You'll see the detailed information for that event (see Figure 9.10).

FIGURE 9.10

Here, I am viewing the detail for an event on my iPod's calendar.

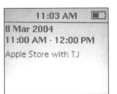

6. Use the **Menu button** to move back to the list of events or back to the calendar.

The iPod calendar also picks up event alarms for the events you place on it. To configure the event alarm, open the **Calendars** menu and scroll until you see the **Alarms** option. Set this to **Beep** to hear the beep sound for an event alarm, **Silent** to see a silent alarm, or **Off** to turn the event alarm off.

To delete an event from your iPod, remove the event file from the Calendars folder on the iPod if you are using a file-based method (such as with Outlook). If you are using iCal, just remove the event from the iCal calendar and synchronize.

> **tip**
>
> If you are looking at an event several months prior to or after the current date, the easiest way to get back to the current date is to use the Menu button to move up to the Calendars menu again and then select the calendar.

Using an iPod to Keep an Address Book

The iPod's Contact Manager is analogous to the calendar, except that it is probably more useful because you mostly just refer to contact information rather than needing to manage it as you typically do with a calendar. Storing contacts on an iPod makes accessing phone numbers, email addresses, and other information fast and easy.

Configuring Your iPod Contacts

As with the calendar, the first step you need to do is to move contact information from your computer to the iPod. You can do this manually if you use a Windows computer or automatically if you use a Mac. After that, you can configure how contact information is displayed on your iPod.

Moving Contact Information from Outlook to an iPod (Windows)

Exporting contacts from Outlook is done with the same steps you use to export calendar information. The one difference is that you choose the vCard file format for contacts. The vCard file format is a standard format used for virtual cards that can be exported from or imported into most contact managers, including Outlook and Address Book.

After you have exported contact information from Outlook, the steps to import those contacts onto your iPod are very similar as well. Instead of using the Calendars folder on the iPod, you place contacts in the Contacts folder.

See "Moving Calendar Information from Outlook to an iPod (Windows)" on page **142** for the detailed steps to export information from Outlook and then import it to the iPod.

Moving Contact Information to an iPod Using iSync and Address Book (Mac)

Use the steps in the section "Moving Calendar Information to an iPod Using iSync and iCal (Mac)" on page **143** to move your contact information onto an iPod.

Configuring How Contacts Appear

When it comes to displaying contact information on an iPod, you have two options. To select an option, choose **Main menu**, **Settings**, **Contacts**. You'll see the Contacts preferences screen. This screen has two options. Use the **Sort** option to choose how contacts are sorted on the screen. Use the **Display** option to determine how contacts are displayed on the screen. In both cases, your choices are First Last, which lists the first name followed by the last name, and Last First, which places the last name first and the first name last.

To select an option, choose the setting and press the **Select button** to toggle the option.

Viewing Your Contacts

To view your contacts, perform the following steps:

1. Choose **Main menu**, **Extras**, **Contacts**. You'll see the list of contacts sorted by your sort preference (see Figure 9.11).

2. To view a contact's detailed information, highlight the contact in which you are interested and press the **Select button**. You'll see a screen showing all the information for that contact (see Figure 9.12).

tip

To remove a contact from your iPod, remove the contact's vCard file from the Contacts folder on the iPod's hard drive. Or, remove the contact from the Address Book application and synchronize.

FIGURE 9.11

This screen displays a list of contacts stored on your iPod.

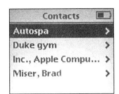

FIGURE 9.12

The 555 prefix should always tip you off to a bogus phone number.

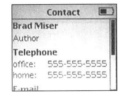

3. Scroll down the screen to see all the information for the contact.

Using the iPod to Store and Display Text

You can also store and display text files on your iPod. For example, you might want to store instructions to perform a task that you have trouble remembering how to do or the directions to a location on your iPod for easy reference.

Creating Notes for an iPod

To create a note on an iPod, use any word processor or other application that can create a text file (filename extension should be .txt). Create the text you want to store on the iPod and save it as a TXT file.

Moving Notes to an iPod

Connect your iPod to your computer and place the text file you created in the **Notes** folder on the iPod's hard drive. (To do this, you need to configure your iPod so it can be used as a hard drive.)

Reading Notes on an iPod

After you have placed text files in the Notes folder, you can read them by choosing **Main menu**, **Extras**, **Notes**. You'll see the Notes screen, which contains a list of all the text files in the Notes folder on your iPod. To read a note, highlight it and press the **Select button**. You'll see the note's text on the screen (see Figure 9.13). Scroll down the screen to read all of the text if you need to.

FIGURE 9.13

Hopefully, you'll put your iPod's Notes feature to better use than I did.

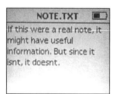

NOTE.TXT

If this were a real note, it might have useful information. But since it isnt, it doesnt.

note

In case you are wondering, there isn't a typo in the word *isn't* in the figure. The iPod didn't display the apostrophes in this note. I have heard that it does display them fine in some cases.

tip

If you use mapquest.com to generate driving directions, you can download those directions to your iPod so that you can view them there. One of the best tools to use to do this is an application called PodQuest. To learn about this useful tool, visit www.mibasoft.dk/podquest.html.

The Absolute Minimum

Although the features in this chapter aren't a good reason to buy and use an iPod, they are a nice bonus that you can take advantage of without too much work on your part. Check out this list of features:

- You can use your iPod as a clock and even as an alarm clock. This is probably the most useful extra feature, at least in my book (which you happen to be reading right now).

- You can store calendar events on your iPod's calendar to make it a handy way to keep track of where you are supposed to be and when you are supposed to be there.

- Forget carrying around a paper list of contact information; store the names, addresses, email addresses, and phone numbers of people you need to contact on your iPod, and they will be with you whenever your iPod is.

- Although the iPod's screen is too small to make reading long sections of text pleasant, you can store short text notes on your iPod and read them while you are on the move.

- Lest you think these extra features are all work and no play, check out **Main menu**, **Extras**, **Games**. Sure, none of these iPod games will challenge Halo on the Xbox for the Best Game Ever title, but they might help you kill a few minutes of time.

IN THIS CHAPTER

- Maximize your iPod's battery life and durability.
- Update or restore your iPod's software.
- Identify and solve iPod problems.

Maintaining an iPod and Solving Problems

The iPod is a well-designed device, and it is more likely than not that you won't ever have any trouble with it, especially if you practice good battery management and keep its software up to date. In this chapter, you'll learn how to do those two tasks, plus you'll learn how to handle any problems in the unlikely event they do occur.

Maintaining Your iPod's Power

Like any other portable electronic device, your iPod literally lives or dies by its battery. When not connected to a power source, your iPod's battery is the only thing standing between you and a musicless life. Fortunately, working with your iPod's battery isn't very difficult, but it is something you need to keep in mind.

Monitoring and Maximizing Battery Life

The Battery icon in the upper-right corner of the screen gives you a general idea of your battery's status at any point in time.

When your iPod is running on battery power, the amount of shading within the icon provides a relative—and I do mean relative—indication of your battery's current state (see Figure 10.1). As you use battery power, the "filled in" part of the battery will decrease until your iPod runs out of gas. When it does, you'll see an icon of a battery with an exclamation point that indicates your iPod is out of power, and the battery will have to be charged before you can use the iPod again.

> **note**
>
> The iPod's battery is rated for 12 hours while the iPod mini's battery is rated for eight hours. Of course, these ratings are based on ideal conditions, which means that the iPod plays straight through for these periods with no controls being used, no backlighting, and so on. Should you expect to get that much time under actual conditions? Probably not. Later in this section, you'll learn how to test your iPod's battery to make sure it is in good condition.

Battery icon

FIGURE 10.1

Keep an eye on the battery icon to make sure you don't run out of juice while you are on the move.

To maximize your iPod's playing time per battery charge, you can do the following:

- Keep the iPod's software up to date (you'll learn how later in this chapter).
- Use the Hold switch to prevent your iPod from being unintentionally turned on when you carry it around. You'd be amazed how easy it is for the iPod to be turned on and start to play without you knowing it, especially if you carry it in your pocket, backpack, or computer bag. (It's no fun trying to listen to

r

ur
t

tip

When an iPod is turned off, it still uses some power. For example, its internal clock keeps "ticking." And, it takes some power to maintain the iPod's memory. If you don't use your iPod for 14 days or more, you should charge its battery to keep it ready to play.

f,
t

cklighting is very helpful to be able
...............low-light conditions. However, it does use additional power, so you should use it only as needed to maximize battery life. When you don't need it, such as in daylight conditions, turn it off. When you do need it, set it such that it remains on only a few seconds when you press a control.

- Minimize track changes. Each time you change tracks, the iPod uses more power than it would just playing tracks straight through.
- Turn the Equalizer off. The Equalizer uses more power than playing music without it.
- Every 30 recharges or so, fully drain and recharge the battery.
- Keep the iPod at a comfortable temperature. Using the iPod in very cold or very hot conditions lowers its battery life.

Charging an iPod's Battery

Fortunately, there are a number of ways to charge your iPod's battery, including the following:

- Use the included FireWire power adapter.
- Connect the iPod to a six-pin FireWire port either directly with a cable or via a Dock.
- Use a power adapter designed for 12-volt sources, such as the power outlets in your vehicle.

note

You can't charge an iPod using a four-pin FireWire connector.

There are two different ways that the iPod lets you know it is charging.

When your iPod's battery is charging via a FireWire connection to a computer, the Battery icon will include a lightning bolt symbol and will include a filling motion from the left to the right of the icon (see Figure 10.2). When the battery is fully charged, the icon will be completely filled and the motion will stop.

Battery being charged

FIGURE 10.2
This iPod is getting its battery charged via a FireWire cable.

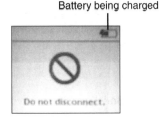

Do not disconnect.

When you charge your iPod's battery through a separate power adapter only, the battery icon fills the iPod's screen and flashes (see Figure 10.3). When the process is complete, the battery icon remains steady.

FIGURE 10.3
This iPod is being charged with the power adapter.

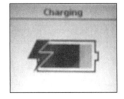

Charging

According to Apple, it takes only an hour to charge a drained iPod mini battery and two hours to charge a drained iPod battery to 80% of its capacity. It takes about four hours to fully charge a drained battery.

Getting More Life Out of an iPod's Battery

The iPod uses a lithium-ion battery. Any battery, including the iPod's, will eventually wear out and no longer provide the power it once did. In my research, most lithium-ion batteries are rated for 300–500 charges. In this context, a charge can't be precisely defined, but it does include a full discharge and then a full recharge. A partial charge doesn't "count" as much, but the precise relationship between amount of charge and how much that charge "counts" can't be specified.

Batteries like that in the iPod actually last longer if you don't let them fully discharge before you recharge them. Frequent "topping off" will not reduce the battery's life and in fact is better for your battery than letting it run very low on power before you recharge it.

Every 30 recharges or so, do run your iPod until it is completely out of power and then perform a full recharge. This will reset the battery's power gauge, which tends to get more inaccurate if the battery is never fully discharged.

note

The fact that the iPod's battery will eventually wear out is nothing unique to the iPod. All batteries die eventually and must be replaced. However, some early iPods (the Original iPod) did have major battery problems that have left the iPod a now-undeserved reputation for having defective batteries.

It doesn't hurt the battery to do frequent and short recharges, such as by placing the iPod in a Dock every day after you are done using it.

However, you should make sure to run the iPod on battery power for significant periods of time. If you constantly run the iPod from the power adapter or while it is in the Dock connected to a power source, the iPod's battery's performance will degrade.

Solving Battery Problems

Frankly, your iPod's battery will eventually wear out. Fortunately, this won't happen until you have used the iPod for many, many hours and have recharged it hundreds of times. You'll know when the end of its useful life is approaching because the time it can play on battery power will become shorter and shorter.

Testing Your iPod's Battery

If your iPod doesn't seem to play for a reasonable amount of time, you should test it to get an
idea of what its current battery life is. Test your iPod by performing the following steps:

1. Fully charge your iPod.

2. Remove the iPod from the charger so that it is running on battery power.

3. Make a note of the current time.

caution

Because fully discharging and then recharging an iPod's battery causes wear on it, you shouldn't do this test frequently. Only do it if you suspect that your iPod's battery is having problems.

4. Use the **Settings** commands to turn off the **Equalizer** and **Backlight**.

5. Set **Repeat** to **One**.

6. Select an album or playlist and play it.

7. Let the iPod play until it runs out of power. While the iPod is playing, don't use any of its controls. Anytime you cause the iPod to perform an action, you cause it to use additional power. In this test, you are attempting to determine what its maximum life is so you can compare it to the rated life.

8. When the iPod stops playing and the low power icon appears in the display, make a note of the time.

9. Calculate the battery life by figuring out how much time passed since you started the iPod playing (compare the time you noted in step 8 with what you noted in step 3).

If your iPod mini plays for four hours or longer or your iPod plays for six hours or longer on a full charge, Apple considers that its battery life is acceptable. If the iPod won't play for more than four hours, it likely has a problem and needs to be replaced.

Getting Help from Apple for iPod Battery Problems

If your iPod doesn't play for the expected time, the battery probably needs to be replaced. If the iPod is still under warranty (one year without the AppleCare Protection Plan or two years with it), Apple will replace the battery for free. If the iPod is not under warranty, Apple will replace the battery for you (currently this costs $99 plus $6.95 shipping). To get more information and start this process, go to www.apple.com/support/ipod/power/ and click the **iPod battery service request form** link.

If you are comfortable working with electronic devices yourself, you can replace the iPod's battery on your own. How to do this is beyond the scope of this book, but you can purchase a battery and get help on the

note

Batteries are manufactured items, which means they aren't always made just right. You should test your new iPod's battery life to make sure yours is performing up to snuff prior to the warranty expiring.

Keep in mind that battery life is dependent on many factors, such as temperature, what features are being used, and so on. The guidelines are pretty loose because the conditions under which an iPod is used are so variable.

caution

According to Apple, your iPod will be replaced with an equivalent model rather than just the battery being replaced. Make sure you have all the data you need off your iPod before you send it in for service.

Web at places such as www.ipodbattery.com and www.ipodresq.com. Replacement batteries cost from $60 to $80, including tools and instructions. Although being a bit more expensive, sending the unit back to Apple is probably a better way to go in most situations. (Who knows, if you have an old iPod, you might get a better unit back in return!)

Updating or Restoring an iPod's Software

Apple is continually improving the iPod's software to add features, make it even more stable, and so on. You should periodically check for new iPod software and, when you find it, install it on your iPod—this is called *updating* the iPod's software.

When you are having major problems with your iPod or just want to completely reformat it, you can also *restore* its software to return it to factory settings.

tip

To see the current version of iPod software installed on your iPod, choose **Main menu**, **Settings**, **About**. On the About screen, you will see the version of iPod software you are currently using next to the Version label.

You do both of these tasks in the same way, as the following steps show:

1. Open a Web browser and move to www.apple.com/support/ipod/. You'll see the iPod Support page (see Figure 10.4).

FIGURE 10.4

Apple's iPod Support page provides access to the latest iPod software.

2. Locate and click the link for the latest iPod or iPod mini software for your computer's OS, such as Mac OS X or Windows XP. You'll move to the iPod Software Update page.

3. Complete the **form**, click the **radio button** for your OS, and click **Download Update**. The update will be downloaded to your computer. Notice the name of the application you download and where you store it on your computer.

4. Launch the **iPod Update application**—in some cases, it will run automatically after you download it. On the Mac, you'll see the iPod Software Updater application (see Figure 10.5). On Windows PCs, you will have to restart your computer after running the Setup application. Then, choose **Start menu**, **iPod**, **System Software**, **Updater**. You'll then see the Updater application for Windows.

tip

If you use Mac OS X, you don't need to do this process because the Software Update feature will notify you when new iPod software is available, and then you can use the Software Update application to download and install it.

note

If your iPod's software is the most current version, you'll see "(up to date)" next to the Software Version text in the iPod Updater window, and the Update button will be disabled.

FIGURE 10.5

You use the Updater application to update your iPod's software or to restore it to original condition.

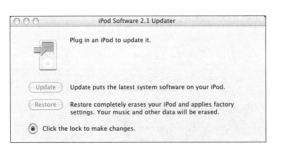

5. Connect the iPod you want to update or restore to your computer.

6. If you want to install the latest version of the iPod software on your iPod, click the **Update** button. If you want to restore your iPod, click **Restore** instead.

7. Follow the onscreen instructions to complete the update or restore process.

After you have updated your iPod, you can continue using it as you did before the update.

If you restored your iPod, you will have to perform an update from iTunes to load your music back onto it. You'll also have to replace any calendar or contact information you want to store on it.

Identifying and Solving iPod Problems

Okay, I admit it. The iPod isn't perfect. Once in a while, it might not act the way you expect it to. Hey, no one or no technology is perfect after all. In this section, you'll read some information that will help you in the event you do experience problems.

> **caution**
>
> When you restore an iPod, all of its data is erased, including its music, calendar data, contacts, and so on. If you have stored files on the iPod that aren't stored elsewhere too, make sure you copy the files you want to save from the iPod to another location before you restore it.

Solving iPod Problems

Troubleshooting iPod problems isn't all that different from troubleshooting other kinds of problems. First, observe exactly what is happening. Determine what you are doing and how the iPod is responding or not responding, as the case may be. Then, use the information in the following sections to see if you can solve the problem yourself.

Checking the Basics

We all do things that can be classified as dumb once in a while. And using the iPod can result in a few of these events, so use the following list to make sure you haven't done anything to shoot yourself in the foot:

- If the iPod won't respond to any controls, make sure the Hold switch isn't active. The Hold switch does just what it is supposed to—it prevents the iPod's controls from doing anything. It can be rather embarrassing to panic that your precious iPod has suffered a major failure only to realize that the Hold switch is on. (Of course you understand that this has never happened to me.)

- If the iPod won't turn on, connect it to the power adapter or to a computer using a six-pin FireWire connection. It might simply be that the battery is out of power. Remember that the iPod uses some battery power even when you aren't using it, and after 14 days or so, it might not have enough battery power to wake up. Sometimes the empty battery icon will appear when you try to turn on a fully discharged iPod and sometimes it won't.

- Try connecting the iPod to a computer. If it mounts, you probably just need to do a minor reset to get it to work again.

Resetting an iPod

If you can't get an iPod to do anything (and you've checked the Hold switch) or if it is behaving badly, try resetting it. When you reset an iPod, its temporary memory is cleared, but your data won't be affected. Follow these steps:

1. Connect the iPod to the power adapter using the FireWire cable and then plug the power adapter into a wall outlet or connect your iPod to your computer using a six-pin FireWire connector.

2. Move the **Hold switch** to the On position and then slide it to the Off position again.

3. Press and hold both the **Menu** and **Select buttons** down for about five seconds until you see the Apple logo on the iPod's screen. This indicates that the reset process is complete.

4. Try to use the iPod to do what you were trying to do when you noticed a problem.

If resetting your iPod solves your problem, you are home free. If not, you might want to try restoring it.

Restoring an iPod

As you read earlier, you can also use the iPod Software Update application to restore an iPod. When you restore an iPod, its hard drive is erased and a clean version of its software is installed. The purpose is to configure the iPod with factory settings that will likely solve many problems you are having.

For the steps to perform a restore, see "Updating or Restoring an iPod's Software" on page **157**.

Getting Help with iPod Problems

Although I could have added a lot more pages to this book with specific problems you might encounter and potential solutions to those

caution

If your iPod is mounted on your computer (check on the desktop or in iTunes), eject it before you reset it to prevent any damage to its data.

note

The buttons to reset an older iPod are slightly different; press the Play/Pause and Menu buttons in Step 3.

caution

Restoring an iPod also deletes any data that you have stored on its hard drive, so make sure you have any data that is unique to the iPod backed up before you restore it. You don't have to worry about its music because that will be replaced the next time you connect it to your computer to perform an update from iTunes (assuming all the iPod's music is stored in your iTunes Library of course).

problems, that would have been kind of wasteful for two main reasons. One, it is likely you won't ever experience the problems I would include. Two, Apple maintains an extensive iPod Web site from which you get detailed information about iPod problems. You can use this information to solve specific problems you encounter (that aren't solved with the information in the previous sections, such as a reset).

To access this help, use a Web browser to move to www.apple.com/support/ipod. On this page, you can search for help, read FAQs, and get other information that will help you solve iPod problems (see Figure 10.6).

tip

Feel free to write to me with questions about your iPod or to ask for help with problems you are having with your iPod. You can reach me at

bradmacosx@mac.com.

There are a number of other Web sites that might be helpful to you as well. These include www.ipodlounge.com and www.ipodhacks.com. You can also use www.google.com to search for other iPod information; you'll find no shortage of it.

FIGURE 10.6

Need iPod help? You got it.

Hacking the iPod

FIGURE 10.7

Original iPod,
Third
Generation iPod,
iPod Mini.

The term "hacking" is now used many times in negative connotations. The reality is that hacking is simply a means of either understanding how something works, using reverse engineering, or making something work differently than its intended use.

Replacing Your iPod Battery

When, not if, your iPod no longer accepts a charge, it is time to replace your battery. The battery in your iPod is similar to many cell phone batteries. There are different batteries in the first two-generation iPods than the third, and the iPod Mini is a different model all together. So, what do you do when your iPod decides it wants a new battery? Besides shipping it off to Apple, which will set you back up to $100, your only other option is to replace the battery yourself.

> # caution
>
> Danger!
>
> Be aware that hacks could void your iPod's warranty. In other words, if you damage your iPod performing a hack, you are out of luck. Apple Computer, Inc. will not help you fix it, or if they do, the cost for the repairs will come out of your pocket. As a general rule, before hacking anything, I always ask myself a simple question: Can I afford to buy a new one if I make a mistake? If the answer is no, simply enjoy your iPod as it was intended. Otherwise, hack away!

Unfortunately, replacing the iPod battery is not as simple as your cell phone. If you take a close look at your iPod, you notice that there are no screws, latches, or indentations that give you a clue on how they put the iPod together, or how you can take it apart. But fear not, we have the answers for you!

Battery Replacement—First and Second Generation iPod

The first two generations of iPods uses a 3.7 Volts 1200 mAh battery. What does that mean? You don't really care, do you? You just want your iPod to work again. So let's skip the electrical class and go right to the point. Order the 3.7 Volt 1200 mAh batteries. Expect to pay around $30 for one.

FIGURE 10.8

Tools Required   The only tools you need are a small, hard plastic wedge tool. Think of it as the end of a regular flathead screwdriver, but it is plastic and not metal. Yes, you can use a regular flathead screwdriver, but you take an awful risk of scratching your iPod with the metal on metal contact. One of the nice things about an iPod is how cool it looks, so why take a chance of ruining its look?

Look around online before buying the iPod battery. Many times, the company selling you the battery will include an iPod battery tool with the sale. If not, you will want to purchase one. I have seen them for as low as six dollars online. However, any hard plastic (or nylon) sharp-edged wedge tool will work.

Begin by using the wedge tool to carefully pry the case apart, starting at the top. The case is in two parts; the back metal and the front plastic. As the gap widens, work your way down the side of the iPod, and you will find case clips hidden inside the iPod. Use your tool to unclip each case clip as you find them.

After you have one side completely unclipped, you can easily swing the back metal cover off the iPod.

The old battery is actually glued in place. You can use your tool, if it is sturdy enough, to pry the battery free. Be aware, however, that the battery is connected to the iPod by small wires and a connector. Take great care not to break these.

The final task is to unclip the battery wires from the iPod itself. After this is done, install the new battery, snap the case back together, charge the new battery, and your iPod is as good as new!

Battery Replacement—Third Generation iPod

The third generation of iPods uses a different battery than the first two. This is a 3.7 Volts 850 mAh battery. It is much smaller than the original iPod $30 range online.

Tools Required   The tools required for taking apart the iPod are a ruler with metric measurements and a plastic wedge, as described in the Tools Required section for the first two-generation iPods. You can use a small regular flathead screwdriver as well, such as the type used for eyeglass repair. However, you do run the risk of scratching your iPod, so be careful if you go that route!

FIGURE 10.9

The first step is to measure, using the ruler, 6cm (60MM) down either side of the iPod. This is where you start prying the plastic and metal case apart.

Insert your wedge or screwdriver, and carefully pry open the case working back and forth in the seam. This allows even pressure in the crease so that you don't run the risk of breaking any of the clips that hold the two pieces together.

After you have separated the two halves of the case, you need to work your way around the entire case to unclip each and every clip. Do this by pushing each clip inward toward the center of the iPod. After the silver case is loose, it will still be attached by a ribbon cable.

DO NOT pull the two pieces apart quickly. Look for the ribbon after the two halves are separated. Do not break this ribbon. Gently lay the metal half of the iPod case down, with the ribbon cable still attached. Be aware that these ribbons are very sensitive and can break or crack, and you don't want that!

With the front of the iPod (where the controls are) laying flat, you will see the tiny hard drive surrounded by blue rubber. Remove the hard drive by lifting all the blue rubber. There is a ribbon cable connecting the hard drive to the motherboard of the iPod. You need to disconnect this ribbon from the motherboard via the tab at the end of the ribbon. Gently lift the tab and disconnect the hard drive. Set aside the hard drive.

Next, you need to remove that old, dead battery. To do so, simply lift it out, being careful of the power cable running from the battery to the motherboard. You will also notice that the battery cable actually runs underneath the motherboard. Be certain to carefully pull it out, taking note of its position so that when you install the new battery, you can tuck the new power cable back out of the way in the same spot.

After the cord is out from under the motherboard, pull up on the connector to disconnect the power cord from the motherboard.

To install, simply plug in the new battery, tuck the wire back underneath the motherboard, replace the hard drive (don't forget to plug it back in as well!), and reassemble the iPod.

Charge up your battery, and you are back in the music business!

Battery Replacement—iPod Mini

FIGURE 10.10

The battery replacement in an iPod Mini is more involved and complex than in any of its larger brethren. The iPod case is one solid metal form, unlike the two-piece cases for the iPod. As such, the steps to disassemble the iPod Mini are very different.

The iPod Mini uses a very small Li-ion model #EC003 battery. Of all the iPod batteries, these are the most expensive, starting at around $40.

Tools Required   To disassemble the iPod, you need a small, regular flathead screwdriver and a small Phillips-head screwdriver. These must be small, such as the eyeglass repair type.

First, use the tip of the flathead screwdriver to carefully pry the top white plastic cover, where your headphones plug in, from the top of the Mini. There is a small amount of glue holding the plastic cover, so take care not to crack or pry too hard in any one spot. Move around the edge, gently but firmly lifting the white top up and away.

When the top is removed, you see two tiny Phillips screws. Use the Phillips screwdriver to remove these two screws.

Next, use the flathead screwdriver to remove the plastic cover from the bottom of the Mini. Glue is also holding this piece in place, so as in the top, take your time and gently remove the plastic. Be certain not to do any damage to the docking port on the bottom of the Mini!

tip

Have an empty drinking glass handy to put your screws in so you don't lose them!

After the plastic cover is off, you will find a small metal clip. Using the tip of your flathead screwdriver in each corner of this metal clip, gently pry the clip free.

You will notice a small connector behind this bottom metal clip. Using the flathead screwdriver, you need to disconnect this clip from its socket. Don't forget to reattach this clip when you reassemble your iPod Mini!

After the connector has been removed, you can gently push the guts of your iPod Mini up from the bottom. The innards will slide up and out of the metal case.

The battery can now be lifted from its spot on the motherboard, unclipped, and replaced with your new battery.

Reverse the preceding steps, charge your new battery, and your iPod Mini is ready to go!

The Absolute Minimum

The iPod is what we hope most technology will be—it just works and works well. Here are some points to help you keep your iPod in tune:

- Understand your iPod's battery and use the practices described in this chapter to keep it maintained properly.

- Keep your iPod's software current by using the update software that Apple releases periodically.

- If you do run into problems, check the last section in this chapter for help in solving them. Fortunately, it is unlikely that you will have problems; if you do, a reset or restore usually fixes them. If not, you have a lot of help available.

PART II

iTunes

IN THIS CHAPTER

- Figure out why iTunes will rock your world.
- Learn to speak in three-letter acronyms (TLAs), such as MP3 and AAC.
- Visit the Library.
- Learn the best three places to get music for your Library.
- Play with playlists.
- Meet the digital music triumvirate.

Touring iTunes

With not-very-sincere apologies to Mr. Edison, Apple's iTunes is the best thing to happen to music since the phonograph. This amazing application enables you to do things with your music you might have never dreamed possible. Of course, you can use iTunes to listen to audio CDs, but that is certainly nothing to write home (or a book) about. Any two-bit boom box can do that. That basic task is barely a warm-up for iTunes. If you have never used iTunes before, prepare to be impressed (and if you have used iTunes before, be impressed anyway).

What You Can Do with iTunes

I could fill a book (or at least Part II of this book) with all the great things you can do with iTunes. Following are some examples just to whet your appetite:

- Listen to audio CDs.
- Listen to Internet radio.
- Store all the music you like in a single place so you never need to fuss with individual CDs again.
- Search and organize all this music so that listening to exactly the music you want is just a matter of a few mouse clicks (and maybe a few key presses).
- Create custom albums (called *playlists*) containing the specific songs you want to hear.
- Create custom albums (called *smart playlists*) that are based on a set of criteria, such as all the Jazz music you have rated at four or five stars.
- Use the iTunes built-in Equalizer to make your music just right.
- Burn your own music CDs to play in those oh-so-limited CD players in your car, a boom box, or in your home.
- Share your music collection with other people over a wired or wireless network; you can listen to music other people share with you as well.

Audio File Formats You Might Encounter When You Use iTunes

As you work with digital music and other audio files, you'll encounter a number of different file formats that you need to understand. This is important because each of these formats offers specific benefits and limitations that impact what you do with your music. For example, some file formats offer better music quality versus file size than others. You definitely don't need to have all the specifications for each of these formats committed to memory (nor will you find them in this book); instead, all you need to be able to do is to distinguish between them and to be able to choose the format that is the most appropriate for what you are trying to do.

Most audio file formats are *encoded*. What this means is that specific compression algorithms (because this is a computer book, I am required by contract to use that word at least once) are used to reduce the size of the audio file without, hopefully anyway, lowering the quality of the resulting sound very much. The higher the compression that is used, the lower the quality of the resulting music when it is played back. Note that the words *higher* and *lower* are relative. Often, it takes a musical expert to tell the difference between encoded and unencoded music, but even if it is imperceptible to us mere mortals, it does exist.

When it comes to digital audio files, one trade-off always has to be made. And that is *file size* versus *sound quality*. When you add thousands of songs to your iTunes Library, you can easily consume gigabytes of disk space. Although you might have a humungous hard drive in your computer, you might also have other files you want to store on it, such as photos, Word docs, and so on. Even I realize that computers can be used for more than just music.

To keep the amount of disk space required to store your music to a minimum, you will encode it. When you do, you choose the settings you want to use to encode that music. The more encoding you apply, the less space the music will consume, but the lower quality the playback will be. You will quickly find a happy medium between file size and how the music sounds to you.

You'll learn about this in more detail later in the book, but for now, you should read the following sections so you can become comfortable with the various audio file formats you will encounter.

CD Audio

The CD Audio format was the world's first widely used entry in the digital audio format life cycle. The creation of this format was the start of the CD revolution. Instead of vinyl albums, which were a pain to deal with and included lots of hisses, pops, and other distractions when played, listeners began enjoying digital music. In addition to being much easier to handle than LPs, CDs provided a much better listening experience and were—and are— much more durable than records. They also sounded much better than cassettes and could be just as portable.

Eventually, CD Audio made its way to computers, which now can provide all the music-listening enjoyment of a home stereo plus much more, thanks to applications such as iTunes.

Although you can use iTunes to listen to your audio CDs, typically you will just convert those CDs into one of the newer digital formats and store that content on your computer's hard disk

> **caution**
>
> Some audio CDs use copyright-protection schemes that prevent you from listening to them on a computer (with the idea being that you won't be able to make copies of the songs for illegal purposes). Unfortunately, not only do these CDs not work in your computer, they can actually cause damage. Before playing a CD in your computer, check the CD's label carefully to make sure it doesn't contain any warnings about playing the CD in a computer or state that the CD is copy-protected. If it does have these warnings, don't try to use the CD in your computer.

so you don't have to use a CD when you want to listen to music. You will also make use of this format when you put your iTunes music on your own audio CD so that you can play your iTunes music when you are away from your computer.

MP3

Even if this book is your first foray into the wonderful world of digital music, you have no doubt heard of MP3. This audio file format started, literally, an explosion in music technology that is still reverberating and expanding today.

MP3 is the acronym for the audio compression scheme called *Moving Picture Experts Group (MPEG) audio layer 3*. The revolutionary aspect of the MP3 encoding scheme was that music data could be stored in files that are only about one-twelfth the size of unencoded digital music without a noticeable degradation in the quality of the music. A typical music CD consumes about 650MB of storage space, but the same music encoded in the MP3 format shrinks down to about 55MB. Put another way, a single 3.5-minute song shrinks from its 35MB on audio CD down to a paltry 3MB or so in MP3 format. The small size of MP3 files opened up a world of possibilities.

note

Because encoded music files are relatively small, storing an entire music collection in a relatively small amount of disk space is possible, thus eliminating the need to bother with individual CDs. Using a digital music application such as iTunes, you can easily store, organize, and access an entire music collection on your desktop or laptop computer.

For example, MP3 enabled a new class of portable music devices. Because MP3 files can be stored in small amounts of memory, devices with no moving parts can store and play a fair amount of music; these were the early MP3 players, such as the Rio. Then came other devices containing small hard drives—can you say iPod?—that can store huge amounts of music, enabling you to take your entire music collection with you wherever you go. These devices are extremely small and lightweight, and their contents can be easily managed.

You will encounter many MP3 files on the Internet, and with iTunes, you can convert your audio CDs into the MP3 format so that you can store them in iTunes and put them on an iPod.

AAC

The newest digital audio format is called *Advanced Audio Coding* or *AAC*. This format is part of the larger MPEG-4 specification. Its basic purpose is the same as the MP3 format: to deliver excellent sound quality while keeping file sizes small. However, the AAC format is a newer and better format in that it can be used to produce files that have better quality than MP3 at even smaller file sizes.

Also, as with MP3, you can easily convert audio CD files into the AAC format to store them on a computer and add them to an iPod. What's more, you can convert

AAC files into the Audio CD or MP3 format when you want to put them on a CD to play on something other than your computer, such as a car stereo.

The AAC format also enables content producers to add some copy-protection schemes to their music. Typically, these schemes won't have any impact on you (unless of course, you are trying to do something you shouldn't).

One of the most important aspects of the AAC format is that all the music in the iTunes Music Store is stored in it; when you purchase music from the store, it is added to your computer in this format.

note

Frankly, you aren't likely to notice any difference between AAC music files and MP3 files, except in one area—some portable digital music players (such as MP3 players) don't support AAC-formatted music. The iPod does, so if you use one (given that you are reading this book, I assume you do), you don't have to be concerned about this difference.

WAV

The *Windows Waveform (WAV)* audio format is a standard on Windows computers. It has been widely used for various kinds of audio, but because it does not offer the "quality versus file size" benefits of the MP3 or AAC formats, it is mostly used for sound effects or clips that people have recorded from various sources. Millions of WAV files are available on the Internet that you can play and download.

You can load WAV files into iTunes, and you can even use iTunes to convert files into the WAV format. However, because MP3 and AAC are much newer and better file formats, you aren't likely to want to do this very often. Occasionally, you might want to add WAV files to your iTunes music collection; this can be easily done, as you will learn later in this book.

tip

If you ever want to find a sound byte from your favorite movie or TV show, you can probably do so at one of the many WAV Web sites on the Internet. One example is www. wavcentral.com. Interestingly enough, even the sound clips on these sites are being largely converted into MP3.

AIFF

The *Audio Interchange File Format (AIFF)* provides relatively high-quality sound, but its file sizes are larger than MP3 or AAC. As you can probably guess from its name, this format was originally used to exchange audio among various platforms.

As with the WAV format, because the MP3 and AAC formats provide better sound quality in smaller file sizes, you aren't likely to use the AIFF format very often. The most likely situation in which you might want to use it is when you want to move some music or sound from your iTunes collection into a different application that does not support the MP3 or AAC format.

Apple Lossless

This encoding format is also new; it is a compromise between the high-quality of WAV and AIFF formats and the small size of AAC files. Apple Lossless files are very high quality (equivalent to AIFF) but are only one-half the file size of those non-compressed formats. If you want the maximum quality of music playback (especially if you create audio CDs), this can be a useful encoder to use. About its only downside is that not all audio applications can play it (iTunes and the iPod can and those are all you really need anyway).

The iTunes Music Library

Earlier, you read that one of the great things about iTunes is that you can use it to store all your music on your computer. This is done with the iTunes Music Library (see Figure 11.1). This is the place in which you store all the music and sound you import into iTunes, such as from audio CDs or other sources. You can then browse or search your Library to find the music you want to listen to or work with.

FIGURE 11.1

The iTunes Library is the one place to go for all the good music in your life.

As you use iTunes, you will frequently be accessing your Library; it will often be your first stop when you work with your music.

Where Does All That Music Come From?

You have three primary sources of the music and sounds from which you will build your iTunes Library:

- **Audio CDs**—You can add music from your audio CDs to the iTunes Library. In iTunes lingo, this process is called *importing*.

- **The Internet**—You can download music and other audio files from the Internet and add those files to your iTunes Library.

- **The iTunes Music Store**—Part III of this book, titled "The iTunes Music Store," is dedicated to this music source, and for good reason. Using the iTunes Music Store, you can search for, preview, and purchase music online and add that music to your Library.

> **note**
>
> iTunes uses a more civilized term (importing) for the process of converting an audio CD into a different format and adding the resulting music to your Library. The more traditional term for converting audio CD music into the MP3 format is *ripping*. I kind of like *ripping* myself, but because *importing* is the term iTunes uses, I guess we will go with that.

Playlists: Customize Your Music Experience

I've saved one of the best features of iTunes for nearly last—*playlists*. Playlists enable you to create custom collections of music from the songs in your iTunes Library. (If you think of a playlist as a custom CD without the disc, you will be very close.)

When you create playlists, you can mix and match music to your heart's content. For example, you can build your own "greatest hits" collections that include multiple artists, music genres, and so on. You can repeat the same song multiple times in the same playlist. You can also get rid of songs you don't like by not including them in the playlists you listen to. What's more, you can create a playlist to include a specific amount of music from a single CD or endlessly repeat all the music in your Library.

Basically, you can use playlists to organize a collection of songs in any way you choose. You can then listen to your playlists, put them on a CD, or move them to an iPod.

You'll learn all you need to know about playlists in Chapter 17, "Creating, Configuring, and Using Playlists."

The Other Members of the Band: The iPod and the iTunes Music Store

When it comes to citizenship, iTunes definitely gets an A+ because it plays so well with others.

If you have read Part I, "The iPod," you know that the iPod might just be the coolest portable electronic device ever to hit the streets. Although the iPod is indeed an awesome piece of technology, it wouldn't get very far without a tool to manage the music it contains. iTunes is that tool. iTunes and the iPod go together like a 1-2 combination punch, peanut butter and jelly, jalapenos on a pizza, Bing Crosby and Bob Hope (well, you get the idea). Using iTunes, you can determine which parts of your music library are on the iPod. iTunes manages moving the music files to the iPod and organizing them, so the process is quite simple (from your perspective anyway). In fact, iTunes will manage the process for you automatically if you prefer; when you connect your trusty iPod to your computer, iTunes will recognize it and then synchronize the music it has in your Library with that on your iPod.

When you get to Part III of this book, you will learn in detail about the last part of the digital music triumvirate: the iTunes Music Store. With the iTunes Music Store, you can shop for music to add to your Library. When you find songs you'd like to have, you can purchase and download them into your iTunes Library with just a couple mouse clicks. And you can do all this from within iTunes itself. It feels like the iTunes Music Store is just an extension of iTunes, which, in fact, it is. You access the iTunes Music Store from within iTunes, and the Store uses an interface that looks very similar to iTunes. So, once you know iTunes, you won't have any problems with the iTunes Music Store.

The Absolute Minimum

Now that you have met iTunes, I hope you are jazzed (pun intended) to get into it and start making its musical magic work for you. In the chapters following this one, you'll learn how to do everything from listening to audio CDs and Internet radio to building playlists to sharing your music over a network. Here are the major topics you learned about in this introduction to iTunes:

- You can use iTunes to do just about anything you want to with your music, from listening to CDs to putting your entire music collection on your hard drive to managing the music on an iPod.

- The primary audio file formats you can use with iTunes are AAC and MP3. However, you can also use WAV, AIFF, and Apple Lossless.

- The iTunes Music Library is where you store and can work with all your iTunes music.

- You can get music for your iTunes Library from audio CDs, the Internet, and the iTunes Music Store.

- You can use playlists to create and listen to customized collections of music.

- iTunes works seamlessly with the iPod and the iTunes Music Store.

Getting Started with iTunes

It's time to put iTunes through it paces so you can see and hear for your-self what it can do. Fortunately, you will find that iTunes is not only well designed once you start using it, but it is also easy to get started with.

In the first part of this chapter, you'll learn how to install and launch iTunes. Although using iTunes on a Windows PC and on a Macintosh are nearly identical, there are slight differences in how you install the applications on each platform. So, I've included an installation section for each kind of computer. It should go without saying, but I will say it anyway just in case: You don't need to read both installation sections. Just read the section that is applicable for the type of computer you use.

After you have installed and launched iTunes, read the section called "Getting to Know iTunes," where you'll get the grand tour of the amaz-ing iTunes features you will be using throughout the rest of this part of the book.

Installing iTunes on a Windows PC

Over the years, Apple has produced a few applications designed for both Windows PCs and Macintoshes. Thank goodness for Windows users that iTunes is also in this group. (None of the others are worthy of much mention, but iTunes is definitely a crossover hit!)

In order to use iTunes on a Windows computer, you must be running Windows 2000 or Windows XP. If you are running Windows 98, Me, or 95, you are out of the iTunes game. (Of course, those older versions of Windows are really old and you should be using a newer version for more reasons than just the ability to run iTunes!)

You have two primary ways to get a copy of iTunes and install it on your computer. (The good news is that neither way will cost you any more money than you have already spent.) First, if you have purchased an iPod, which is a likely case given that you are reading a book about iPods, a copy of iTunes is provided on the CD included with every iPod. Second, if you don't have an iPod or if you don't have the CD that came with it for some reason, you can download iTunes from the Internet.

note

In case you are wondering, about the only other successful application that Apple has produced for Windows computers is the database program FileMaker Pro. This originally was developed by a subsidiary of Apple called Claris. Claris spun out from Apple and is now known as FileMaker, thus giving the company the same name as its most popular product.

Downloading and Installing iTunes on a Windows PC

It can be better to download a copy of iTunes from the Internet to install it on your computer even if you have a copy on the iPod CD. That's because the application is periodically updated. When you download a copy from the Web, you get the latest and greatest version. When you install a copy from the CD, you get the latest and greatest version when the CD was produced, which might not be the current latest and greatest.

If you want to download and install a copy of iTunes, perform the following steps:

1. Open your favorite Web browser, such as Internet Explorer.
2. Move to http://www.apple.com/itunes.
3. Click the **Free Download** link. You will see the Download page.
4. Scroll down the page until you see the **Download iTunes section** (see Figure 12.1).

5. Click the **Windows 2000 or XP** radio button.

6. Enter your email address if you want to sub-scribe to any of Apple's iTunes newsletters; if you don't, you can leave this blank.

7. Enter your first and last name if you want to (this is optional information).

8. Choose the area in which you live in the drop-down list.

9. Check the boxes for the Apple newsletters you want to receive (or uncheck the boxes for any Apple newsletters you don't want to receive). For example, the *New Music Tuesdays* newsletter lets you know about music that has been added to the iTunes Music Store.

10. Click Download iTunes. You'll see the File Download dialog box.

note

For information about installing iTunes from the CD included with iPods, see "Installing the iPod's Software (Including iTunes)" on page **22**. If this is the option you chose, you can skip over the rest of this section and move ahead with launching the application, as I explain in "Launching and Performing the Initial Configuration of iTunes on a Windows PC," on page **184**.

FIGURE 12.1

Downloading iTunes is easy and free; what could be better?

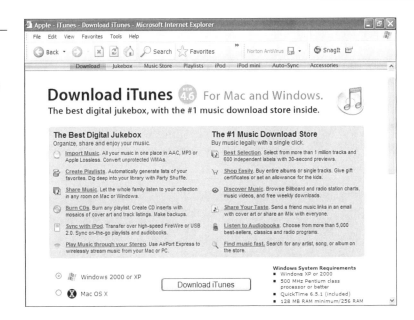

11. Click Save. You'll see the Save As dialog box.

12. Choose the location in which you want to save the iTunes installation program and click **Save**. The download process will begin; you can monitor its progress in the **File Download Progress** dialog box.

13. When the download process is complete, click **Open**. The InstallShield Wizard will open and start the installation process. After a moment or two, you will see the iTunes for Windows window (see Figure 12.2).

FIGURE 12.2

Working through the iTunes Installer is mostly a matter of reading and clicking Next.

14. Read the information in the Installer window and click **Next**. The License Agreement dialog box will appear.

15. If you have a lot of time and patience, read the license agreement; when you are done, click **Yes** if you agree or **No** if you don't. (Of course, if you don't agree, you can skip the rest of these steps and the rest of this part of the book because you won't be able to use iTunes.)

16. In the resulting Information window, you can read information about iTunes, such as what it can do and what you need to install it. Because you have this book, you don't really need to read this information, but it can't hurt to do so. When you are done reading, click **Next**. You'll see the Setup Type window (see Figure 12.3).

> **note**
>
> When I wrote this, the iTunes installation package was about 20MB. If you only have a dial-up connection to the Internet, you might want to install iTunes from the iPod software CD and then update the copy you install.

17. Check the following options to make them active or uncheck them to make them inactive:

   ■ **Install desktop shortcuts**—This option places a shortcut to iTunes on your desktop. Unless you don't like desktop shortcuts for some reason, you should usually leave this option checked.

■ **Use iTunes as the default player for audio files**—This option causes iTunes to be used to play most audio files that you will access on the Internet, your computer, CDs, and so on. If you prefer to use another application, such as Windows Media Player, uncheck this box. However, I recommend that you leave it checked for now. You can always change the default application to be something else after you have become comfortable with iTunes.

FIGURE 12.3

As you install iTunes, you have a couple of options, such as whether you want iTunes to be the default player for audio files.

18. Click **Next**. You'll see the **Choose Destination Location** dialog box.

19. If the default installation location is fine with you, click **Next**. If you don't want to accept the default installation location (which is C:\Program Files\iTunes\), click the **Browse** button and choose the location you do want to use. Then click **Next**. You'll see a window advertising the iPod.

20. Click **Next**. As the Installer starts to work, you will see the Setup Status window. This window provides you with information about the installation process (see Figure 12.4).

    When the process is complete, you will see the Installation Successful window.

21. Click **Finish**. In some cases, you will need to restart your computer and complete the installation process. When your computer restarts, iTunes will be ready for you. If you aren't prompted to restart your computer, iTunes will be ready for you without a restart.

caution

If you have other open applications that contain documents with unsaved changes, make sure you save them before you restart your computer.

FIGURE 12.4

Here, you can
see that the
iTunes Installer
is currently
installing
QuickTime.

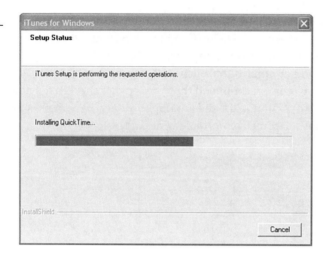

Launching and Performing the Initial Configuration of iTunes on a Windows PC

Whichever path you have taken to this point (installing iTunes from the iPod CD or
from the Internet), I am sure all is well and you are ready to start cutting your teeth
on iTunes.

To open the application and perform the initial configuration (which you need to do
only the first time you open the program), follow these steps:

1. Open iTunes. You have several ways to do this. You can use the iTunes desktop icon to open it (assuming you chose to have an icon placed there). You
   can also choose **Start**, **All Programs**, **iTunes**, **iTunes** to launch the
   application from the **Start** menu. Or, you
   can click the iTunes shortcut that was con-
   veniently placed in the taskbar for you.

   After you have used one of these methods,
   the iTunes window will open. The first time
   you launch the application, the iTunes
   Setup Assistant will appear (see Figure
   12.5). The helpful assistant will guide you
   through the few configuration decisions
   you need to make before you start working
   with the application. As with other assis-
   tants, you will move through the iTunes
   Setup Assistant by reading its information,
   making choices, and using the **Next** button.

   tip

   If you find yourself to
   be opening iTunes every
   time you use your com-
   puter, and you probably
   will, consider adding it
   to the list of startup
   programs so it will
   open automatically when you turn
   your computer on.

FIGURE 12.5

The iTunes Setup Assistant appears the first time you open the application; get a good look at it because you won't be seeing it again.

2. Click **Next** to move to the Find Music Files screen. The purpose of this screen is to indicate whether you want iTunes to search your Music folder to find any existing music and then add that music to your iTunes Library. If you have music in this folder, I recommend that you let iTunes add it to your Library.

   If you want iTunes to search for music in the AAC and MP3 formats on your computer, leave the **Add MP3 and AAC files check box** checked.

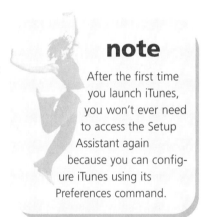

note

After the first time you launch iTunes, you won't ever need to access the Setup Assistant again because you can configure iTunes using its Preferences command.

   If you also want to add any unprotected WMA files to your iTunes Music Library, check the **Add WMA files** check box. This check box will be active only if you have files like this stored on your computer.

   If you don't want to add any of these files, uncheck both check boxes.

   Then click **Next**.

3. Use the Keep iTunes Music Folder Organized window to indicate whether you want iTunes to automatically rename and organize the music in your iTunes Music folder when you change that music's information (such as genre).

   Unless you have a very specific reason not to want this feature, click **Yes, Keep My iTunes Music Folder Organized** and then click **Next**.

   If you do have some reason why you don't want iTunes to rename or move your music files, click **No, I'll Change the File and Folder Names Myself** and then click **Next**.

4. Use the iTunes Music Store window to deter-mine whether you want to move to the iTunes Music Store immediately after the Setup Assistant is done.

Because you will learn about the iTunes Music Store in detail in Part III, "The iTunes Music Store," click the **No, take me to my iTunes Library** radio button and click **Finish**.

The Setup Assistant will run and you will see the iTunes window (see Figure 12.6). If you indicated that you want iTunes to find any music in your Music folder and add it to the iTunes Library, you will see the music that the application found.

note

Now you are ready to learn about the major elements of the iTunes window. Unless you also have a Macintosh that you also want to install iTunes on, you can skip ahead to the section "Getting to Know iTunes" on page **189**. However, because my writing is so scintillat-ing (don't you love that word!), I wouldn't blame you if you read the next section even if you don't have a Mac!

FIGURE 12.6

Okay, so the iTunes window doesn't look so exciting yet; soon, there will be lots of great music to listen to.

Installing and Configuring iTunes on a Macintosh

Because iTunes is developed by Apple, it is as integrated into the Macintosh operating system as much as any application can be. You have a number of ways to get iTunes installed on your Mac, including the following:

■ **Install Mac OS X**. When you install Mac OS X, iTunes is also installed, unless you specifically tell the Installer not to install it. If you have installed OS X on your Mac, you don't need to do any installation, but you should make sure you have the current version installed (to do so, see the section "Keeping iTunes Up to Date on a Macintosh" on page **326**.

■ **Buy a new Mac**. Okay, this might be the most expensive option, but, hey, you get a free Mac with your copy of iTunes!

■ **Install iTunes from the iPod Software CD**. The software installation CD included with an iPod also enables you to install iTunes.

■ **Buy a copy of the Apple iLife suite**. In addition to iTunes, you'll get iMovie, iPhoto, iDVD, and Garage Band.

■ **Download and install iTunes from the Internet**. You can always download and install the latest version of iTunes from the Internet.

If you have installed Mac OS X on your computer, you probably don't need to do any installation because it is likely that you already have iTunes installed on your machine.

To use one of the CD options, just insert the CD, launch the installer, and follow the onscreen instructions.

If you don't already have some version of iTunes installed on your Mac, you can download and install a copy from the Internet. This is often the best option because you are sure to get the most current version of the application.

note

Not to push my other books (okay, to push my other books), but if you need help with Mac OS X in general, see *Special Edition Using Mac OS X, v10.3 Panther* (catchy title, huh?).

note

If you are still using Mac OS 9, you aren't totally out of the iTunes game because you might have an early version installed. However, because Mac OS X is the future (not to mention most of the present) of the Mac platform, I don't cover installing or using iTunes under Mac OS 9 in this book.

The process for downloading and installing iTunes on a Mac is almost identical to what you use to download and install iTunes on a Windows computer. To save a few trees, I haven't included the steps to do this on a Mac. Just refer to the section "Downloading and Installing iTunes on a Windows PC" on page **180**. The most important difference is that you should choose to download the version for Mac OS X (as if you couldn't guess that!). After that, just follow the onscreen instructions.

You have a number of ways to open iTunes on a Mac, including the following:

- Click the **iTunes** icon on the Dock.

- Open the **Applications** folder and double-click the **iTunes** icon.

- Insert an audio CD into your Mac; by default, iTunes is set to launch whenever you mount an audio CD.

> **note**
>
> Because you are probably using Mac OS X and therefore already have iTunes, you should go ahead and make sure you are using the latest version by running the Software Update application. To do so, choose **Apple menu**, **Software Update**. If a more current version of iTunes is available than the one installed on your computer, you will be prompted to download and install it.

The first time you open iTunes, you will need to work through a basic configuration of the application. Following are the steps you need to perform:

1. Launch iTunes. You will see yet another **License Agreement** screen. (I guess Apple was kidding with the others.)

2. Click **Agree**. You will see the iTunes Setup Assistant, which will guide you through the rest of the process (see Figure 12.7).

3. Click **Next**. You will see the Internet Audio Settings window. These settings control whether iTunes is the default application for audio content from the Internet and if iTunes should automatically connect to the Internet when it needs to.

4. Click both **Yes** radio buttons and then click **Next**. You'll see the Find Music Files window.

FIGURE 12.7

The iTunes Setup Assistant lives up to its name.

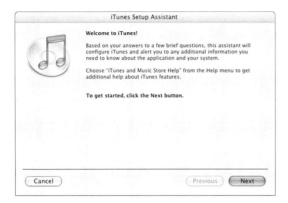

5. If you want iTunes to search for music on your Mac and then add that music to the iTunes Library, click **Yes, Find MP3 and AAC Files in My Home Folder**. If you don't want this to happen, click **No, I'll Add Them Myself Later**. Click **Done**. You'll see the iTunes Music Store window.

The iTunes window will open (see Figure 12.8) and you will be ready to tour the application in the next section.

FIGURE 12.8

There aren't any songs in the Library yet, so this iTunes window looks a bit boring; we'll soon fix that!

Getting to Know iTunes

The required but mundane work of installing iTunes on your computer is done. Now, let's take a quick tour so you get the overall feel of this excellent application. In the following chapters, you'll get down and dirty (well, because we are dealing with electrons here, there isn't really any dirt) with the details.

Seeing Through the iTunes Window

The iTunes window, like the windows on your house, consists of a number of panes (see Figure 12.9). Let's take a quick look at each of these.

FIGURE 12.9
Working with iTunes panes won't cause you any (pain, that is).

On the far left of the iTunes window is the Source List. On this list, as you might suspect from its name, are the sources of music with which you can work. To work with a source, such as a CD or the iTunes Music Store, you select it by clicking it. When you select a source, its contents will appear in the Content pane and Browser (if you have the Browser open for a selected source). In Figure 12.9, I have selected the Library as the source; its contents are shown in the Browser at the top of the window while the list of individual songs that make up the Library is at the bottom of the window.

note

Different sources have different icons in the Source List. For example, the Library has a yellow box containing a music note, whereas playlists have a blue box with a musical note.

You will use many types of sources, including the Library, the Radio, the iTunes Music Store, audio CDs, playlists, and more. As we work though the rest of this part of the book, you will get experience with all these kinds of sources.

The Browser presents the contents of the selected source at a summary level, by genre, artist, and album. You can view the contents of the selected source by clicking it in the appropriate column. For example, in Figure 12.9, I have selected the Rock genre. The Artist column then shows all the artists whose music I have in the selected genre. The Album column shows all the albums for the selected artist.

The Browser can be shown or hidden. For example, take a look at Figure 12.10, which shows the iTunes window with the Browser hidden.

FIGURE 12.10

Where, oh where, has my Browser gone? Where, oh where, can it be?

At the bottom of the iTunes window (or filling it if the Browser is hidden) is the Content pane. This area lists each song in the selected source. For each song, you will see a variety of information, such as Song Name, Track #, Time, Artist, and so on. You can choose the information you see on this list to make it contain the information you find the most useful. The order in which songs are listed in the Content pane is the order in which they will play when you play the selected source.

Going back to Figure 12.9, you can see that several songs by the group 3 Doors Down are listed in the Content pane.

tip

We will get to working with the Browser later, but for now know that you can open and close it by clicking the **Browse** button or by choosing **Edit, Show Browser** or **Edit, Hide Browser**.

Controlling Your Music

Surrounding those panes are the controls you use to work with and get information about your music. At the top of the window, from left to right, you will see the following areas (see Figure 12.11):

Playback controls   Information window   Search tool   Action button

FIGURE 12.11

At the top of the iTunes window, you see a number of controls you can use to play and manage your music.

- **Playback controls**—Here, you can see the familiar Play/Stop, Fast Forward, and Rewind buttons along with the Volume Control slider. These work as you probably expect them to.

- **Information window**—In the center of the iTunes window is the Information window. In this area, you will see a variety of information about what you are doing at any point in time. For example, when you are playing music, you will see information about the music currently being played. When you import music, you will see information about the import process. Later, you'll learn how to choose the information displayed here.

- **Search tool**—You use the Search tool to search for music.

- **Action button**—The Action button changes depending on the context you are in. For example, if you have selected the Library, it becomes the **Browse** button, which you use to open or close the Browser. If you select a playlist, it becomes the **Burn** button, which enables you to burn a CD.

When you move to the bottom of the iTunes window, you will see the following (see Figure 12.12):

- **Add Playlist button**—You can use this button to create your own playlists.

- **Shuffle and Repeat buttons**—You use the Shuffle button to shuffle the music in the selected source so that it doesn't play in the listed order. You can use the Repeat button to cause songs to repeat within a selected source.

- **Show/Hide Album Art button**—Songs can have album art associated with them. When you click this button, you will see the Art Album box at the bottom of the Source pane. In it will appear any art associated with the song that is currently selected.

- **Source information**—This information shows you the number of songs, total playing time, and disk space of the selected source. This becomes especially useful at certain times, such as when you are burning a CD or building a playlist.

- **Equalizer button**—This button opens the Equalizer window, which provides you with a graphic equalizer.

- **Visualizer button**—Okay, this was one of the most promoted features of iTunes when it was initially released, but I didn't get it then, and I still don't today. When you click this, the iTunes window fills with a graphic display reminiscent of the 1960s (see Figure 12.13).

- **Eject button**—When you have selected an ejectable source, such as an audio CD or iPod, you can click this button to eject it.

note

Because I don't see much value (not even entertainment value) in the Visualizer, I won't be mentioning it again in this book. You can play with it by using the Visualizer menu if you want to. Oh, by the way, the images you see in the Visualizer are not related to any music that might be playing anyway. Want proof? Fire up the Visualizer with no music playing; it looks just like it does when music is playing.

FIGURE 12.12

Not to be outdone by the top, the bottom of the iTunes window is chock full of good stuff, too.

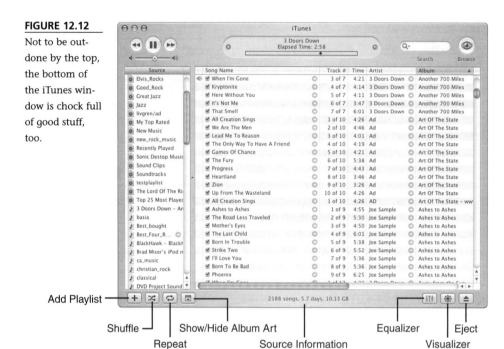

Add Playlist

Shuffle

Repeat

Show/Hide Album Art

Source Information

Equalizer

Eject

Visualizer

FIGURE 12.13

Just because I don't think the Visualizer is groovy, that doesn't mean that you can't dig it.

The Absolute Minimum

You are well on your way to total iTunes nirvana. If you have read this chapter, you should be hip to the following iTunes jazz:

- You have a number of ways to install iTunes on your computer—whether it's a Mac or a Windows PC. The best way is to download and install it from the Internet.

- No matter how you installed iTunes, make sure you keep it up to date (you'll get to that in Chapter 20, "Maintaining iTunes and Solving Problems").

- When you first open iTunes, you work through several configuration settings using the iTunes Setup Assistant. However, you can change these settings at any time using the iTunes Preferences dialog box, which you will be working with throughout the rest of this part of the book.

- The iTunes window is an elegant mix of functionality and good interface design. As you learn more about the application, you will likely be impressed. The primary components of the iTunes window are the controls, the Information area, the Source List, the Browser, and the Content pane.

- Although iTunes is one my favorite applications and I use it constantly, it sports one of the silliest features that was ever part of an application. What is it?

Listening to Audio CDs and Internet Audio with iTunes

The basic reason to have and use iTunes is to listen to music and other audio, such as audio books—not coincidentally, that is the basic point of this chapter. Here, you will learn how to use iTunes to listen to a couple of sources: audio CDs and Internet radio. The good news is that once you know how to use iTunes to listen to these two sources, you know how to listen to other sources you will use as well, such as songs in your Music Library, in playlists, on an iPod, and from shared music.

After you become an iTunes-playing guru, we'll take a look at some of the ways you can configure iTunes to suit your playing preferences.

Listening to an Audio CD

What iTunes has in common with its much less sophisticated cousins the boom box and the standard CD player is the ability to play audio CDs. Although the basic function is the same, iTunes has several tricks in its bag to make listening even better. So, grab a CD and give it a try:

1. Open iTunes.

2. Insert an audio CD into your computer. In a moment, the CD will be mounted on your computer, and it will appear and be selected in the **Source List** (see Figure 13.1). (If it isn't selected by default, click on its icon to select it.)

> **tip**
>
> You might not need to do Step 1 depending on your how computer is configured. If iTunes is set to be the default application for audio CDs, it will open automatically when you insert an audio CD in your computer.

A CD is the selected source

FIGURE 13.1

When a CD appears on the Source List, it awaits your listening pleasure.

Source Information

By default, iTunes will automatically connect to the Internet and attempt to identify the CD you have inserted. If it finds it, it will display the CD's information, including CD name, track names, times, artist, and genre, in the Content pane (in Figure 13.1, you can see the CD's information has been found). This is really cool because iTunes does most of the labeling work for you; this comes in very handy when you want to search or browse for music to create playlists or just to listen to specific tracks.

If iTunes finds information for a CD, it remembers that information and displays it each time you insert the CD.

At the bottom of the iTunes window is the Source Information display. This will show you the total number of songs on the CD, how long it plays, and the total disc space used.

note

If you don't want iTunes to check for a CD's information automatically, you can disable this feature as you will learn a little later in this chapter.

If the CD's information isn't located, you can add it yourself (see Chapter 15, "Labeling, Categorizing, and Configuring Your Music").

3. To play the CD, do any of the following: click the **Play** button in the top-left corner of the window (when a CD is playing, this becomes the **Pause** button), choose **Controls**, **Play**, or press the **spacebar**.

The CD will begin to play. As a song plays, a speaker icon appears next to it in the Content pane to indicate it is the current song, and information about that song appears in the Information window (see Figure 13.2).

FIGURE 13.2

You can tell this CD is playing because of the Pause button and the speaker icon next to the song currently being played.

4. Control the volume of the sound by dragging the Volume slider to the left to turn it down or to the right to turn it up. You can also control the volume by choosing **Controls**, **Volume Up** or **Controls**, **Volume Down**. For yet another option, use the **Ctrl+up arrow** and **Ctrl+down arrow** keys on Windows PCs or the ⌘**+up arrow** and ⌘**+down arrow** keys on Macs to set the volume from the keyboard.

To mute the sound, choose **Controls**, **Mute**. On Windows PCs you can press **Ctrl+Alt+down arrow**, whereas on Macs you can press **Option+⌘+down arrow** to do the same thing.

5. To pause a song, click the **Pause** button, choose **Controls**, **Pause**, or press the **spacebar**.

That's it. You now know everything you need to listen to an audio CD. However, there are lots more ways to control the tunes, some of which are in the following list:

- Double-click any song to play it. When you do that, the speaker icon will jump to the song on which you double-clicked and it will play.

- When a song is playing and you click and hold the **Rewind** or **Fast Forward** button down, the song will rewind or fast forward until you release the button.

- If a song is selected and you press, but don't hold down, the **Rewind** or **Fast Forward** button, the previous or next song, respectively, will be selected. You can also choose **Controls**, **Next Song** or **Controls**, **Previous Song** to move to the next or the previous song. And for yet another method to do the same thing, use the **Ctrl+right arrow** and **Ctrl+left arrow** keys on a Windows PC or the ⌘**+right arrow** and ⌘**+left arrow** keys on a Mac to move to the next or previous song.

tip

When a song is playing, its speaker icon has waves radiating from it to show it is playing. When you pause, the speaker icon remains to show it is the current song, but the waves go away to let you know the song isn't currently playing.

note

Using the Volume slider within iTunes only changes the volume of iTunes relative to your system's volume. If you can't make the music loud or quiet enough, check your system volume level.

- You can set a default action for iTunes to perform each time you insert a CD into your computer. You do this with the **iTunes Preferences** dialog box, which you will be using throughout this part of the book. Choose **Edit**, **Preferences** (Windows) or **iTunes**, **Preferences** (Mac). The **Preferences** dialog box will appear. The **Preferences** dialog box has several panes that you access by clicking the related tab (Windows) or icon (Mac). Click the **General** tab (Windows) or **General** icon (Mac). Use the **On CD Insert** drop-down list to choose the default action iTunes should perform when it recognizes an audio CD. **Show Songs** just displays the list of tracks on the CD. **Begin Playing** starts playing the CD as soon as it is mounted on your computer (this does the same thing as clicking the **Play** button). **Import Songs** adds the selected songs on the CD to your Library. **Import Songs** and **Eject** does the same thing as **Import Songs**, but it ejects the CD when all its tracks have been added to your Library. (You'll see the value of the last two settings in the next chapter.)

- To remove a CD from your computer, select it in the **Source List** and choose **Controls**, **Eject Disc**, press **Ctrl+E** (Windows) or ⌘+**E** (Macintosh), or click the **Eject** button located in the lower-right corner of the iTunes window.

tip
Yet another way to eject a disc is to point to it with the cursor, open its contextual menu, and choose Eject. On Windows machines, you right-click to open this menu. On Macs, you Ctrl-click with a single-button mouse or right-click if you have a two-button mouse (which hopefully you do).

Viewing Information While Listening to Tunes

You can view different information in the Information window, such as the name, artist, and album of the currently playing song. When you first view this window, it contains a timeline bar that represents the total length of the song being played (see Figure 13.3). A black diamond indicates the relative position of the music you are hearing at any point in time compared to the total length of the song.

At the top of the Information window is a line of text. What appears here changes over time; it automatically rotates between the artist's name, album name, and name of the song currently playing. You can freeze this display on a specific attribute, such as song name, by clicking the text. Each time you click, the

note
When you "freeze" information in the Information window, it remains frozen until the next track is played, at which point it starts rotating again.

information will change from album to artist to song name. Whichever one you last clicked on will remain showing in the window.

FIGURE 13.3

The iTunes Information window looks basic, but there is much hidden behind its quiet demeanor.

Current location in the playing song

Artist, album title, or song name

Time

Timeline bar

Underneath the album, artist, and song name line is the time information. This can display elapsed time (the amount of time a song has been playing), remaining time (the amount of time a song has left), or total time (the song's total length). Unlike the name information, this display does not rotate among these values. You can set the value being displayed by clicking the time being displayed; each time you click, a different time value will be shown until you have rotated among all three values.

Finally, if you click the **Change Display** button, the display will become a graphical representation of the volume levels at various frequency groups (see Figure 13.4). You can return to the title information by clicking the button again.

note

The neat thing about the Information window is that it changes based on the context of what you are doing. You have seen how it works when you listen to music. When you add music to your Library, the information and tools in the window become those you use for the import process.

Change Display button   Volume levels

FIGURE 13.4

Why would you want to use the volume level display in the Information window? No real reason, but it does look kind of cool.

Controlling the Tunes

Playing an audio CD from start to finish and controlling the volume are useful and required tasks, but with iTunes you can take control of your music so that you hear only what you want to hear, in the order in which you want to hear it. In the following sections, you'll see how iTunes lets you take control of your tunes. For example, in the next section, you'll learn how to choose the songs you want to hear.

Choosing the Songs You Hear

Let's face it, you probably don't like every song on a CD no matter how much you like the CD on the whole. With iTunes, you can choose the songs that play when you play the CD. You can cause a song to be skipped by unchecking the **Select** check box (see Figure 13.5). When the CD plays, it will skip over every song whose Select check box is unchecked.

To have iTunes include and thus play the song again the next time you play the CD, simply check its **Select** check box.

> **tip**
>
> Along with a CD's information, iTunes remembers the settings you make for a CD and reuses them each time you insert and play the CD. This includes skipping songs, changing the order in which they play, and so on. Cool!

FIGURE 13.5

Here, the song "The Taming of Smeagol" will be skipped because its Select check box is unchecked (of course, this is only for an example; all the songs on this CD are excellent).

Select check box

Choosing the Order in Which Songs Play

iTunes determines the order in which songs play by the order in which they are shown in the Content pane, starting from the top of the pane and moving to the bottom. By default, songs are listed and therefore play in the order they appear on the CD, from track 1 to the last track on the disc. However, you can make songs on a CD play in any order you choose. You have a couple ways to do this.

You can change the order in which songs are listed in the Content pane (and thus the order in which they play) by dragging the songs up or down in the pane (see Figure 13.6). When you change the order of the songs in the pane, you change the order in which they will play.

You can also change the order of tracks by sorting the Content pane by the various attributes shown, such as **Song Name**, **Time**, **Artist**, and so on. You can do this by clicking the column heading of the attribute by which you want to sort the list. When you do so, the tracks will be sorted by that column (see Figure 13.7). To change the direction of the sort (from ascending to descending or from descending to ascending), click the **Sort Order** triangle; the sort direction will be reversed, and the songs will be reordered accordingly. Just like when you manually move songs around, they will play in the order in which they are listed in the pane.

FIGURE 13.6

Order! Order!
Compare the
order of the
songs in this fig-
ure with the pre-
vious one;
listening to the
CD now will be
an entirely
different
experience.

The Content Pane is sorted by this column

Sort Order triangle

FIGURE 13.7

Now the order of
the songs is
based on their
length; in this
case, the longest
song on the CD
will play first,
the next longest
second, and
so on.

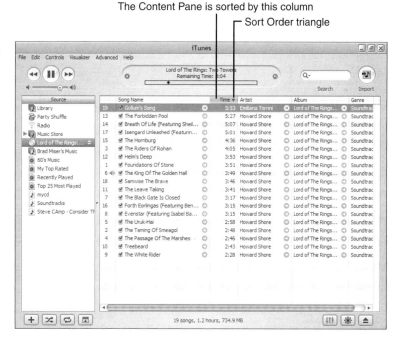

The column by which the pane is sorted is indicated by the column heading being highlighted in blue—this defaults to the first column, which is the track number. (When a CD is the source, the Track Number column is always the first or leftmost column in the Content pane, and it's unlabeled.) When you select a different column, its heading becomes blue to show that it is the current sort column.

You can also tell which column is the sort column as well as the direction of the sort by the **Sort Order** triangle. It only appears in the sort column. When the triangle is pointing down, the sort is descending. When the triangle is pointing up, the sort is ascending.

Getting Random

For a little variety, you can have iTunes play songs in a random order. This feature is called Shuffle. To use this feature, click the **Shuffle** button located at the bottom of the window (second one from the left) or choose **Controls, Shuffle**. As you play music, songs will be selected in a random fashion regardless of how they are listed in the window. Just to add a bit of confusion for you, the order in which the songs are listed in the window doesn't change as you might expect. This is the one case in which the order of the songs in the window is not the order in which they play. The only way you can tell that the Shuffle feature is active is that the Shuffle button will be highlighted.

To return the CD to its natural order, click the **Shuffle** button again or choose **Controls, Shuffle**.

Repeating Tracks

Sometimes, you just can't get enough. In that case, you can set iTunes to repeat an entire CD once or to repeat only a single song. To repeat your tunes, check out these pointers:

tip

To return a CD to the default order, click the first column (which is the Track Number column but is unlabeled for some reason) and then make the Sort Order triangle point down. This returns the CD to play by track number. If you have moved songs around manually too, you will have to drag them up or down the list to return them to their original order. Fortunately, the track number remains associated with the appropriate song, so this isn't too hard.

note

If you have manually ordered a CD by dragging songs, that order is remembered and used when you sort the CD by the first column. To put songs back in their original order, drag them so that track 1 is at the top, track 2 is next, and so on.

- To have iTunes repeat an entire CD, choose **Controls**, **Repeat All** or click the **Repeat** button located at the bottom of the window (third one from the left). The **Repeat** button will become highlighted to show you that it is active, and the CD will repeat when you play it.

- To repeat only the selected song, choose **Controls**, **Repeat One** or click the **Repeat** button a second time. A "1" will appear on the **Repeat** button to indicate that only the current song will be repeated.

- To turn off the repeat function, choose **Controls**, **Repeat Off** or click the **Repeat** button until it is no longer highlighted in blue.

> **note**
>
> If you used the menu to shuffle a disc, you will notice that the Shuffle command on the menu has a check mark next to it. This check mark shows you that the command is currently active. When it isn't, the check mark will disappear. This is true of other settings as well, such as Repeat.

Controlling iTunes from the Desktop

Using the controls you have seen so far is fine, but you might not want to have the iTunes window foremost all the time. You must be able to see iTunes to control it, right? Wrong!

Controlling iTunes from the Windows System Tray

When iTunes is running on a Windows machine, an iTunes icon is displayed in the System Tray. Right-click this icon and you will see an iTunes menu (see Figure 13.8). At the top of the menu, you will see information about the song that is playing (if iTunes is paused, this text will be grayed

> **tip**
>
> Using Repeat, you might hear a song you don't like all that much more than once. Remember to uncheck the Select check box for any songs you don't want to hear. They will be skipped no matter how you play the CD.

out). You can use the commands on this menu just as you can from within iTunes itself. For example, you can skip to the next song by choosing **Next Song**. After you choose a command, you can move off the menu and it will disappear. This is a handy way to control iTunes without having to make its window active or even show it on your desktop.

FIGURE 13.8

You can control iTunes even if you can't see it.

iTunes icon in the System Tray

If you don't want the iTunes icon to appear in the System Tray for some reason, you can remove it. Open the **iTunes Preferences** dialog box (**Ctrl+,**), click the **Advanced** tab, uncheck the **Show iTunes Icon in System Tray** check box, and click **OK**. The icon will no longer appear in your System Tray.

Controlling iTunes from the Mac's Dock

The iTunes icon on the Mac OS X enables you to control iTunes when it is in the background, when its window is minimized, or when the application is hidden. When you Ctrl-click the **iTunes Dock** icon (or right-click if you have a two-button mouse), the **iTunes** menu will appear (see Figure 13.9). At the top of this menu, you will see information about the song currently

tip

To keep iTunes out of the way, open it and select a source, such as an audio CD. Then configure and play the source. Minimize (Windows) or hide (Mac) the iTunes window so it no longer appears on your desktop. Then, you can use the iTunes System Tray icon menu (Windows) or iTunes Dock icon menu (Mac) to control it—for example, to pause when you receive a phone call.

playing (the text is grayed out if iTunes is paused). You control iTunes by choosing a command on this menu. For example, you can pause the music by choosing **Pause**. After you choose a command, the menu will disappear, and you can get back to what you were doing.

FIGURE 13.9

On the Mac, you use its Dock menu to control iTunes even when you can't see it.

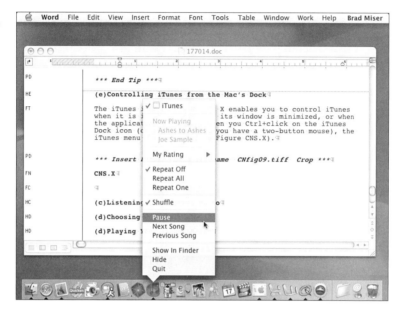

Listening to Internet Radio

iTunes supports Internet "radio" stations; you can choose one of the available stations and listen to its content similarly to how you listen to a radio station over the air. (The stations are actually Web sites that offer streaming MP3, but they are analogous to radio, so using that as a model is a good way to think about them.) iTunes offers a number of genres from which you can choose, such as Pop, Classic Rock, Jazz, and so on. Listening to one of these stations is much like listening to a CD (or any other source for that matter).

note

This is likely obvious to you from the title of this section, but your computer must be able to connect to the Internet to be able to listen to Internet radio.

Playing Your iTunes Radio

To tune in iTunes radio, perform the following steps:

1. Open iTunes and select the **Radio** source by clicking it. The Content pane will contain the list of genres available to you. The column headings will be updated to be appropriate to the content. For example, you will see **Stream**, **Bit Rate**, and **Comment**.

2. Click the **expansion triangle** for the genre in which you are interested (see Figure 13.10). iTunes will connect to the Internet to update the list of channels for the genre you selected, and the genre will expand. You will see the various channels it contains. Look at the stream name, bit rate, and comment for the channels to decide which you want to try. Usually, the comment will provide a description of the kind of music the stream contains.

> # note
>
> When you view the Content pane with Radio source, Stream provides the names of the channels available to you. Bit Rate is a measure of the quality of a channel. The higher the bit rate, the better the quality, but the higher bandwidth connection you need to play it successfully. The Comment column contains a description of each channel.

Radio source

Expansion triangle

Expanded genre

FIGURE 13.10

Most of these radio stations (called streams) don't include commercials.

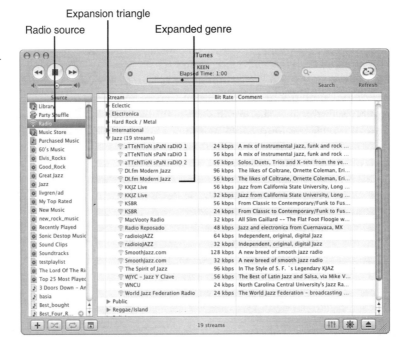

3. To play a channel, select it and click
   Play or double-click the stream you want
   to hear. The channel will begin to play
   (this will be instantaneous if you have a
   fast connection to the Net, or there will
   be a slight delay if you use a dial-up
   connection). Just like when you play a
   song on a CD, the speaker icon will appear
   next to the channel to which you are
   listening.

   Also just like when you listen to a CD,
   information about the channel will
   appear in the Information window (see
   Figure 13.11). This includes the stream
   name, the song currently playing, and
   the Web site with which the channel is
   associated.

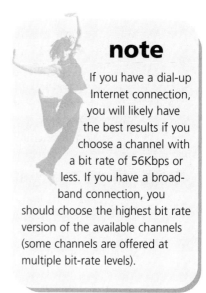

note

If you have a dial-up
Internet connection,
you will likely have
the best results if you
choose a channel with
a bit rate of 56Kbps or
less. If you have a broadband connection, you
should choose the highest bit rate
version of the available channels
(some channels are offered at
multiple bit-rate levels).

FIGURE 13.11

Smooth Jazz is
an appropriate
name for this
stream.

You can use the Volume slider to change the volume level and the **Stop** button to stop playback. The **Rewind** and **Fast Forward** buttons work a little differently than you might expect. Rather than moving you in the selected stream, they instead take you to the previous or next stream, which makes sense when you think about each stream as being like a track on a CD.

Refreshing Your Radio

When you choose the **Radio** source, the **Action** button becomes the **Refresh** button. When you click this, all the genres are refreshed with the latest content. If you leave the **Radio** source selected for a long time, you might want to click the **Refresh** button once in a while to see if new channels become available. (Each time you select the **Radio** source, it is refreshed, so you don't need to click the **Refresh** button if you have recently selected the **Radio** source.)

Configuring iTunes for a Slow Internet Connection

If you use a slow Internet connection, such as a dial-up account, traffic on the Internet can cause the stream of music to slow or even stop, resulting in pauses in the music, even if you choose a lower bit-rate channel, such as 32Kbps. If this is a problem for you, perform the following steps:

1. Choose **Edit**, **Preferences** (Windows) or **iTunes**, **Preferences** (Mac). The **Preferences** dialog box will appear.

2. Click the **Advanced** tab (Windows) or the **Advanced** icon (Mac). The **Advanced** pane will appear (see Figure 13.12).

3. On the **Streaming Buffer Size** drop-down list, choose **Large**. This increases the amount of buffer space used to store a stream before it actually starts to play.

4. Click **OK**. The dialog box will close.

tip

The name of the song currently playing is especially useful when you hear a song you like that you might want to add to your collection. Make a note of the song's name and artist. Then, you can look for CDs containing that song or, even better, buy it from the iTunes Music Store.

note

There are more than just tunes on the iTunes Radio. You can also hear talk, news, and other audio content.

tip

A faster way to open the Preferences dialog box is to press **Ctrl+,** (Windows) or ⌘**+,** (Mac).

FIGURE 13.12

The iTunes Preferences dialog box is very useful, and you will be coming back here again and again.

Hopefully, this will eliminate any pauses in the streams to which you like to listen. If not, choose a different stream or one with a lower bit rate.

Playing Around with Internet Audio

You can do a couple other things with Internet audio using iTunes.

If you want iTunes to be used to play Internet audio by default, open the **Preferences** dialog box (**Ctrl+,** on Windows computers or ⌘**+,** on Macs). Open the General pane. Then check the **Use iTunes as the Default Player for Audio Files** check box (Windows) or click the **Set** button (Mac). When your browser hits an audio file that iTunes supports, iTunes should play it.

You can also play audio streams for which you have a URL within iTunes. To do this, use the following steps:

1. Find the URL pointing to the stream to which you want to listen. Hopefully, you can copy the URL from the Address bar of the Web browser because that is a lot easier than trying to remember the URL or writing it down and then typing it in.

tip

If you want to play the content to which the URL points more than once, download it to your computer and add it to the Library. You'll learn how to do this in the next chapter. You can also add a stream to a playlist by selecting it and choosing **File**, **New Playlist from Selection**.

2. Choose **Advanced**, **Open Stream**. The **Open Stream** dialog box will appear.

3. Paste in or type the URL in the **URL** field (see Figure 13.13).

FIGURE 13.13

Here, I've pasted in a URL to an MP3 file that contains a line from the movie *The Matrix*.

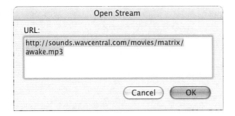

4. Click **OK**. The stream will play.

Customizing the iTunes Window

You can configure iTunes in various ways to suit your preferences. You can also change the size of the iTunes window in different ways.

Setting General iTunes Preferences

On the General pane of the **Preferences** dialog box are several settings you might want to use (see Figure 13.14):

FIGURE 13.14

The General pane of the iTunes Preferences dialog box provides…, well, general preferences.

■ **Source Text**—Use this drop-down list to change the size of the font of the sources shown in the **Source List**. The options are **Small** (default) or **Large**.

■ **Song Text**—This setting changes the size of the text used in the Content pane. Again, your options are **Small** or **Large**.

■ **Show Party Shuffle**—Party Shuffle is a special playlist that you'll learn about later. You use this check box to show or hide this playlist. If the check box is checked, the Party Shuffle playlist will be shown; if unchecked, the playlist won't appear on the Source List.

■ **Show Radio**—This check box determines if the Radio source is shown or not. Uncheck it if you never use the Radio and don't want it to appear on the Source List.

■ **Show Genre When Browsing**—Earlier, you learned about the Browser. This check box controls whether the **Genre** column appears in the Browser (the check box is checked) or not (the check box is not checked). I like the **Genre** column, so I leave this checked, but if you don't, you can uncheck the check box.

■ **Group Compilations When Browsing**—Compilations are CDs that feature more than one artist or composer, such as a theme CD (you know, something like Great TV Theme Songs of the 1970s). If you check this check box, iTunes will show Compilations as an option when you browse by Artist. The compilations in your collection can be browsed by choosing this option (this will make more sense when you learn to browse your music collection in the next chapter). If you uncheck this check box, compilations aren't shown.

■ **Show Links to Music Store**—If you check this box, arrows will appear next to each song, artist, and album in your music collection. When you click these arrows, iTunes will move to the Music Store and will attempt to find the song, artist, or album in the Store. You'll learn more about this in Part III of this book.

■ **On CD Insert**—This determines what iTunes does when you insert an audio CD into your computer. You learned about its options earlier in this chapter.

■ **Connect to Internet When Needed**—If you don't want iTunes to try to connect to the Internet automatically, such as when you are using it on a laptop, uncheck this check box. Because iTunes uses the Internet to get CD information, provide Internet radio, and access the iTunes Music Store, you should leave this check box checked whenever you are using iTunes on a computer that can connect to the Internet.

■ **Check for iTunes Updates Automatically**—This option enables iTunes to check for updates automatically. You'll learn more about this later in this part of the book.

■ **Use iTunes As Default Player**—You learned about this already. This determines if iTunes is used as the default player for various types of audio files.

Changing the Size of the iTunes Window

Like the windows of other applications, you can change the size of the iTunes window. For example, you might want to make the window smaller so that it doesn't consume so much desktop space (remember that you can minimize or hide the window and use its System Tray or Dock controls to control it).

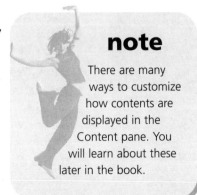

note

There are many ways to customize how contents are displayed in the Content pane. You will learn about these later in the book.

Changing the Size of the iTunes Window on a Windows PC

As you use iTunes, keep in the mind the following tips for keeping the window out of your way:

■ **You can minimize/maximize the window**. Use the standard Minimize and Maximize controls in the iTunes window to hide it or make it full-screen size.

■ **You can make the window smaller**. If the iTunes window is in the resize mode (click the Maximize button so the window's size is maximized, then click it again), you can drag its **resize handle** to make the window smaller until it reaches the smallest possible size (see Figure 13.15). Then, you can slide the window out of the way.

tip

You can change the relative width of the Source List versus the Content pane/Browser by dragging the resize pane handle to the left or right (see Figure 13.15).

Resize pane handle

FIGURE 13.15

Smaller is some-
times better,
when it comes
to window size
that is.

Resize window handle

To shrink the iTunes window down even further, choose Advanced, Switch to Mini
Player. The window will collapse so that you can see on the window and playback
controls and the Information area (see Figure 13.16).

FIGURE 13.16

The Mini Player
version of the
iTunes window is
aptly named,
don't you think?

When the Mini Player window is being used, make it even smaller by dragging the
Resize handle. Then, you can only see the window and playback controls (see Figure
13.17).

FIGURE 13.17

Just when you
think the iTunes
window can't
get any smaller,
you find out
that it can.

To get the iTunes window back to "normal," click the Window Zoom/Maximize box. Then use the Resize handle to make the window the size you want it to be.

Changing the Size of the iTunes Window on a Mac

When you use iTunes on a Mac, you can change the window's size in the following ways:

- **You can hide the application**. Press ⌘+**H** to hide the application. Its window will be hidden from the desktop. You can control iTunes by using its Dock menu. Click the **iTunes Dock** icon to show the window again.

- **You can toggle the size of the window**. If you click the Toggle Size button (the green "light") on the window's title bar, the iTunes window will collapse so that only the playback controls and the Information window are shown (see Figure 13.18). Click the button again to open the window to its full size.

> **tip**
>
> You can change the relative width of the Source List versus the Content pane/Browser by dragging the resize pane handle (the dot located in the center of the bar between the Source List and the Content pane/Browser) to the left or right.

- **You can change the size of the window**. In either the full or collapsed state, you can change the size of the window by dragging its resize handle located in the bottom-right corner of the window.

FIGURE 13.18

On the Mac, you can quickly collapse the iTunes window to this handy size by clicking the Green Zoom button.

Tumbling Tumbleweeds
Elapsed Time: 0:08

Setting iTunes Audio Preferences

You can use iTunes Audio preferences to control how your music plays. For example, you can get rid of the gap of silence between songs or make songs play back at a consistent volume level. You can take advantage of these features by using the Audio pane of the iTunes Preferences dialog box. On this pane, you can configure the following audio settings for your music (see Figure 13.19):

- **Crossfade playback**—This effect causes one song to fade out and the next one to fade in smoothly, eliminating the gaps of silence between songs. To activate it, check the Crossfade Playback check box and use the slider to see the amount of fade time. If you move the slider to the left, songs will fade out more quickly. If you set it to 0, there is no fading, and as soon as one song ends, the next one starts. If you move the slider to the right, the fades will last longer. Click OK and the effect will take effect.

- **Sound Enhancer**—This effect is iTunes' attempt to "add depth and enliven" the quality of your music. The actual result of this effect is a bit difficult to describe, so the best thing to do is try it for yourself. Check the **Sound Enhance** check box and use the slider to set the relative amount of enhancement. Click **OK** and then listen to some music. It if sounds better to you, increase the amount of the effect. If not, decrease it or turn it off.

- **Sound Check**—This effect sets the relative volume level of all songs the same. It is useful if you have changed the relative volume level of songs (perhaps you cranked up your favorite classical tunes) and want to have all your music play at the same volume level. To implement this effect, check its check box and click **OK**.

- **AirTunes Settings**—You can use the AirPort Express Base Station to broadcast your iTunes music over a wireless network (this is called AirTunes). You'll learn about using this cool feature in Chapter 19, "Sharing iTunes Music over a Network." You use the bottom two check boxes in the Audio preferences pane to turn the AirTunes feature on and to disable the iTunes volume control for the remote speakers.

tip

If you toggle the window to its reduced size and then make it even smaller with the resize handle, the window will contain only the window and playback controls.

note

This Crossfade setting does not impact audio CDs. Because there is a physical gap between tracks on the CD, iTunes can't do anything about it. This setting applies to other sources, such as your Library and playlists. (So why cover it in the CD chapter you ask? Because this seemed like the place to cover the other effects, so I added this one here, too.)

FIGURE 13.19

Audio preferences enable you to fine tune your music experience.

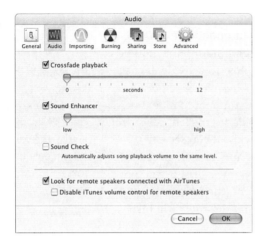

note

You'll learn how to change the relative volume level of songs later in this part of the book.

The Absolute Minimum

By learning how to use iTunes to play audio CDs and Internet radio, you've picked up a lot more knowledge than you might realize. That's because you use the same steps and controls to listen to other music sources, such as your Library, playlists, and so on. In the next couple chapters, you'll learn about these other sources; once you do, you'll be able to use the techniques you picked up in this chapter to work with them.

For now, keep the following tidbits in mind:

- Many of the controls in the iTunes window work just like similar controls on a CD player.

- The iTunes Information window doesn't look like a lot, but you'll learn to really love it when you are building your Library in the next chapter.

- If a song's Select check box is checked, it will play. If it's not checked, the song won't play.

- You determine the songs you want to hear and the order in which you want to hear them for all your sources by the order in which they appear in the Content pane (except for the Radio source, which you have to take as it comes). Each time you insert a CD, iTunes remembers the settings you used last time and uses those settings again. Just wait until you get to playlists— you can take this concept to the extreme!

- You can repeat or randomize the music in any source, such as a CD or playlist.

- Don't forget about the iTunes System Tray (Windows) or Dock (Mac) menu. This is a great way to keep iTunes music going while not consuming any of your valuable desktop real estate.

- You can change the width of columns within the iTunes window, and you can also resize the iTunes window to make it the size you want. As you work through later chapters, you'll also learn how to customize the information you see inside the window as well.

- Listening to the Radio source provides access to lots of music available on the Internet.

- You can use iTunes Audio preferences to control the gap between songs, to equalize the relative volume of songs, and to enhance the sound you hear.

- Know the sources of all iTunes music.

- Find out where your iTunes music will be stored and change the location if it suits your fancy.

- Maximize your music's quality/file size ratio by choosing encoding options and quality levels when you import audio CDs.

- Build your iTunes Library by importing audio CDs into it.

- Browse and search your Library like a master librarian.

- Dump music you don't want cluttering up your digital shelves.

Building, Browsing, Searching, and Playing Your iTunes Music Library

Are you ready for some real iTunes? If the material in the previous chapters covered good features of iTunes, which it did, then this chapter starts the coverage of the amazing, awesome [insert your own superlative here] features that make iTunes something to write a book about. Here is where we start taking your iTunes game to the next level, hitting some home runs, scoring touchdowns, and some other sports clichés that all good books use. It's time to start working with that mysterious Library I have mentioned a number of times but into which, until now, you have only had glimpses.

The iTunes Library is where you can store all your music, such as that from your audio CDs and the Internet, and where any music you purchase from the iTunes Music Store is stored. After you have added music to your Library, you never have to bother with individual CDs again because you can access all your music from the Library. And, you can use the music in your Library in many ways, such as to create playlists, burn CDs, and so on.

Right now, your iTunes Library is probably sort of sad. Like a book library with no books in it, your iTunes Library is just sitting there gathering dust on its digital shelves. You will change that shortly. The first step is to add music to the Library. Then, you'll learn how to browse, search, and listen to the tunes you have added there.

Gathering Your Music from All the Right Places

If you are going to add music to your Library, you have to get it from somewhere, right? The following are the three main sources of tunes for your Library:

- **Audio CDs**—Who wants to bother with audio CDs? Wouldn't it be nice if you could store all of the content of your CD collection in one place so you can listen to any music you want to at any time just by browsing or doing a quick search? Obviously, that is a loaded question because you already know you can use iTunes to do just that. In this chapter, you'll learn how to copy the music from audio CDs into your Library (as you'll remember from Chapter 12, "Touring iTunes," this is called *importing*) so that you never have to use the original CDs again.

- **MP3 and other audio files**—You can add audio files in just about any format to your Library. For example, there are lots of free and legal MP3 files on the Web that you can add to your own Library. In this chapter, you will learn how to add music to your Library in this way too.

- **iTunes Music Store**—With the iTunes Music Store, you can browse and search among hundreds of thousands of songs. When you find music you like, you can purchase an entire CD's worth of songs or you can buy individual songs (can you say one-hit wonders!). When you buy a song, it is downloaded and added to your iTunes Library. Instead of ordering a CD or, even worse, buying one in a physical store, your music is available to you instantly, and you don't even have to import it. Because the iTunes Music Store is so cool, I have devoted an entire part of this book to it (Part III, "The iTunes Music Store"). In that part, you will see how to build your Library by purchasing music online.

Determining Where and How the Music Library Music Is Stored

It is much easier to organize an empty room, so it is good practice to set up the organization of your iTunes Library before you fill it with music. In this section, you'll learn how iTunes organizes the music in your Library. If its standard practices aren't good enough for you, you can change its ways to suit your own organizational preferences.

Working with the iTunes Music Folder

As you import music into the Library, files are created for each song you add (whether it's from a CD, downloaded from the iTunes Music Store, or imported from an existing file). When you first started the application, iTunes created a folder in which it stores all the music it manages for you.

The default location of this folder depends on the kind of computer you are using. On Windows computers, the folder will be stored in a folder called iTunes Music, located within your My Music folder. On Macs, this folder is also called iTunes Music, but it is located in the Music folder within your Home folder.

To see the current location of the iTunes folder on your computer, open the **iTunes Preferences** dialog box and then open the **Advanced** pane (see Figure 14.1). At the top of this dialog box, you will see the iTunes Music Folder Location box. Within this box, you will see the path to your iTunes Music folder.

tip

In case you don't remember from the last chapter, you access the iTunes Preferences dialog box by pressing **Ctrl+** (Windows) or ⌘**+** (Macs).

FIGURE 14.1

The current location of your iTunes folder is shown on the Advanced pane of the iTunes Preferences dialog box.

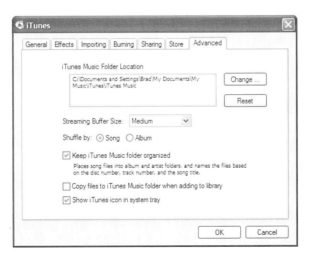

Just for fun, go ahead and open your iTunes Music folder so you can see it for yourself. Use the path you see on the Advanced pane to find it. If you haven't added any music to your Library yet, it might be pretty dull. To see what a full folder looks like, check out Figure 14.2.

FIGURE 14.2

Don't be envious—soon your iTunes Library will soon be as full of good tunes as mine is.

As you can see, within the iTunes Music folder is a folder for each artist (in the figure, my B.B. King folder is highlighted). Within the artists' folders, each album from which you have added music is shown. Within each of those folders, the tracks you have added are individual files (see Figure 14.3). If you take a close look at Figure 14.3, you can see that the files have the extension .mp3, which means these files were imported in the MP3 format.

FIGURE 14.3

In this folder, you can see all the songs contained on the album *The Best of BB King* (which is an excellent album by the way, not that I am qualified to be a music critic).

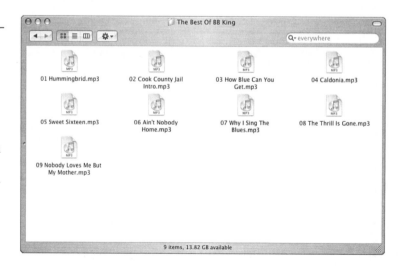

Configuring the Location of the Music Folder

In most cases, the default location of your iTunes Music folder will be fine, and you don't have to do anything about it. However, there are some cases in which you will want to change the location of this folder. For example, suppose you have several hard drives in your computer and the one on which the folder is currently stored doesn't have a lot of room. Even though individual song files are relatively small, you are likely to end up with thousands or tens of thousands of them in your Library. That can add up to a lot of disk space. You might want to change the location of your iTunes Music folder so that it is on a drive with more room.

> **note**
>
> If you already have music in your Library, changing the location of the iTunes Music folder won't hurt you. When you select a new folder, iTunes will remember the location of any previous music you have added to the Library and will update its database so that music will still be part of your Library.

To change the location of this folder, do the following:

1. Open the **Advanced** pane of the iTunes Preferences dialog box.

2. Click the **Change** button. On a Windows PC, you will see the Browse For Folder dialog box (see Figure 14.4). On a Mac, you will see the Change Music Folder Location dialog box (see Figure 14.5).

FIGURE 14.4

You use the Browse For Folder dialog box to move to or choose a new home for your iTunes Music folder.

3. Use the dialog box to move to and select the folder in which you want your iTunes Music folder to be located.

4. Click **OK** (Windows) or **Open** (Mac). You'll return to the Advanced pane, and the folder you selected will be shown in the iTunes Music Folder Location area.

5. Click **OK** to close the iTunes Preferences dialog box.

FIGURE 14.5

The Change
Music Folder
Location dialog
box looks a bit
different from its
Windows coun-
terpart, but the
purpose is
exactly the
same.

Setting Other Organization Preferences

The location of the folder in which your music
will be stored is likely the most important part
of the organization preferences. However,
you'll need to understand a couple more preferences. These are also located on the
Advanced pane of the iTunes Preferences dialog box:

- **Keep iTunes Music Folder
  Organized**—This preference causes
  iTunes to organize your music as
  described earlier—that is, by artist,
  album, and song. Because this is a logical way to organize your music files, I
  recommend that you leave this option
  active by making sure this check box is
  checked.

- **Copy Files to iTunes Music Folder
  when Adding to Library**—This preference causes iTunes to make a copy of
  audio files that already exist on your computer (such as MP3 files you have
  downloaded from the Internet), and it places those copies in your iTunes
  Music folder, just like files you create by importing them from a CD. If this
  preference is inactive, iTunes uses a pointer to song files you are adding
  instead of making a copy of the files; it doesn't actually place the files in your
  iTunes Music folder. I recommend that you make this preference active by
  checking its check box. This way, all your music files will be in the same
  place, no matter where they came from originally. If you don't have iTunes
  make copies when you add songs to your Library and then you delete or
  move the song files you added, iTunes will lose track of the song and you will
  experience the "missing song file" problem. To learn how to solve that problem, see "Solving the Missing Song File Problem" on page **329**.

caution

If you have iTunes copy
files to your iTunes Music
folder when you add
them to your Library, be
aware that it does actu-
ally make a copy of the file
you are adding. This means
you will have two files for each
song you add to the Library. After
you have successfully added songs
to your Library, you should delete
the song files from their original
location so that you aren't wasting
disk space.

Understanding Encoding and Other Important Format Options

In Chapter 11, you learned about the major music file formats that you need to be aware of as you use iTunes. As you will recall, the two primary formats you use when dealing with music are AAC and MP3, but the Apple Lossless format is useful if you want only the highest quality from your music. When you add music to your Library, you choose the format and then you choose the specific configuration of that format.

> **note**
>
> Just in case you don't remember, AAC is a newer and better file format than MP3 because it produces higher quality files with smaller file sizes.

Choosing a Format Option

Although I am sure that going into the specifications for each kind of format would make for fascinating reading, there isn't really any need to get into that detail. Frankly, the benefit of using an application such as iTunes is that it manages all this complexity for you so that you don't have to be concerned with it. If you are like me, you just want to work with the music, not diddle around with complicated settings.

Generally, when you add music to your Library, you should use either the AAC or MP3 format. Because the AAC format is better (with *better* meaning that it provides higher quality music in smaller file sizes), it is usually the best choice.

> **note**
>
> About the only case I can envision where MP3 would be a better option is if you use a portable music player that can only play MP3 music. But because you are reading this book, you are probably using an iPod, and iPods are designed to work with the AAC format as well as the MP3 format (and all the other formats explained in this chapter as well, such as the Apple Lossless format).

Picking Quality Levels

After you select a format, you decide the quality with which the music will be encoded. Higher quality levels mean better-sounding music, but larger file sizes. If file size is not a problem, then choosing a higher quality setting is the way to go. If you have relatively little disk space, you might want to experiment to see which is the lowest quality setting you can choose that results in music that still sounds good to you. If you demand the absolute best in music quality and have hard drive space to spare, Apple Lossless is a good option for you.

Note that when it comes to music, quality is in the ear of the beholder. Also, it heavily depends on the type of music you listen to as well as how you listen to it. For example, if you listen to heavy metal rock using a low-quality pair of speakers (in other words, cheap speakers), quality will be less of an issue for you because you likely won't hear any difference anyway. However, if you listen to classical music on high-quality speakers, the differences in quality levels will likely be more noticeable.

The trade-off for quality is always file size. The higher the quality setting you choose, the larger the resulting files will be. If you don't have disk space limitations and have a discriminating ear, you might want to stick with the highest possible quality setting. If disk space is at a premium for you, then consider using a lower quality setting if you can't detect the difference or if that difference doesn't bother you.

> **note**
>
> Nothing against heavy metal rock, of course (I like some of it myself). It's just that it usually includes lots of distortion and constant noise, which means that minor flaws in the encoded music won't be as noticeable.

Configuring iTunes to Import Music

When you add music to your Library, you start by choosing the import options (mainly format and quality levels) that you want to use. Here are the steps to follow:

1. Open the **Importing** pane of the iTunes Preferences dialog box (see Figure 14.6).

FIGURE 14.6

Here, you can see that the AAC format (the AAC encoder) is selected.

2. Select the format in which you want to add music to your Library on the Import Using menu. For example, to use the AAC format, choose **AAC Encoder**. To use the MP3 format, choose **MP3 Encoder**. Or, choose **Apple Lossless Encoder** to maximize the quality of your music. The other encoder options are WAV and AIFF, you probably won't use those options except for special circumstances, such as when you are going to use the music you encode in a different application, in which case the AIFF encoder might be a good choice.

3. Choose the quality level of the encoder you want to use on the Setting menu. The options you see in this list depend on the format you selected in step 1. If you chose AAC Encoder, you have two quality options: High Quality and Custom. If you chose MP3 Encoder, you have four options: Good Quality, High Quality, Higher Quality, and Custom. If you choose the Apple Lossless Encoder, you have only the Automatic option.

   In the Details box, you will see a summary of the settings you have selected. For example, you will see the data rate of the encoder, such as 128Kbps, and the processor for which the encoder has been optimized. (Do you need to worry about these details? Not really.)

   If you use the AAC encoder, the High Quality setting will likely be all you ever need.

> **note**
>
> The Custom option enables you to configure specific settings that the encoder will use. Because you don't typically need to do this, we won't explore doing so in this chapter. If you want to check it out, choose Custom on the Setting menu and explore the options you see.

4. If you want music you add to your Library to play while it is being added, check the **Play songs while importing** check box. This is a personal preference, and it doesn't impact the encoding process significantly.

5. If you want the files that iTunes creates when you import music to include the track number in their filenames, check the **Create filenames with track number** check box. Because this helps you more easily find files for specific songs, I recommend that you keep this preference active.

6. The **Use error correction when reading Audio CDs** check box causes iTunes to more closely control the encoding process. You should use this option only if you notice problems with the music you add to your Library, such as cracking or popping sounds. If that happens, check this check box and try the import process again.

7. Click **OK** to close the dialog box.

Adding Music from Audio CDs to Your iTunes Music Library

Now that you know all you need to about configuring iTunes to build your Library, you are ready to start adding your own audio CDs to your Library.

Adding Audio CDs to Your Library

Use these steps to add a CD to your Library:

1. Configure the encoder you want to use for the import session (see the section "Configuring iTunes to Import Music" on page **230**).

2. Insert the CD you want to add to your Library. iTunes will attempt to identify it. When it does, the CD will appear in the Source List and will be selected (see Figure 14.7). Notice that the Action button in the upper-right corner of the screen is now the Import button.

3. If there are songs that you don't want to add to the Library, uncheck their **Select** check boxes. Only songs with their check boxes checked will be imported. Unless you really hate a song or disk space is at a premium for you, it is generally better to import all the songs. You can use the Select check box in another source, such as in your Library, to cause those songs to be skipped when you play that source.

4. Click the **Import** button. It will become highlighted, and the import process will start (see Figure 14.8).

   If you left the Play songs while importing preference active, the music will begin to play as it is imported.

> **tip**
>
> You can also choose **File**, **Import** or press **Shift+Ctrl+O** (Windows) or **Shift+⌘+O** (Mac) to start the import process. You will see a dialog box that enables you to move to and select the CD you want to import.

The Information window will show information related to the import process, such as the name of the song currently being imported and the rate at which the import process is happening. The rate of the import process depends on the hardware you are using and the import settings. In most cases, the import process will occur at a much greater rate than the playing process. For example, with moderate hardware, you can usually achieve import rates of 10×, meaning 10 minutes of music will be imported in 1 minute of time.

FIGURE 14.7
iTunes is ready
to add this CD to
the Library.

Song currently being imported

Imported songs

Import information

Stop button

FIGURE 14.8
You can see that
the import
process is really
moving; it is cur-
rently moving
along at 10×
speed.

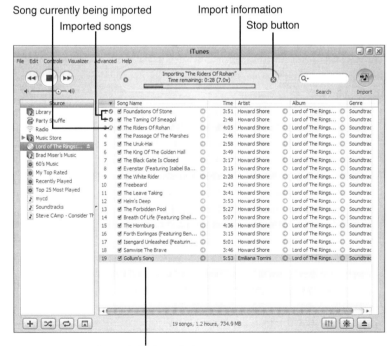

Songs to be imported

An orange circle with a "squiggly" line inside it marks the song currently being imported. When a song has been imported, it is marked with a green circle containing a check mark.

If you want to stop the import process for some reason, click the **Stop** button (the small "x" within a circle) in the Information window.

When the process is complete, you will hear a tone, and all of the songs will be marked with the "import complete" icon.

If you have the Play songs while importing preference active, the music will keep playing long after the import process is complete (because importing is much faster than playing is). Listen for the complete tone or keep an eye on the screen to determine when all the music on the CD has been imported.

5. Eject the CD.

Building Your iTunes Music Library in a Hurry

The import process moves along pretty quickly, but you can make it even faster by following these steps:

1. Gather a pile of your CDs in a location close to your computer.

2. Set the import preferences (encoder and quality) for the import session.

3. Open the **General** pane of the iTunes Preferences dialog box.

4. Choose **Import Songs and Eject** on the **On CD Insert** menu (see Figure 14.9). This causes iTunes to immediately begin the

import process when you insert a CD. When the import process is complete, the CD will be ejected automatically.

5. Click **OK** to close the dialog box.

6. Insert the first CD you want to import. iTunes will start importing it automatically. When the process is complete, the CD will be ejected automatically.

7. Insert the next CD you want to import. Again, iTunes will import the music and eject the disc when it is done.

8. Repeat step 7 until all the CDs have been imported. You'll be amazed at how quickly you can build a Library, even if you have a large number of CDs. When you are done batch importing your CDs, you might want to reset the On CD insert menu to **Show Songs** to prevent unintentionally importing a CD.

FIGURE 14.9
Choosing the Import Songs and Eject option makes adding lots of CDs to your Library as fast as possible.

Importing Audio Files into Your Library

Another potential source of music for your Library is the Internet. There are millions of audio files there, and you can download these files and add them to your Library.

Or, you might have lots of MP3 files on your computer already. You can add all these to your iTunes Library so that you can use that music from within iTunes as well.

You can add music that is stored on your hard drive to your iTunes Library by following these steps:

1. Locate the files you want to add to your Library. For example, find the MP3 files on your hard drive or go to a Web site that has audio files, such as MP3 files, and download them to your computer.

caution

Make sure that you don't download and add illegal files to your Library. In addition to this being the wrong thing to do, you can get prosecuted for downloading files illegally. Make sure any Web sites from which you get files have those files legally with permission of the files' creators.

2. Using iTunes on a Windows computer, choose **File**, **Add File to Library** to add individual music files or **File**, **Add Folder to Library** to add a folder full of music files. On a Mac, choose **File, Add to Library**. If you used the Add Folder to Library command, you'll see the Browse For Folder dialog box. If you used the Add File to Library command, you'll see the Add to Library dialog box.

> ## tip
> On a Mac, you can choose a folder containing files you want to import using the Add to Library dialog box.

3. Use the dialog box to move to and select the folder containing the files you want to add or to select the files you want to add to the Library.

4. Click **Open**, **OK** or **Choose** (the name of the button you see depends on the command you use). The files you selected will be imported into your Library. If you selected a folder, all the songs it contains will be added to your Library. You can also add song files to your iTunes Library by dragging them from the desktop onto the Content pane. This does the same thing as using one of the Add to Library commands.

Browsing and Searching Your Music Library

It won't be long until you have a large Library with many kinds of music in it. In fact, you are likely to have so much music in the Library that you won't be able to find songs you are interested in just by scrolling up and down the screen. In this section, you'll learn how to find music in your Library, first by browsing and then by searching.

Browsing in the Library

You've already seen the Browser a couple of times. Now it is time to put it to work:

1. Select the **Library** on the Source List.

2. If the Browser isn't showing, click the **Action** button, which is now labeled Browse (it looks like an eye). The Browser will appear (see Figure 14.10). The Browser has three columns: Genre, Artist, and Album. The columns start on the left with the most general category, Genre, and end on the right with the most specific category, which is Album.

FIGURE 14.10

The Browser offers a good way to find songs in your Library.

The contents of the "path" selected in the Browser are shown in the Content pane that now occupies the bottom part of the right side of the window. At the top of each column is the All option, which shows all the contents of that category. For example, when All is selected in the Genre column, you will see the contents of all the genres for which you have music in the Library. In Figure 14.10, you can see that I have selected All the Genre column, AD in the Artist column, and All in the Albums column. The causes the Content pane to show all the albums I have by the group AD in the Content pane.

At the bottom of the screen, you will see Source Information for the selected source. Again, in Figure 14.10, you can see that the 13 songs shown in the Content pane will play for 56.7 minutes and consume 57.4MB of disk space.

tip

If you don't see the Genre column in the Browser, open the General pane of the iTunes Preferences dialog box and check the Show Genre When Browsing check box.

You can also open and close the Browser by choosing **Edit**, **Show Browser** or **Edit**, **Hide Browser**. Pressing **Ctrl+B** (Windows) or ⌘+**B** (Mac) also works.

3. To start browsing your Library, select the genre in which you are interested by clicking it. When you do so, the categories in the other two columns are

scoped down to include only the artists and albums that are part of that genre (see Figure 14.11, which shows the Jazz genre in my Library). Similarly, the Content pane now includes only jazz music. Notice in Figure 14.11 that the Source Information has been updated, too. It now shows that I can listen to one day of jazz before I run out of music.

FIGURE 14.11

Because Jazz is selected in the Genre column, the Artist and Album columns contain only the jazz that is in my Library.

FIGURE 14.12

Now I am browsing all my music in the Jazz genre that is performed by Dave McKenna.

4. To further limit the browse, click an artist in which you are interested in the Artist column. The Album column will be scoped down to show only those albums for the artist selected in the Artist column (refer to Figure 14.12). Also, the Content pane will show the songs on the albums listed in the Album column.

5. To get down to the most narrow browse possible, select the album in which you are interested in the Album column. The Content pane will now show the songs on the selected album.

6. When you have selected the genre, artist, and album categories in which you are interested, you can scroll in the Content pane to see all the songs included in the group of songs you are browsing.

tip

You can change the size of the Browser relative to the Content pane by dragging the resize handle (the small circle located in the center of the bar between the two panes) up or down to make the Browser larger or smaller. Of course, making the Browser larger makes the Content pane smaller, and vice versa. Remember that you can also make the Source List narrower or wider by dragging its resize handle to the left or right.

To make the browse results less narrow again, choose **All** in one of the Browser's columns. For example, to browse all your music again, click **All** in the Genre column.

Hopefully, you can see that you can use the Browser to quickly scan your Library to locate music that you want to hear or work with. As you use the Browser more, you will come to rely on it to get you to a group of songs quickly and easily.

Searching Your Music Library

You can use iTunes Search tool to search for specific songs. You can search for songs by any of the following criteria:

- All (searches all possible data)
- Artists
- Albums
- Composers
- Songs

tip

If you want to search by all data at the same time, you don't need to perform step 2 because All is the default selection.

To search for music in your Library, perform the following steps:

1. Select the source you want to search (for example, click the **Library** source). As you might surmise, you can search any source in the Source List, such as a CD, playlist, and so on, by selecting it and then performing a search.

2. Click the **magnifying glass** icon in the **Search** tool (see Figure 14.13). You will see a menu containing the list of data by which you can search.

FIGURE 14.13

By selecting Artists on the menu, you can search the Artist field for all the songs in the selected source (in this case, the Library).

Data for which you can search
Search tool

3. Select the data for which you want to search in the menu. When you release the mouse button, the data you selected will appear in gray inside the search box and in regular text underneath it so you can see which data you are searching for. For example, choose **Artists** to search by the Artist field.

4. Type the data for which you want to search in the field. As you type, iTunes searches the selected source and presents the songs that meet your criterion in the Content pane. It does this on the fly so that the search narrows with each keystroke. As you type more text or numbers, the search becomes more specific (see Figure 14.14).

5. Keep typing until the search becomes as narrow as you need it to be to find the songs in which you are interested.

FIGURE 14.14

Because I selected Artist and typed "lyn" in the Search tool, the Content pane shows all songs whose artist includes the text "lyn," as in The Lyndhurst Orchestra, Lynyrd Skynyrd, and so on.

After you have found songs, you can play them, add them to playlists, and so on.

To clear your search, click the **Clear Search** button that appears in the Search tool after you have typed in it (refer to Figure 14.14). The songs shown in the Content pane will again be determined by your selections in the Browser.

Playing Music in Your Music Library

Remember earlier when I said that you use the same listening techniques to listen to music in your Library as you do when listening to a CD? Now it's time to prove my words.

When you listen to music in your Library, you start by choosing the scope of the music you want to hear. You do this by browsing or searching for music (if you don't know how to do this, here's a hint: Read the previous two sections).

note

When you are listening to your Library, I don't recommend that you uncheck a song's Selected check box in the Library or move songs up and down in the list to control how they are played. Use playlists for that kind of customized listening instead (playlists are explained in Chapter 16, "Creating, Configuring, and Using Playlists"). Changes you make to songs in the Library can result in unexpected things happening if you forget to undo a change before making a playlist, burning a CD, and so on.

After you have the group of songs to which you want to listen showing in the Content pane, use the listening tools you learned about in the previous chapter to listen to your music. For example, you can click **Play** to play the songs, use the Repeat button to repeat them, sort the Content pane by one of the column headings to change the order in which the songs play, and so on.

Removing Tunes from the Music Library

Not all that glitters is gold, nor are all tunes that are digital good. Sometimes, a song is so bad that it just isn't worth the hard disk space it consumes.

To remove songs from your Library, ditch them with the following steps:

1. Find the songs you want to delete by browsing or searching.

2. Select the songs you want to trash. They will become highlighted to show you they are selected (see Figure 14.15).

tip

Remember that you can stop a song from playing by unchecking its Select check box in the Content pane. If you aren't sure you want to dump a song permanently, use that method instead so that you can always use the song again should you change your mind.

FIGURE 14.15

If I hit the Delete key now, "Sirius (MP3)" will be removed from my Library.

3. Press the **Delete** or **Backspace** key. You will be prompted to confirm that you really want to delete the song you have selected.

4. Click **Yes** to confirm the deletion. You will see another prompt asking if you want the selected files to be moved to your Recycle Bin (Windows) or Trash (Mac).

5. Click **Yes**. The selected songs will be deleted from your Library, and their song files will be moved to the appropriate trash receptacle on your computer. The next time you empty that receptacle, they will be gone forever.

Of course, songs you delete probably aren't really gone forever. You can always add them back to the Library again by repeating the same steps you used to place them in there the first time. This assumes that you have a copy somewhere, such as on a CD or stored in some other location. If you imported the music from your hard disk and had iTunes move the songs files to your iTunes Music folder, your only copy will reside in your iTunes Library, so make sure you have such music backed up before you delete it if you might ever want it again.

tip

In many of the prompts iTunes presents to you, you have the option of telling the application not to present those prompts to you again. Just look for the appropriate **Do Not Ask Me Again** check boxes in such prompts and check them to hide those prompts in the future.

caution

You should never delete music that you purchased from the iTunes Music Store unless you are absolutely sure you will never want it again or you have that music backed up elsewhere. You can only download music you purchased from the store one time. After that, you have to pay for it to download it again.

The Absolute Minimum

Although it might not smell like a book library, your iTunes Library is at least as useful and is a heck of a lot easier to get to. In this chapter, you learned how to build and use your iTunes Library. Before we move on to the next great thing about iTunes, check out some related points of interest (well, my interest anyway; hopefully, they will be yours, too):

continues

■ Through the Audible.com service (accessible via the iTunes Music Store), you can also add audio books to your iTunes Library to listen to them on your computer and you can add them to an iPod. Working with audio book content is very similar to working with music. Unfortunately, covering the details of doing so is outside the scope of this book.

■ You learned that you can choose the import encoder and quality settings when you import music from audio CDs to your Library. You can import the same songs at different quality levels to experiment with various settings or to create different versions of the same song. For example, you might want a high-quality version to play from your computer and a lower-quality version with a smaller file size for a portable device. To create another version of a song, you can change the import settings and import it from a CD again. You can also reimport a song already in the Library by setting the encoding settings and adding its file (which will be located in the iTunes Music folder) to the Library, just like other music files stored on your computer.

■ Although we focused on the AAC and Apple Lossless Encoder formats in this chapter, in some cases you might want to use the WAV or AIFF format. For example, suppose you want to use part of a song as a sound byte in an application that doesn't support either of the primary formats, but does support WAV files. You could choose the WAV format and then import the song you want to use in that format. The WAV file, which would be located in your iTunes Music folder, could then be added to the other application you are working with.

■ If you are listening to music while doing something else, such as browsing your Library, you might move away from the song that is currently playing. If you want to move back to it again, choose **File**, **Show Current Song** or press **Ctrl+L** (Windows) or ⌘**+L** (Mac).

■ If you like to shuffle while you listen, you can determine whether iTunes shuffles by song or by album. It can be interesting when listening to the Library if you shuffle by album because iTunes will pick an album and play a song from it, then pick another album, play a song, and so on, rather than just randomly picking songs on the same album. To set this behavior, open the **Advanced** pane of the iTunes Preferences dialog box and click the **Album** radio button next to the Shuffle by text. (The default option is **Song**.)

■ You can use the Browser with any source, although it defaults to being closed with CDs and some playlists because it usually isn't that useful in those contexts (especially when the source is a single CD). Just select the source you want to browse and open the Browser.

IN THIS CHAPTER

- Get to know and love tags.

- Get the details for your music.

- Label your music so that you can do cool things with it, such as creating playlists based on a song's information.

- Rate your songs, set the relative volume level, and hear only the parts you want to hear.

- Don't miss out on album artwork just because you have gone digital.

- Work the Content pane like a pro.

Labeling, Categorizing, and Configuring Your Music

It's confession time. I admit it. This topic might not seem too exciting at first glance. Who wants to spend their time labeling and categorizing music? That is a fair question; I hope by the time you read through this chapter, you answer that question with an enthusiastic "I do, that's who!" Of course, I would be almost as happy even if your response is, "It might not be as fun as building my Library, but it will make my iTunes world a lot better." Think of this chapter as learning the nuts and bolts of how iTunes works so that you can become an iTunes wizard later on.

After you have worked through the labeling content in this chapter, I think you will find the ability to configure the songs in your Library to be pretty exciting because that is where you start really bending iTunes to your will (which isn't as dramatic as it sounds because iTunes is really pretty easy to command).

Understanding Song Tags and Knowing Why You Should Care About Them

In the previous chapter, you saw how you can browse your iTunes music collected by genre, artist, and album. This makes finding music fast and easy, even if you have thousands of songs in your Library. This functionality is enabled because each song in your Library has information—also called *tags*—that categorizes and identifies those songs for you. Genre, artist, and album are just three of the possible tags for each song in iTunes. There are many more items of information that iTunes manages.

These types of data fall into two groups: data that iTunes assigns for you and that you can't change, and data that you or iTunes assigns and that you can change.

> **note**
>
> Not all songs have all the data fields listed. You will only see data that is applicable to a specific song. For example, only music purchased from the iTunes Music Store has information about the purchase.

Data that iTunes assigns and that you can view but can't change include the following:

- **Kind**—The type of file the song is, such as AAC, MP3, and so on.
- **Size**—The amount of disk space required to store the song.
- **Bit Rate**—The quality level at which the song was encoded. Larger numbers, such as 128Kbps, are better.
- **Sample Rate**—The rate at which the music was sampled when it was captured.
- **Date Modified**—The date on which the song file was last changed.
- **Play Count**—The number of times the song has been played.
- **Last Played**—The last time the song was played.
- **Profile**—A categorization of the song's complexity.
- **Format**—The format in which the song was encoded, such as MPEG-1, Layer 3, and so on.
- **Channels**—Whether the track is stereo or mono.
- **Encoded With**—The tools used to encode the song, such as iTunes, QuickTime, and so on.
- **ID3 Tag**—Data formatted according to a set of specifications. If a song's data has been formatted with this specification, the ID3 version number will be shown.

- **Purchase By** and **Account Name**—Information that identifies who purchased the music from the iTunes Music Store and what account was used.

- **FairPlay Version**—For music purchased from the iTunes Music Store, this identifies the version of protection software that was used to encode it.

- **Where**—A path to the song's file on your computer along with the file's name. (Actually, you can change this by changing the location of the song. The reason it is on this list is because you don't manipulate the data itself using the iTunes information tools.)

Data collected for songs that you can change includes the following:

- **Name**—The name of the song.

- **Artist**—The person who performs the song.

- **Album**—The name of the album from which the song comes.

- **Grouping**—A label you can assign to group songs together in some fashion.

- **Composer**—The person who is credited with writing the song.

- **Comments**—A free-form text field in which you can make comments about a song.

- **Genre**—A song's musical genre, such as jazz or classical.

- **Year**—The year the song was created.

- **Track Number**—The song's position on the CD from which it came, such as "2 of 12."

- **Disc number**—The number of the CD. This is meaningful only for multiple CD sets.

- **BPM**—The song's beats per minute.

- **Compilation**—An indicator of whether the song is part of a compilation CD; that being one with music from a variety of artists, such as a theme CD (perhaps something like the best love songs used in action movies).

note

When you insert a CD, iTunes attempts to get that CD's information from the CDDB (the online CD database), which is why it connects to the Internet. If iTunes finds the CD in this database, the information for that CD is applied to the CD and carried into the Library if you import the songs from that CD into iTunes. If you purchase music from the iTunes Music Store, it also contains many of these tags.

When you add a song to your Library, iTunes will add as much of this data as it can find for each song. However, you can add or change the data in the previous list.

So, why should you care about all this data? There are a couple of reasons.

The first is that, as you already know because you learned how to browse and search your Library in the previous chapter, this data can be used to find music in which you are interested. That reason alone should be enough to convince you that these types of data are important to you.

The second reason is, when it comes time to create playlists (which you will learn about in Chapter 16, "Creating, Configuring, and Using Playlists"), you can use song tags to determine which songs are included in your playlists. For example, you can configure a playlist to include the last 25 songs you have played from the Jazz genre. This is just a basic example—you can get much more sophisticated than that. In fact, you can include lots of different combinations of these types of data as criteria in playlists to create very interesting sets of music to listen to.

Viewing Song Information

Now that you understand the types of data that can be associated with songs in your Library, it's time to learn how to view that information. You have three basic areas in which to view song information: the Browser, the Content pane, and the Info window.

Viewing Tags in the Browser

If you read through the previous chapter, you have already used this technique. When you view the Browser, you see the genre, artist, and album tags associated with the songs you are browsing. For example, in Figure 15.1, the songs currently being shown in the Content pane have the Genre set to Rock and the Artist set to 3 Doors Down.

Viewing Tags in the Content Pane

Although you might not realize it, you have also seen tags in the Content pane. The column headings you see in the Content pane are actually the tags associated with the songs you are viewing (see Figure 15.2).

You can customize the columns (tags) shown in the Content pane, as you will learn later in this chapter.

FIGURE 15.1

Each column in the Browser is a tag associated with songs in your Library.

FIGURE 15.2

Each column heading in the Content pane is a tag.

Viewing Tags in the Info Window

The Info window is probably the only area in which you haven't seen tags yet. To view the Info window, select a song in your Library and choose **File**, **Get Info** or press **Ctrl+I** (Windows) or ⌘**+I** (Mac). The Info window will appear (see Figure 15.3).

This window has four panes that you will be using throughout the rest of this chapter. The Summary pane provides a summary view of the song's information, starting at the top with any album art associated with the song and including its name, artist, and album. In the center part of the pane, you see the data iTunes manages (you can view this data, but you can't change it). At the bottom of the pane, you can see the path to the song's file on your computer.

When you click the Info tab, you will see the tags that you can change (see Figure 15.4). You'll learn how to change this data in the next section.

FIGURE 15.3

The Info window enables you to view the tags associated with a song, and you can change many of them.

FIGURE 15.4

Although you can't change the tags shown on the Summary pane, you can change the ones on the Info pane.

The other two panes of the window, Options and Artwork, are used to configure specific aspects of a song (again, we'll get to these topics in a few pages).

You can view information for other songs without closing the window. Click **Next** to move to the next song in the source you are viewing (such as your Library) or **Previous** to move to the previous song. When you do, that song's information will be displayed in the Info window.

To close the window, click **OK**.

Labeling Your Music

Typically, if you have imported a CD or purchased music from the iTunes Music Store, you shouldn't change most of the data that came from the source, such as name, artist, album, track number, and so on. Occasionally, a CD's information will come in incorrect (such as a misspelling in the artist's name); you'll probably want to fix such mistakes. Also, you can certainly add data in those fields that are empty. There are a couple of places in which you can change a song's tags.

Labeling a Song in the Info Window

You can use the Info window to change a song's tags, as you can see in the following steps:

1. Open the **Info** window for the song whose information you want to change.

2. Click the **Info** tab. The Info pane will appear.

3. Enter or change the information shown in the various fields. For example, you can change the song's name or artist. Or you might want to add comments about the song in the Comments box.

   One of the more useful tags is Genre. This can be used for browsing and also in playlists.

4. To change a song's genre, select the new genre on the Genre menu.

5. When you are done entering or changing tags, click **OK**. The Info window will close, and any changes you made will be saved.

tip

If a genre isn't listed on the menu, you can add it to the menu by choosing Custom on the menu and then typing the genre you want to add. That genre will be added to the menu and associated with the current song. You can use genres you add just like those included by the default.

Labeling Multiple Songs at the Same Time

> **tip**
>
> To select multiple songs that are next to each other, hold the **Shift** key down while you click songs. To select multiple songs that aren't next to each other, hold the **Ctrl** (Windows) or ⌘ (Mac) key down while you click songs.

You can change some tags, such as Genre, for a group of songs at the same time. This can be a faster way to enter data because you can change multiple songs at the same time. Here are the steps to follow:

1. Select the songs whose data you want to change.
2. Open the **Info** window. You'll be prompted to confirm that you want to change the information for a group of songs.
3. Click **Yes** to clear the prompt. (You might also want to check **Do not ask me again** so that you don't see this prompt each time you view info for multiple songs.) The Multiple Song Information window will appear (see Figure 15.5). The information and tools in this window work in the same way as they do for individual songs. The difference is that the information and settings apply to all the songs you have selected.
4. Enter data in the fields, make changes to existing data, or use the other tools to configure the songs you have selected. As you change information, the check box next to the tag will become checked to show that you are changing that data for all the selected songs.
5. When you are done making changes, click **OK**. The window will close and the changes you made will be saved.

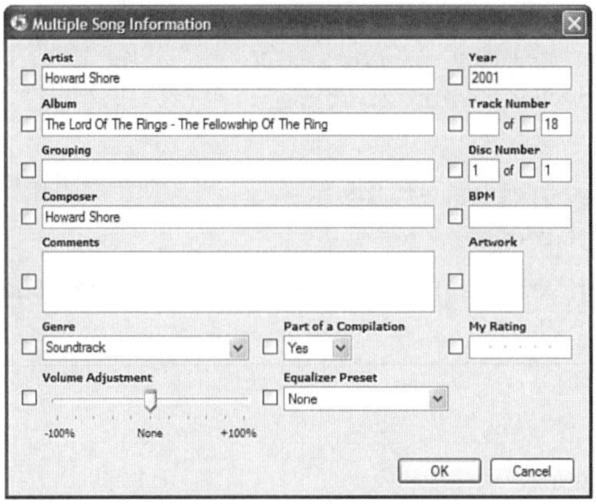

FIGURE 15.5
You can use this window to change the data for multiple songs at the same time.

Labeling a Song in the Content Pane

You can also edit tags within the Content pane:

1. When you are viewing the song you want to label in the Content pane, click once on it to select it. It will become highlighted to show that you have selected it.

2. Click once on the tag you want to edit. The tag will become highlighted to show that it is ready to be edited (see Figure 15.6).

3. Type the new information.

4. Press **Enter** (Windows) or **Return** (Mac). The changes you made will be saved.

FIGURE 15.6

You can also change tags from the Content pane.

Configuring a Song's Options

You can configure a number of options for the songs in your Library, including the following:

- **Relative Volume**—You can change a song's relative volume so that it is either louder or quieter than "normal." This is useful if a song was recorded at a relatively high or low volume level that makes it either jarring or difficult to hear when you play it with other songs.

- **Equalizer Preset**—You can use the iTunes Equalizer to configure the relative volume of sound frequencies. You'll learn about the Equalizer in Chapter 18, "Equalizing Your Music."

- **My Rating**—You can give tunes a rating from one to five stars. You can use ratings in various ways, such as to create criteria for playlists (such as include only my five-star songs) or to sort the Content pane.

- **Start and Stop Time**—You can set songs to start or stop at certain points in the track. This can be useful if you don't want to hear all of a track, such as when a song has an introduction that you don't want to hear each time the song plays.

note

Remember that you can use the Sound Check feature to have iTunes try to equalize the volume of the songs you play.

tip

The Start Time setting is particularly useful for live albums on which the artist has introductions to one or more songs. If you listen to the album frequently, hearing the introductions over and over again can be annoying. Use the Start Time setting so that the song starts playing at the music and you won't have to wait for the introduction to be done before you get to the good stuff.

Configuring Song Options in the Info Window

You can configure a song's options in the Info window by performing the following steps:

1. Select the song whose options you want to set.

2. Open the **Info** window.

3. Click the **Options** tab (see Figure 15.7).

4. To change the song's relative volume, drag the **Volume Adjustment** slider to the left to make the song quieter or to the right to make it louder.

5. To rate the song, click the dot representing the number of stars you want to give the song in the My Rating field. For example, to give the song three stars, click the center (third) dot. Stars will appear up to the point at which you click. In other words, before you click you'll see a dot. After you click a dot, it becomes a star.

6. To set a start time, check the **Start Time** check box and enter a time in the format minutes:seconds. When you play the song, it will start playing at the time you enter.

A good way to figure out where to start a song is to play it while watching the elapsed time in the Information area. When you get to the point at which you want the song to start playing, make a note of the elapsed time setting and use that for the start time.

7. To set a stop time, check the **Stop Time** check box and enter a time in the format *minutes:seconds*. When you play the song, it will stop playing at the time you enter.

8. Click **OK**. The window will close and your changes will be saved.

FIGURE 15.7

Using the Options tab, you can configure a number of settings for a song.

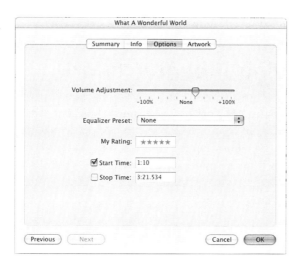

Ratings Songs in the Content Pane

You can also rate songs in the Content pane. To do so, follow these steps:

1. Scroll in the Content pane until you see the **My Rating** column (see Figure 15.8).

2. Select the song you want to rate. Dots will appear in the My Rating column for that song.

3. Click the dot representing the number of stars you want to give the song. The dots up to and including the one on which you clicked will become stars.

Adding and Viewing Album Artwork

Many CD and album covers are works of art (though many aren't!), and it would be a shame never to see them just because your music has gone digital. With iTunes, you don't need to miss out because you can associate artwork with songs and display that artwork in the iTunes window. You can also print CD case labels that include an album's artwork so that you can produce CDs that look just like those you purchase. (You'll learn about printing CD case labels in Chapter 18, "Burning Your Own CDs or DVDs.")

Most of the music you purchase from the iTunes Music Store will include artwork that you can view. You can also add artwork to songs that you obtain from other sources and view and use those graphics in the same way.

Viewing Album Artwork

To view a song's artwork, do one of the following:

- Click the **Artwork** button located under the Source list. The Artwork pane will appear and display the artwork associated with either the currently playing song or the currently selected song (see Figure 15.9). At the top of the artwork, you will see **Selected Song**, which indicates you are viewing the artwork associated with the selected song, or **Now Playing**, which indicates you are viewing artwork associated with the song currently playing.

■ Click the artwork to see a larger version in a separate window (see Figure 15.10). The title of the window will be the name of the song the artwork is associated with.

FIGURE 15.9

You can view the artwork associated with a song in the Artwork pane.

Artwork button

FIGURE 15.10

You can view a large version of a song's artwork in a separate window.

- To choose between viewing artwork associated with the selected song or the song currently playing, click the text at the top of the Artwork pane. The artwork will change to the other option (for example, if you click Now Playing, it will become Selected Song), and you will see the artwork for that song.

- If you choose the Now Playing option, the artwork will change in the Artwork pane as the next song begins playing (unless, of course, the songs use the same artwork).

- If the song has more than one piece of artwork associated with it, click the arrows that appear at the top of the Artwork pane to see each piece of art.

note

If you view the artwork in a separate window, it does not change with the music. When you open the artwork in a new window, it is static, meaning you can only view the image you clicked.

Adding Artwork for Songs

You might want to associate artwork with a song. For example, if a song doesn't have album art associated with it, you can add the art yourself. Or, you might want to add the artist's picture or some other meaningful graphic to the song. You can add one or more pieces of art to songs by using the following steps:

1. Prepare the artwork you are going to associate with a song. You can use graphics in the usual formats, such as JPG, TIFF, GIF, and so on.

2. Select the song with which you want to associate the artwork.

3. Open the **Info** window and then click the **Artwork** tab (see Figure 15.11). If the selected song has artwork with it, you will see it in the Artwork pane.

You can use the slider under the image box to change the size of the previews you see in the window. Drag the slider to the right to make the image larger or to the left to make it smaller. This doesn't change the image; instead, it only impacts the size of the image as you currently see it in the Info window. This is especially useful when you associate more than one graphic with a song because you can see them all at the same time.

tip

You can also add artwork to a song by dragging the image file from your desktop onto the Artwork pane of the Info window.

FIGURE 15.11

You use the
Artwork pane to
add artwork to a
song.

FIGURE 15.11

You use the
Artwork pane to
add artwork to a
song.

4. Click **Add**. A dialog box that enables you to choose an image will appear.

5. Move to and select the image you want to associate with the song.

6. Click **Open** (Windows) or **Choose** (Mac). The image will be added to the window (see Figure 15.12).

7. Continue adding images to the Artwork pane until you have added all the images for a song.

   The default image for a song is the one on the left of the image box.

8. To change the order of the images, drag them in the image box.

9. Click **OK**. The window will close and the images will be saved with the song (see Figure 15.13).

FIGURE 15.12

This song now
has two images
associated
with it.

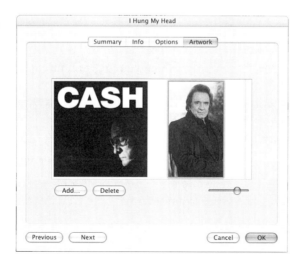

FIGURE 15.13

You can tell this song has multiple images associated with it by the arrows at the top of the Artwork pane. Click an arrow to see the other images.

View previous image

View next image

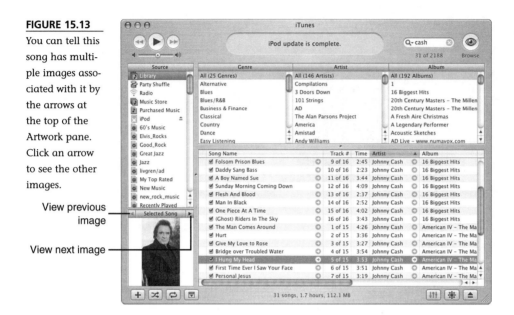

Customizing the Content Pane

There are a number of ways to customize the columns (tags) that appear in the Content pane. What's more, you can customize the Content pane for each source. The customization you have done for a source (such as a CD or playlist) is remembered and used each time you view that source.

You can choose the tags (columns) that are shown for a source by using the following steps:

1. Select the source whose Content pane you want to customize. Its contents will appear in the Content pane.

2. Choose **Edit**, **View Options** or press **Ctrl+J** (Windows) or ⌘**+J** (Mac). You will see the View Options dialog box (see Figure 15.14). At the top of the dialog box, you see the source for which you are configuring the Content pane. (In Figure 15.14, it is a playlist called Johnny Cash.) You also see all the available columns that can be displayed. If a column's check box is checked, that column will be displayed; if not, it won't be shown.

3. Check the check boxes next to the columns you want to see.

4. Uncheck the check boxes next to the columns you don't want to see.

5. Click **OK**. When you return to the Content pane, only the columns you selected will be shown (see Figure 15.15).

FIGURE 15.14

You can set the columns shown in the Content pane with the View Options dialog box.

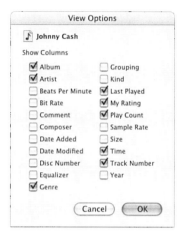

If you can't see all the columns being displayed, use the horizontal scrollbar to scroll in the Content pane. You can also use the vertical scroll bar to move up and down in the Content pane.

FIGURE 15.15

If you could view all the columns in this Content pane, you would see that they correspond to the check boxes checked in the previous figure.

Following are some other ways to customize the Content pane:

■ You can change the width of columns by pointing to the line that marks the boundary of the column in the column heading section. When you do, the cursor will become a vertical line with arrows pointing to the left and right.

Drag this to the left to make a column narrower or to the right to make it wider. The rest of the columns will move around to accommodate the change.

■ You can change the order in which columns appear by dragging a column heading to the left or to the right. When you release the mouse button, the column will assume its new position and the other columns will move to accommodate it.

■ As you learned when playing a CD, you can sort the Content pane using any of the columns by clicking the column heading by which you want the pane to be sorted. The

note

The only column you can't change (width or location) is the first one (which usually displays the track if you are viewing a CD or playlist and is empty when you are viewing your Library).

songs will be sorted according to that criterion, and the column heading will be highlighted to show it is the current sort column. To change the direction of the sort, click the **sort order triangle**, which appears only in the Sort column. When you play a source, the songs will play according to the order in which they are sorted in the Content pane, starting from the top of the pane and playing toward the bottom.

The Absolute Minimum

Hopefully this chapter turned out to be more exciting than you might have expected based on its title. Although labeling your music might not be fun in itself, it does enable you to do fun things. Setting options for your music enables you to enhance your listening experience, and adding and viewing artwork is fun. Finally, you saw that the Content pane can be customized to your preferences. As we leave this chapter, here are some nuggets for you to chew on:

- If iTunes can't find information about a CD, you can enter that information yourself by using the Info window that you learned about in this chapter.

- If you want to check for information about a CD on command, choose **Advanced**, **Get CD Track Names**. (You can also use this command if you turned off the preference that allows iTunes to perform this task automatically.) iTunes will connect to the Internet and attempt to get the CD's information.

- Occasionally, iTunes will find more than one CD that seems to be the one it looked for. When this happens, you will see a dialog box that lists each candidate that iTunes found. Select the information you want to apply to the CD by clicking one of the candidates.

- You can submit track names for a CD. Label the CD and select it. Then choose **Advanced**, **Submit CD Track Information**. The CD's information will be uploaded into the CDDB and will be provided to other people who use the same CD.

- When adding artwork to songs, you aren't limited to just the related album cover. You can associate any kind of graphics with your songs. For example, you can use pictures of the artists, scenes that relate to the music, pictures you have taken that remind you of the music, and so on.

- If you have looked at the figures in this chapter, you should be able to guess who one of my favorite artists is. Can you remember that far back?

IN THIS CHAPTER

● Learn why playlists might just be the best
  of iTunes' many outstanding features.

● Collect your favorite music in a standard
  playlist so you hear only the music you
  want to hear when you want to hear it.

● Change your playlists whenever the spirit
  moves you.

● Become an iTunes master by creating your
  own smart playlists to make iTunes choose
  music for you to listen to based on your
  criteria.

● Use iTunes' special playlists.

Creating, Configuring, and Using Playlists

Of all the cool features that iTunes offers (and as you have seen, there are lots of cool features), this chapter's topic—playlists—just might be the coolest of them all. Playlists enable you to listen to exactly the music you want to hear, when and how you want to hear it. Do you love a CD but hate a song or two on it? Fine, just set up a playlist without the offensive song. Wish that you could hear different songs from a variety of albums? No problem. Ever thought that it would be neat if you could pick a style of music and hear your favorites tunes in that style? How would you like it if the tunes you hear are selected for you automatically based on your preferences? With iTunes playlists, you can do all this and more.

Understanding Playlists

Simply put, playlists are custom collections of songs that you create or that iTunes creates for you based on criteria you define. After a playlist has been created, you can listen to it, put it on a CD, move it to your iPod, share it over a network, and more.

There are two kinds of playlists: standard playlists and smart playlists.

The Standard-But-Very-Useful Playlist

A standard playlist (which I'll call just *playlist* from here on) is a set of songs you define manually. You put the specific songs you want in a playlist and do what you will with them. You can include the same song multiple times, mix and match songs from many CDs, put songs in any order you choose, and, basically, control every aspect of that music collection (see Figure 16.1).

note

In the Source List, the playlist icon is a blue box with a musical note in its center (see Figure 16.1). A smart playlist has a purple box with a gear inside it (see Figure 16.2).

FIGURE 16.1

Here is a standard playlist that contains a wide variety of tunes from an assortment of artists.

Playlists are very useful for creating CDs or making specific music to which you might want to listen available at the click of the mouse. With a playlist, you can determine exactly what songs are included and the order in which those songs play. Playlists are also very easy to create and they never change over time—unless you purposefully change them of course.

The Extra-Special Smart Playlist

A smart playlist is smart because you don't put songs in it manually. Instead, you tell iTunes what kind of songs you want included in it by the attributes of that music, such as genre or artist, and iTunes picks those songs for you (see Figure 16.2). For example, you can create a playlist based on a specific genre, such as Jazz, that you have listened to in the past few days. You can also tell iTunes how many songs to include.

> # caution
>
> Creating smart playlists depends on your music being properly tagged with information, such as genre, artist, song names, and so on. Sometimes music you add to your Library, such as by adding MP3 files that are stored on your hard drive to it, won't have all this information. Before you get going with smart playlists, make sure you have your music properly labeled and categorized. Chapter 15, "Labeling, Categorizing, and Configuring Your Music," explains how you do this.

FIGURE 16.2

On the surface, a smart playlist doesn't look all that different from a playlist, but when you take a closer look, you will see that a smart playlist lives up to its name.

The really cool thing is that smart playlists can be dynamic, meaning that the songs they contain are updated live, based on your criteria. As you add, listen to, or change your music, the contents of a smart playlist can change to match those changes; this happens in real time so that the songs included in a smart playlist can change too. Imagine that you have a smart playlist that tells iTunes to include all the music you have in the Jazz genre that is performed by Kenny G, the Pat Metheny Group, Joe Sample, and Larry Carlton. If you make this a "live" smart playlist, iTunes will automatically add any new music from any of the artists to it as you add that music to your Library. The content of a live smart playlist changes over time, depending on the criteria it contains.

> **note**
>
> Whether it's a standard playlist or a smart playlist, the playlist is the staring point for some iTunes activities such as burning a CD. And much of the time, a playlist makes listening to specific music easy and fast.

Building and Listening to Standard Playlists

Although they aren't as smart as their younger siblings, standard playlists are definitely very useful because you can choose the exact songs included in them and the order in which those songs will play. In this section, you will learn how to create, manage, and use playlists.

Creating a Standard Playlist

You have two ways to create a playlist. One is to create a playlist that is empty (meaning that it doesn't include any songs). The other is to choose songs and then create a playlist that includes those songs.

The place you start depends on what you have in mind. If you want to create a collection of songs, but aren't sure which specific songs you want to start with, create an empty playlist. If you know of some songs that you are going to included, choose them and create the playlist. Either way, creating a playlist is simple and you end up in the same place.

> **tip**
>
> You should create standard playlists for CDs that you burn because you always can be sure of the songs a standard playlist contains.

Creating an Empty Standard Playlist

You can create an empty playlist from within iTunes by using any of the following techniques:

- Choosing **File**, **New Playlist**.
- Pressing **Ctrl+N** (Windows) or ⌘**+N** (Mac).
- Clicking the **Create Playlist** button (see Figure 16.3).

FIGURE 16.3
This playlist has been created and is ready to be renamed.

New playlist

Create playlist

Whichever method you use will result in an empty playlist whose name will be highlighted to show you that it is ready for you to edit. Type a name for the playlist and press **Enter** (Windows) or **Return** (Mac). The playlist will be renamed and selected. The Content pane will be empty because you haven't added any songs to the playlist yet. You will learn how to do that in the section called "Adding Songs to a Playlist" on page **271**.

Creating a Standard Playlist with Songs in It

If you know some songs you want to place in a playlist, you can create the playlist so that it includes those songs as soon as you create it. Here are the steps to follow:

tip

Remember that you can choose a group of songs that are next to one another by holding down the Shift key while you click them. You can choose multiple songs that aren't next to one another by holding down the **Ctrl** key (Windows) or the ⌘ key (Mac) while you click them.

1. Browse or search the Library to find the songs you want to be included in the playlist. For example, you can browse for all the songs in a specific genre or search for music by a specific artist.

2. In the Content pane, select the songs you want to place in the playlist.

3. Choose **File**, **New Playlist from Selection**. A new playlist will appear on the Source List and will be selected. Its name will be highlighted to indicate that you can edit it, and you will see the songs you selected in the Content pane (see Figure 16.4).

tip

You can also create a new playlist containing one or more songs by selecting the songs and pressing **Ctrl+Shift+N** (Windows) or ⌘**+Shift+N** (Mac).

iTunes will attempt to name the playlist by looking for a common denominator in the group of songs you selected. For example, if all the songs are from the same artist, that artist's name will be the playlist's name. Similarly, if the songs are all from the same album, the playlist's name will be the artist's and album's name. Sometimes iTunes picks an appropriate name, and sometimes it doesn't.

FIGURE 16.4

Because I created a playlist from selected songs, the new playlist contains the songs I selected when I created it.

4. While the playlist name is highlighted, edit the name as needed and then press **Enter** (Windows) or **Return** (Mac). The playlist will be ready for more songs.

Adding Songs to a Playlist

The whole point of creating a playlist is to add songs to it. Whether you created an empty playlist or one that already has some songs in it, the steps to add songs are the same:

1. Select the Library as the source.

2. Browse or search the Library so that songs you want to add to the playlist are shown in the Content pane.

3. Select the songs you want to add to the playlist by clicking them (remember the techniques to select multiple songs at the same time). To select all the songs currently shown in the Content pane, press **Ctrl+A** (Windows) or ⌘**+A** (Mac).

4. Drag the selected songs from the Content pane onto the playlist to which you want to add them. When the playlist becomes highlighted and the cursor includes a plus sign (+), release the mouse button (see Figure 16.5). The songs will be added to the playlist.

5. Repeat steps 2 through 4 until you have added all the songs you want to include in the playlist.

6. Select the playlist on the Source List. Its songs will appear in the Content pane (see Figure 16.6). Information about the playlist, such as its playing time, will appear in the Source Information area at the bottom of the iTunes window.

tip

For still another way to create a playlist, try this: Select a group of songs and drag them onto the Source List. When you do so, iTunes will do the same thing as it does when you create a playlist using the New Playlist from Selection command.

tip

You can also move songs from one playlist to another one. Just select a playlist instead of the Library in step 1.

You can select and add the same song to a playlist as many times as you'd like to hear it.

note

The Source Information area becomes very important when you are creating a CD because you can use this to make sure a playlist will fit onto a CD.

FIGURE 16.5

You add songs to a playlist by dragging them onto the playlist in the Source pane.

FIGURE 16.6

This playlist, called (in a burst of creativity) "Big Band Boogie," contains music from an album of the same name.

Removing Songs from a Playlist

If you decide that you don't want one or more songs included in a playlist, select the songs you want to remove in the playlist's Content pane and press the **Delete** key. A warning prompt will appear. Click **Yes** and the songs will be deleted from the playlist. (If this dialog box annoys you like it does me, check the **Do not ask me again** check box and you won't ever have to see it again.)

Setting the Order in Which a Playlist's Songs Play

Just like an audio CD, the order in which a playlist's songs play is determined by the order in which they appear in the Content pane (the first song will be the one at the top of the window, the second will be the next one down, and so on). You can drag songs up on the list to make them play earlier or down in the list to make them play later.

Listening to a Standard Playlist

After you have created a playlist, you can listen to it by selecting it on the Source List and using the same controls you use to listen to a CD or music in the Library. You can even search in and browse playlists just as you can the Library or CDs. (That's the real beauty of iTunes; it works the same way no matter what the music source is!)

Deleting a Standard Playlist

If you decide you no longer want a playlist, you can delete it by selecting the playlist on the Source List and pressing the **Delete** key. A prompt will appear; click **Yes** and the playlist will be removed from the Source List. (Make sure to check the **Do not ask me again** check box if you don't want to be prompted in the future.) Even though you've deleted the playlist, the songs in the playlist remain in the Library for your listening pleasure.

tip

You can also change the order in which songs will play by sorting the playlist by its columns. You do this by clicking the column title in the column by which you want the Content pane sorted. You can set the columns that appear for a playlist by using the **Edit**, **View Options** command, as you learned to do in the previous chapter.

You can use the iTunes Shuffle and Repeat features with playlists just like you can use them with other sources. For example, to hear the songs in a playlist in a random order, select the playlist you want to hear and click the Shuffle button. The songs will play back in random order. The setting of these buttons, just like song order and view options, is remembered with the playlist. So if you set a playlist to Shuffle, it will shuffle whenever you play it until you unshuffle it again.

Becoming a Musical Genius with Smart Playlists

The basic purpose of a smart playlist is the same as a standard playlist—that is, to contain a collection of songs to which you can listen, put on a CD, and so on. However, the path that smart playlists take to this end is different from standard playlists. Rather than choosing specific songs as you do in a standard playlist, you tell iTunes the kind of songs you want in your smart playlist, and it picks out the songs for you and places them in the playlist.

note

When you delete a song from a playlist, it *isn't* deleted from the Library. It remains there so you can add it to a different playlist or listen to it from the Library.

For example, suppose you want to create a playlist that contains all of your Classical music. Rather than picking out all the songs in your Library that have the Classical genre (as you would do to create a standard playlist), you can use a smart playlist to tell iTunes to choose all the Classical music for you. The application then gathers all the music with the genre Classical and places that music in a smart playlist.

Understanding Why Smart Playlists Are Called Smart

You create a smart playlist by defining a set of criteria based on any number of different attributes. After you have created these criteria, iTunes chooses songs that meet those criteria and places them in the playlist. An example should help clarify this. Suppose you are a big-time Elvis fan and regularly add Elvis music to your Library. You could create a playlist and manually drag your new Elvis tunes to that playlist. But by using a smart playlist instead, you could define the playlist to include all your Elvis music. Anytime you add more Elvis music to your Library, that music would be added to the playlist automatically.

note

iTunes includes several smart playlists by default. These include 90's Music (music based on the Year attribute being 1990 to 1999), My Top Rated (all the music you have rated three stars or above), Recently Played (songs you have played within the past two weeks), and Top 25 Most Played (the 25 songs you have played most often). To see the songs that meet these conditions, select a smart playlist and you will see its songs in the Content pane.

You can also base a smart playlist on more than one attribute at the same time. Going back to the Elvis example, you could add the condition that you want only those songs you have rated four stars or higher so that the smart playlist contains only your favorite Elvis songs.

As the previous example shows, smart playlists can be dynamic; iTunes calls this *live updating*. When a smart playlist is set to be live, iTunes changes its contents over time to match the criteria. If this feature isn't set for a smart playlist, that playlist will contain only those songs that meet the criteria at the time the playlist was created.

Finally, you can also link a smart playlist's conditions by the logical expression All or Any. If you use an All logical expression, all the conditions must be true for a song to be included in the smart playlist. If you use the Any option, only one of the conditions has to be met for a song to be included in the smart playlist.

Creating a Smart Playlist

You can create a smart playlist by performing the following steps:

tip

You can also create a new smart playlist by pressing **Ctrl+Alt+N** (Windows) or **Option+⌘+N** (Mac).

1. Choose **File**, **New Smart Playlist** or hold down the **Shift** (Windows) or **Option** (Mac) key and click the **New Playlist** button, which becomes the **New Smart Playlist** button when the **Shift** or **Option** key is pressed down. You will see the Smart Playlist dialog box (see Figure 16.7).

Operand menu   Remove Condition

Attribute menu   Condition box   Add Condition

FIGURE 16.7

The Smart Playlist dialog box enables you to create playlists based on a single attribute or many of them.

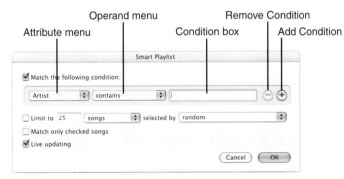

2. Choose the first attribute on which you want the smart playlist to be based in the Attribute menu. For example, you can choose Artist, Genre, My Rating, Year, and so on. The Operand menu will be updated so that it is applicable to the attribute you selected. For example, if you choose Artist, the Operand menu will include Contains, Does Not Contain, Is, Is Not, Starts With, and Ends With.

3. Choose the operand you want to use in the **Operand** menu. For example, if you want to match data exactly, choose Is. If you want the condition to be more loose, choose Contains.

4. Type the condition you want to match in the **Condition** box. The more you type, the more specific the condition will be. As an example, if you choose Artist in step 1, Contains in step 2, and type **Elvis** in this step, the condition would look like the one shown in Figure 16.8 and would find all songs that include Elvis, Elvis Presley, Elvis Costello, Elvisiocity, and so on. If you typed **Elvis Presley** in the Condition box and left the Contains operand, iTunes would only include songs whose artist includes Elvis Presley, such as Elvis Presley, Elvis Presley and His Back-up Band, and so on.

note

As you make selections on the Attribute menu and type conditions in the Condition box, iTunes will attempt to automatically match what you type to data from the songs in your Library. If your Library includes Elvis music and you use Artist as an attribute, iTunes will enter Elvis Presley in the Condition box for you as you start to type "Elvis."

FIGURE 16.8

This smart playlist is getting smarter.

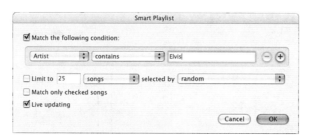

5. To add another condition to the smart playlist, click the **Add Condition** button (the plus sign). A new, empty condition will appear (see Figure 16.9). At the top of the dialog box, the All or Any menu will also appear.

FIGURE 16.9

This smart playlist now contains two conditions; both are currently based on Artist.

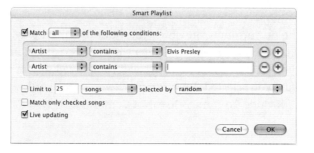

6. Choose the second attribute on which you want the smart playlist to be based in the second condition's **Attribute** menu. For example, if you want to include songs from a specific genre, choose **Genre** on the menu.

> **tip**
>
> If you want to remove a condition from a smart playlist, click the Remove button (the minus sign) for the condition you want to remove.

7. Choose the operand you want to use in the **Operand** menu, such as Contains, Is, and so on.

8. Type the condition you want to match in the **Condition** box. If you selected Genre in step 6, type the genre that the music in the playlist should come from. As you type, iTunes will try to match the genre you type with those in your Library.

9. Repeat steps 6 through 8 to add more conditions to the playlist, until you have all the conditions you want to include (see Figure 16.10).

FIGURE 16.10

This smart playlist is approaching the genius level; it now includes four conditions.

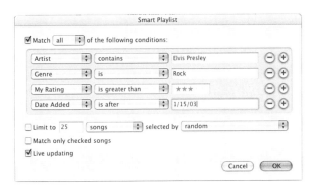

10. Choose **All** on the menu at the top of the dialog box if all the conditions must be met for a song to be included in the smart playlist, or choose **Any** if only one of them must be met. For example, you could create a smart playlist based on multiple Artist conditions, and the playlist would feature music by those artists. In this case, you would choose Any so that if a song is associated with *any* of the artists for which you created the condition, it would be included in the playlist. As a contrasting example, if you want the playlist to include songs you have rated as three stars or better by a specific artist, you would include both of these conditions and then choose All in the menu so that both conditions would have to be met for a song to be included.

You can limit the length of a smart playlist based on a maximum number of songs, the time it plays, or the size of the files it includes. You set these limits using the Limit to check box and menus.

11. If you want to limit the playlist, check the **Limit to** check box. If you don't want to set a limit on the playlist, leave the check box unchecked and skip to step 15.

12. Choose the attribute by which you want to limit the playlist in the first menu; by default, this menu has Songs selected (see Figure 16.11). Your choices include the number of songs (songs on the menu), the time the playlist will play (in minutes or hours), or the size of the files the playlist contains (in GB or MB).

FIGURE 16.11

You can choose to limit a smart playlist to a number of songs, a length of time, or by disk space.

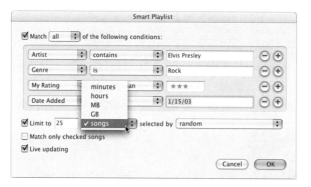

13. Type the data appropriate for the limit you selected in the **Limit to** box. For example, if you selected Minutes in the menu, type the maximum length of the playlist in minutes in the box. If you selected Songs, enter the maximum number of songs that can be included in the playlist.

14. Choose how you want iTunes to choose the songs it includes based on the limit you selected by using the **selected by** menu. This menu has many options, including to choose songs randomly, based on your rating, how often the songs are played, and so on (see Figure 16.12).

FIGURE 16.12

These options tell iTunes how you want it to choose songs for a smart playlist when you limit that playlist's size.

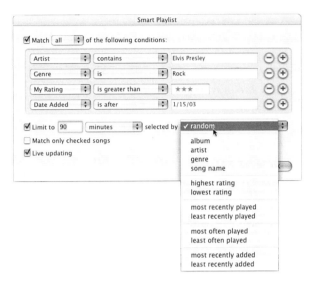

15. If you want the playlist to include only songs whose Select box in the Content pane is checked, check the **Match only checked songs** check box. If you leave this check box unchecked, iTunes will include all songs that meet the playlist's conditions, even if you have unchecked their Select check box in the Content pane.

16. If you want the playlist to be dynamic, meaning that iTunes will update its contents over time, check the **Live updating** check box. If you uncheck this check box, the playlist will include only those songs that meet the playlist's conditions when you create it.

17. Review the playlist to see whether it contains the conditions and settings you want (see Figure 16.13).

FIGURE 16.13

This playlist will include up to 90 minutes of the best of my Elvis music from the Rock genre; as I add music to my Library, it will also be added to this playlist if it meets these conditions.

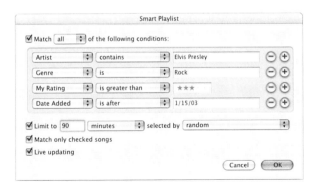

18. Click **OK** to create the playlist. You will move to the Source List, the smart playlist will be added and selected, and its name will be ready for you to edit. Also, the current contents of the playlist will be shown in the Content pane.

19. Type the playlist's name and press **Enter** (Windows) or **Return** (Mac). The smart playlist is complete (see Figure 16.14).

Listening to a Smart Playlist

Listening to a smart playlist is just like listening to other sources: You select it on the Source List and use the playback controls to listen to it. The one difference is that if a smart playlist is set to be live, its contents can change over time.

Changing a Smart Playlist

To change the contents of a smart playlist, you change the smart playlist's criteria (remember that iTunes actually places songs in a smart playlist). Use the following steps to do this:

1. Select the smart playlist you want to change.

2. Choose **File**, **Edit Smart Playlist**. The Smart Playlist dialog box will appear. The playlist's current criteria will be shown.

3. Use the techniques you learned when you created a playlist to change its criteria. For example, you can remove conditions by clicking their Remove button. You can also add more conditions or change the other settings for the playlist.

4. Click **OK**. Your changes will be saved and the contents of the playlist will be updated to match the current criteria (see Figure 16.15).

note

The smart playlist I built as an example (shown in Figure 16.13) in these steps can be interpreted as follows: Include songs by Elvis Presley in the Rock genre that I have rated at three stars or more and that I added to my Library after 1/15/03. Limit the playlist to 90 minutes, and if I have more songs that meet the conditions than this time limit allows, randomly choose the songs to include. Include only songs I haven't skipped and keep adding songs that meet the conditions as I add them to my Library.

note

Just like other sources, when you select a smart playlist, its information will be shown in the Source Information section at the bottom of the window. This can be useful if you want to create a CD or just to see how big the playlist is (by number of songs, time, or file size).

FIGURE 16.14

If you compare the songs in this smart playlist to the criteria shown in the previous figure, you will see why these songs are included in this playlist.

FIGURE 16.15

I changed the conditions on this smart playlist so that only five-star songs are included.

You can also change a smart playlist using the same techniques you use on other sources, such as sorting it, choosing the columns you see when you view it, and so on.

Using Some Very Special Playlists

On the Source list, you'll see a couple of special playlists. In this section, you'll get the details on one and an overview of the other.

Doing the Party Shuffle

The Party Shuffle is a special playlist because you can use it to create interesting sets of music on the fly. You can choose different sources of music and that music will play in random fashion (thus the word "shuffle" in the playlist's title). This is a great tool for quickly playing music in an order that will be fresh and interesting each time you play it.

First, configure the Party Shuffle by using the following steps:

1. Select **Party Shuffle** on the Source List. You'll see a dialog box that explains the Party Shuffle tool to you.

2. Click the **Do Not Show This Message Again** check box and then OK. You'll see the Party Shuffle tool in the Content pane (see Figure 16.16).

3. Select the source of music that you want to listen to on the Source pop-up menu. On this menu, you'll see your Library along with all of the playlists you see in the **Source List**.

   When you choose a source, the songs in that source will be shown in the Content pane. For example, in Figure 16.16, the Purchased Music playlist (read more about this in the next section) is selected and so the Content pane displays songs from this playlist. Because this is the Party Shuffle, these songs appear in random order.

> **tip**
>
> You can also edit a smart playlist by selecting it and opening the Info window (which also opens the Smart Playlist dialog box). For yet another path to the same place, you can open the playlist's contextual menu by right-clicking (Windows or Mac) or Ctrl-clicking it (Mac) and choosing Edit Smart Playlist.

> **tip**
>
> To delete a smart playlist, select it on the Source List and press Delete. Confirm the deletion at the prompt, and the playlist will be removed from the Source List. Again, the songs in the playlist will remain in the Library or other playlists. Only the playlist itself is deleted.

FIGURE 16.16

The Party Shuffle playlist enables you to hear music from selected sources in a random and interesting way.

Song currently playing

Songs that have played

Upcoming songs

Now Playing

Source pop-up menu

4. If you want songs you have rated higher to play more frequently, check the **Play Higher Rated Songs More Often** check box. If you don't check this, all songs in the selected source will have the same probability of being included. If it is checked, songs with higher ratings will have a higher probability of being included.

5. Choose the number of songs that have already played that you want to be displayed toward the top of the Content pane on the **Display __ Recently Played Songs** pop-up menu. For example, if you want to see the last 10 songs played, choose 10.

6. Choose the number of upcoming songs that you want to be displayed on the Display __ upcoming songs pop-up menu. In Figure 16.16, you can see that this is set to 75, which means that the next 75 songs that will be played are shown in the Content pane.

Now, play the Party Shuffle. The first song on the list will play. When it is done, it will be grayed out on the list to indicate that it has already played and the next song on the list will start to play. Each song on the list will play in turn.

When more than the number of songs you chose in Step 5 have played, the first song will disappear from the Content pane and the next song will be added to those that are coming up (the songs that aren't grayed out).

That's all there is to it. The Party Shuffle is a cool way to listen to music because you can add variety to any music source by quickly randomizing it.

Working with Purchased Music

The Purchased Music playlist is one of iTunes's default playlists; its purpose is to contain music you have purchased from the iTunes Music Store (which is, I suppose, how it got its name). You'll learn a lot more about this special playlist is Part III of this book, which explains how to work with the iTunes Music Store.

The Absolute Minimum

Playlists are a great way to customize the music in your Library for listening purposes, to create a CD, or to manage the music on an iPod. As you learned in this chapter, playlists include a specific collection of songs that you choose, whereas iTunes chooses the songs in a smart playlist based on the conditions you specify.

Playlists are a great way to select specific music to which you want to listen. You can make them as long or as short as you like, and you can mix and match songs to your heart's content.

Use the Party Shuffle playlist to keep your music sources fresh.

Like the Party Shuffle, smart playlists can really enhance your listening experience. Following are some ideas you might find interesting for smart playlists:

- Be diligent about rating your songs. Then create a smart playlist for one of your favorite genres that also includes a rating condition. Enable this playlist to be updated live. Such a playlist would always contain your favorites songs in this genre, even as you add more songs to your Library.

- Create a smart playlist based only on genre and allow it to be updated live. This playlist would make it easy to listen to that genre, and it would always contain all your music in that genre.

■ Create a smart playlist that includes several of your favorite artists (remember to choose **Any** in the top menu) and limit the number of songs to 20 or so. Have iTunes choose the songs in random order. Playing this playlist might provide an interesting mix of music. If you include a My Rating condition, you can cause only your favorite music to be included in this group. Make a dynamic list, and it will change over time as you add music to your Library.

■ If you like to collect multiple versions of the same song, create a playlist based on song name. Allow it to be updated live, and this playlist will contain all the versions of this song you have in your Library.

Equalizing Your Music

In addition to the great tools iTunes provides to enable you to choose which music you want to listen to, the application also enables you to control *how* that music sounds. You do this with the Equalizer. Using this feature, you can customize how music sounds to suit your system, hearing, and listening preferences.

Touring the iTunes Equalizer

Like a hardware graphic equalizer, the iTunes Equalizer enables you to change the relative volume levels of various frequencies of the sounds of which music is made (see Figure 17.1).

Preset menu

FIGURE 17.1
The Equalizer puts you in charge of how your music sounds.

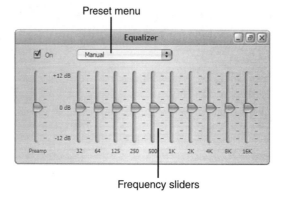

Frequency sliders

To open the Equalizer, click the **Equalizer** button on the right side of the bottom of the iTunes window (it contains three blue sliders). On Macintoshes, you can also open the Equalizer by choosing **Window, Equalizer** or by pressing ⌘+2. The Equalizer window will appear.

At the top of the window, you will see the On check box. When this is checked, the Equalizer is active and will affect how your music sounds. If the check box is not checked, the Equalizer settings don't impact the way your music sounds. When you see the values in the Equalizer window, remember that they are all relative and only change the volume of frequencies relative to one another, not the volume of your system.

Along the left side of the window is the Preamp slider. The Preamp setting changes the relative volumes of all the frequencies at the same time. For example, if a song is recorded at a low volume level, you can drag the Preamp slider up to make its relative volume louder. Similarly, you can drag the slider down to make a song's relative volume level lower.

note

If you don't see the individual frequencies as shown in Figure 17.1, click the Maximize button in the Equalizer window. The window expands and you see the frequency controls.

note

The abbreviation dB stands for *decibels*, which is a measure of the power of sound. Sounds with higher decibels are louder. The decibel measurements are on a logarithmic scale, which means they do not follow a linear progression. In other words, 100 dB is not 10 times louder than 10 dB. To give you an example of this, normal human conversation is about 60 dB, whereas a jet engine at close range is about 150 dB.

The bulk of the window consists of a set of sliders that control the relative volume of a number of sound frequencies that are listed underneath the sliders, from 32Hz to 16KHz (kilohertz). The left end of the range represents lower or bass sound, whereas the middle is the mid-range and the right end is the higher or treble sound. The sliders all have a range of –12 to +12 decibels (dB). Again, this is relative to 0, which means the volume level is not affected.

Above the frequency sliders and to the right of the On check box is the Presets menu. Presets are collections of slider settings, and you can choose to apply them without having to adjust each slider individually. iTunes includes a number of presets, and you can create and save your own presets in the menu.

You can use the Equalizer in a couple of ways: You can set it for all the music you are listening to at a specific time, or you can associate a specific preset with a song so those settings will be used each time that song plays. As you play with the Equalizer, realize that there are no right or wrong settings. It is entirely up to your listening pleasure. If some adjustment makes the music sound "worse" to you, go onto something else. You might find that some of the default presets don't help the way the music sounds at all. It is all relative to your speakers, the music to which you are listening, and your musical ear.

Configuring the Equalizer Manually

To configure the Equalizer manually, perform the following steps:

1. Select some **music**, such as a playlist, and play it.

2. Open the Equalizer.

3. Check the **On** check box, if it isn't checked already. This makes the Equalizer active.

4. Choose **Manual** on the Presets slider. This puts the Equalizer in the Manual mode.

5. If you want to change the relative volume of all the songs you are playing, drag the Preamp slider up to make the music louder or down to make the music quieter.

6. Set each of the frequency sliders to change the relative volume of that frequency. Drag a slider up to make its frequency louder or down to make it quieter. For example, to make music more bassy, drag the sliders for the lower end of the frequency scale up. This will increase the volume of lower sounds and make the bass components of music more prominent. Adjust the other

tip

If you make an adjustment to any of the sliders, the Equalizer will switch to the Manual mode automatically.

sliders to change the relative volumes of their frequencies until the music sounds "better" to you (see Figure 17.2).

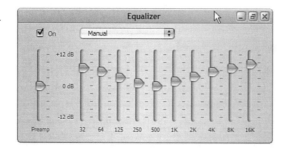

7. When you are done making changes, you can click in the iTunes window to make it active or close the Equalizer to get it out of the way (it continues to work even if you can't see it).

Working with Presets

Dragging all the sliders up and down is lots of fun and all, but it isn't something you are likely to want to do a lot. Presets are collections of slider settings that you can apply just by choosing one on the Presets menu. You can use iTunes' default presets or you can create your own.

Selecting a Default Preset

Working with iTunes' default presets is a snap, as you can see from the following steps:

1. Play some music.

2. Open the Equalizer and turn it on.

3. Open the Presets menu (see Figure 17.3). At the bottom of the menu, you will see the set of default presets available to you.

4. Choose the preset you want to apply. When you return to the Equalizer window, the sliders will be set according to the preset you selected (see Figure 17.4).

5. Continue choosing presets until the music sounds just right.

The specific slider and preset settings you should use depend on many factors, including your sound system, the music to which you are listening, and last, but certainly not least, your personal preferences. For example, if you use speakers that have poor bass performance, you might want to consistently use higher bass settings (assuming you like to hear lots of bass, of course). If you have a system with a powerful subwoofer, you might not need any bass enhancement.

FIGURE 17.3

Are there enough presets for you?

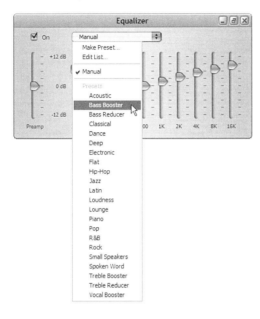

FIGURE 17.4

The Bass Booster preset does just what it sounds like it will.

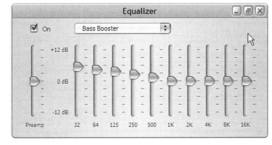

Creating Your Own Presets

If none of the default presets are quite right, you can create your own presets so that you can return to a specific Equalizer configuration easily and quickly. This is useful when a preset of your own making is just what you like and you want to be able to go back to it easily. A good way to create custom presets is to choose one of the default presets and make changes to it. Then, you can save the preset with your changes as a new preset. To create a preset, follow these steps:

1. Open the Equalizer, turn it on, and set its sliders to the settings you want to reuse.

2. Open the Presets menu and choose **Make Preset**. You'll see the Make Preset dialog box (see Figure 17.5).

3. In the New Preset Name box, type a name for your preset.
4. Click **OK**. The preset will be added to the Presets menu, and you can choose it just like one of the defaults (see Figure 17.6).

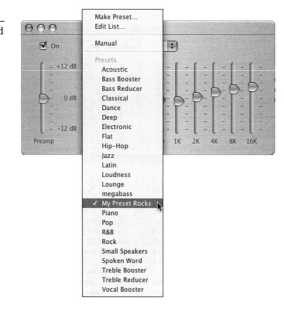

Configuring the Preset Menu

As you saw in the previous section, you can add presets to the Presets menu. You can also remove presets from it to create a custom Presets menu. For example, you might want to get rid of presets you will never use so that the menu offers fewer choices. Or, you might want to rename a preset. To do these tasks, use the following steps:

1. Open the Presets menu and choose **Edit List**. The Edit Presets dialog box will appear (see Figure 17.7).

FIGURE 17.7

You can cus-
tomize the
Presets menu so
it contains only
those presets
that are useful to
you.

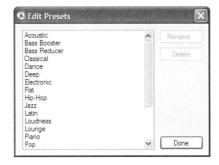

2. To remove a preset from the menu, select it, click **Delete**, and confirm your
   decision at the prompt by clicking **Yes**. You will see a prompt asking you if
   you want to remove the preset from the songs that are set to use it as well
   (you'll learn about this in the next section); click **Yes** if you want to remove
   the preset from the songs or **No** if you want to retain the settings even
   though the preset will be removed from the menu. The preset will be removed
   from the menu.

3. To rename a preset, select it and click **Rename**. The Rename dialog box will
   appear. Type a new name for the preset and click **OK**. It will be renamed on
   the menu.

Setting the Equalizer for Specific Songs

You can apply specific Equalizer presets to individual songs so that those songs will
always play with the settings you associate with them. You can do this from the Info
window or from the Content pane.

There are several situations in which you might want to set the Equalizer for specific
songs. One case might be for songs whose recording level is so low that you have a
hard time hearing it—you can use a preset so that its volume level is adjusted automatically each time you play it. Or, you might like to use different presets with different types of music. By applying a preset to the songs of a specific type, that preset
will be used whenever those songs are played. Suppose you like to listen to both
Classical and Rock and have a preset for each. By associating a preset with the
Classical music and another with the Rock music, the appropriate preset will be used
when you play that music.

Setting the Equalizer in the Info Window

To configure the Equalizer for a specific song, perform the following steps:

1. Select the song to which you want to apply Equalizer settings and open the Info window.
2. Click the **Options tab**.
3. Choose the preset you want to apply to the song in the Equalizer Preset menu (see Figure 17.8).

FIGURE 17.8

Remember the preset "My Preset Rocks" from earlier in the chapter? It's back....

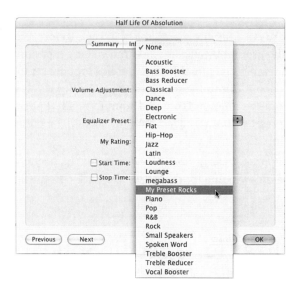

4. Click **OK**. The Info window will close and the preset will be associated with the song.

Assuming that the Equalizer is turned on, the preset you associate with a song will be used each time that song plays.

Using the Equalizer from the Content Pane

You can also configure the preset for a song from the Content pane. First, show the Equalizer in the Content pane. Then, you can choose a preset for the song.

Showing the Equalizer in the Content Pane

To show the Equalizer in the Content pane, you use the View Options dialog box to show its column. In case you don't remember how, the following steps will lead the way:

1. Select the source for which you want the Equalizer column to be displayed, such as the Library or a playlist.

2. Open the View Options dialog box by selecting **Edit, View Options**.

3. Check the Equalizer check box and close the dialog box. The Equalizer column will be added to the Content pane for the selected source.

> **tip**
>
> If you can't see the Equalizer column, scroll in the Content pane until you do. Or, drag the Equalizer column to the left in the Content pane so that you can see it more easily.

Setting the Equalizer in the Content Pane

After you have added the Equalizer column to the Content pane, you can easily associate a preset with a song. For the song with which you want to associate a preset, click the button that appears on the left side of the Equalizer column. The Presets menu will appear (see Figure 17.9). Choose the preset you want to apply to the song. It will be used each time the song is played. To change the preset, select a different one or choose **None** to remove the preset from the song.

FIGURE 17.9

Does this menu look familiar to you?

The Absolute Minimum

You can use the iTunes Equalizer to fine-tune your music to suit your system, your listening tastes, and the kind of music you listen to. Before we leave this topic, here are a few Equalizer tidbits for you:

- You can reduce the Equalizer window so that you see only the On check box and the Presets menu. This makes it easier to keep the window out of your way, but you can still change its settings by choosing presets to apply. To do this on Windows computers, click the **Resize** button on the window's title bar. On Macs, click the **Zoom** button.

- You can apply the same preset to multiple songs at the same time by selecting the songs to which you want to apply the preset and opening the Info window (which becomes the Multiple Song Information window). Choose the preset you want to apply to the selected songs on the Equalizer Preset menu and click **OK**. The preset will be applied to all the songs you selected.

- Which is more decibels, a jet plane engine up close or a typical rock concert in front of the speakers? In general, the noise levels in these environments are roughly the same. Noises at this level can be damaging to your hearing. So if you are hanging out next to jet engines or are planning on going to a rock concert, consider wearing hearing protection. After all, you want to protect your hearing so you can take advantage of iTunes, right?

Burning Your Own CDs or DVDs

When you are at your computer, you'll likely use iTunes to listen to your music because you can easily get to the specific music to which you want to listen, such as by using your Library, creating playlists and smart playlists, and so on. When you are on the move, you'll probably use your iPod to listen to your tunes. At other times, you might want to put music on a CD to take with you, such as when you are traveling in a car with a standard CD player. Or, you might want to back up your music on a DVD to keep your collection safe. Using iTunes, you can quickly and easily burn CDs or DVDs so that they contain any collections of music you want them to.

Understanding the Types of Discs You Can Burn

You can burn several different types of disc formats with iTunes. Each of these formats is useful for specific purposes. With iTunes, you can burn the following types of discs:

- **Audio CD**—When you burn a CD in this format, you can play it in any CD player, such as the one in your car, a boom box, or a home theater. And that is the primary benefit of this format; CD players are ubiquitous, so you can play audio CDs just about anywhere.

- **MP3 CD**—You can place your tunes on a CD in the MP3 format and then play those discs using any player than can handle MP3 music. Many newer CD players for cars and home theater systems can play MP3 CDs, so this is a good thing. The benefit of using the MP3 format is just what you might think it is—you can put about three times as much music on a single disc as you can with a disc that uses the Audio CD format.

- **Data CD or DVD**—This format is the same that's used to store music files on your computer's hard drive. In fact, when you choose this format, you simply replicate songs as they are on your computer on a disc. The primary purpose of this format is to back up your music in order to protect it from loss should something go horribly wrong with your computer.

Getting Your Computer Ready to Burn

In order to burn CDs or DVDs, your computer must have a drive that is capable of writing to CD or DVD. Fortunately, most computers include a CD-RW (CD-Rewritable) drive that you can use to burn CDs. Many also include a DVD-R (DVD Recordable) or DVD-RW (DVD Rewritable) drive that you can use to create DVDs.

To determine if your computer is ready to burn, open the **iTunes Preferences** dialog box and open the **Burning** pane (see Figures 18.1 and 18.2). At the top of this pane, you'll see the text "CD Burner." If iTunes can find one or more drives capable of burning CDs or DVDs, they will be shown here. If iTunes does recognize a drive, you are good to go and can proceed to the next section.

note

In Figure 18.2, you might notice that a menu appears next to the CD Burner text. That's because the machine used for this screenshot includes two drives capable of burning CDs. In this case, you can select from the menu the drive you want iTunes to use to create a disc.

FIGURE 18.1

This Windows computer has a CD burner that is ready to go.

FIGURE 18.2

This Macintosh includes a DVD-RW drive that can be used to burn CDs or DVDs.

If a drive is not shown on this pane, there are two possibilities. One is that a capable drive is installed but is not functioning correctly, so it's not recognized by iTunes. The other is that your computer doesn't have a capable drive at all.

If your computer does have a drive that is capable of writing to a disc, but it is not recognized by iTunes, it is likely that your drive is not working at all. You'll have to use troubleshooting techniques to repair and configure the drive to get it working again. I don't have room in this book to cover this topic because it can be complicated. If you don't know how to do this or you don't know someone who does, you can consult one of the many books available on this topic to help you get the drive working properly.

Selecting and installing a CD-RW or DVD-RW drive in your computer is beyond the scope of this book. If your computer doesn't have at least a CD-RW drive, it is likely a fairly old machine because these drives have been standard on most computers for a couple of years. If you don't want to purchase a new computer that includes a writable drive, you can purchase an external or internal CD-RW drive and install it in your computer fairly easily.

Burning Discs

Burning a disc from iTunes is quite straightforward, as you will see from the information in this section.

Preparing Content to Burn

The first phase in the process is to choose the content you want to place onto a disc. You do this by creating a playlist. In Chapter 16, "Creating, Configuring, and Using Playlists," you learned everything you need to know about creating and using playlists, so I don't need to repeat that information here.

One thing you need to keep in mind as you create a playlist for CD or DVD is the size of the playlist. Obviously, you can't put more music on a CD or DVD than there is room to store files on the disc. How large a playlist can be to be put on a disc depends on the format you will be using. If you are burning an Audio CD, you can get about 70 minutes of music on the disc. If you are creating an MP3 disc, you can store about 210 minutes on a disc. If you are creating a data DVD, you can store at least 5.2GB of files on a disc.

When you are creating an Audio CD, use the play time to judge the size of the playlist; keep it to 70 minutes plus or minus a couple minutes. For the other formats, use file size (for example, a CD can typically hold 750MB).

note

In many cases, a drive that doesn't work properly can be fixed by updating the driver software for that drive. If you use a Windows computer, you might need to download and install the proper driver from your drive's manufacturer; some drivers will be updated automatically when you run Windows Update. If you use a Mac that includes such a drive, the drivers will be updated when you use the Software Update application.

note

If you choose to burn a playlist that contains more music than will fit on the type of disc you are trying to burn, iTunes will warn you about the situation. Then, you can choose to cancel the burn or you can choose to have iTunes burn the playlist across multiple discs.

In any case, use the Source Information area to check the playlist to make sure it will fit on the type of disc you are going to create (see Figure 18.3).

FIGURE 18.3

This playlist contains 1.2 hours of music, which will be just right for a CD in the Audio CD format.

Source Information

The name of the playlist will become the name of the CD or DVD, so if you don't want the current playlist name to be used, change it to be what you do want the CD to be called. (To do this, click the playlist name once. It will be highlighted to show you can change it. Type the new name and press **Return** or **Enter**.)

Preparing for a Burn Session

Next, configure the burn session during which you will create a disc by opening the **Burning** pane of the iTunes Preferences dialog box. Choose the format you want to use for the burning session by clicking the appropriate radio button (see Figure 18.4).

If you choose **Audio CD**, there are two options you can configure. One is the gap between songs, which you choose by making a selection on the **Gap Between Songs** menu. Your options are **None**, which causes one song to begin immediately after the previous one ends; **1 second**, which places 1

note

The exact amount of music you can fit on a disc depends on your drive and the discs you use. The best way to figure out a maximum limit is to experiment until you find the upper limit for your system and the discs you use.

second of silence between tracks; **2 seconds**, which places 2 seconds of silence between songs; and so on, up to **5 seconds**. The other option is the **Use Sound Check** box. If you check this box, iTunes applies its Sound Check feature to the music that it places on a disc. (If you don't remember from earlier in the book, this feature causes iTunes to attempt to set the relative volume of the songs you play to the same level.)

To choose either the MP3 CD or the Data CD or DVD format, simply click the appropriate radio button.

Click **OK** to close the iTunes Preferences dialog box and prepare the burn session.

note

If your system doesn't include a DVD-R or DVD-RW drive, the third option will be just Data CD. If your system does include a DVD burner, this option will be Data CD or DVD.

FIGURE 18.4

Because the MP3 CD radio button is selected, the next CD will be burned in that format.

Burning a Disc

After you have selected the content and prepared the burning session, actually burning the disc is rather anticlimactic. You burn a disc with the following steps:

1. Make sure the playlist you want to burn is selected.

2. Click the **Burn Disc** button. The drive that is configured on the Burning pane of the iTunes Preferences dialog box will open, you will see a prompt in the Information window, and the Burn button will go radioactive (see Figure 18.5).

3. Insert the appropriate disc into the drive. If you selected the Audio CD or MP3 CD format, use a CD. If you selected the Data format, use a CD or DVD. iTunes will check the disc you inserted. If everything is ready to go, you will see the "Click Burn Disc to start" prompt in the Information area.

4. Click the **Burn Disc** button again. iTunes will start the burn process and will display information about the process in the Information area (see Figure 18.6).

   When the process is complete, iTunes will play a tone to let you know. The CD will appear on the Source List and will be selected (see Figure 18.7).

5. To eject the disc, click the **Eject** button. You can then use the CD in any player or drive that is compatible with its format.

tip

If you are putting live music on a disc, make sure you choose None on the Gap Between Songs menu. Otherwise, the roar of the crowd will be interrupted by the silent gaps, which causes the live feeling of the tracks to be lost.

caution

You may ruin the disc if you click stop before the burn process is finished.

tip

To stop the burn before it completes, click the Stop button. If you do this, the disc you are trying to burn might be ruined.

FIGURE 18.5

iTunes is ready
to burn.

Track currently being burned   Stop button

FIGURE 18.6

The playlist
Soundtracks is
being put on
CD.

FIGURE 18.7

The Soundtracks
playlist has
become the
Soundtracks CD.

FIGURE 18.7

The Soundtracks playlist has become the Soundtracks CD.

Labeling Your Discs

Now that you can create your own CDs and
DVDs, you will probably want to make labels
for them to keep them organized and to make
them look cool. The good news is that iTunes
can do some of this for you. The bad news is
that it can't do all of it.

Printing Disc Labels

Unfortunately, iTunes can't help you print disc
labels—yet. Hopefully, this capability will be
added in a future version. For now, if you want
to label your discs, you'll need to use a different
application. You can use just about any graphics application to create a CD or DVD label and
you can also use a word processor to do so.
However, to make the process easier and the
results better, consider investing in a dedicated
disc label creator. If you use a Windows computer, there are many labeling applications
available, such as AudioLabel CD Labeler. If you use a Mac, Discus will enable you
to create just about any disc label that you can imagine (see Figure 18.8).

caution

Any music you purchase
from the iTunes Music
Store should be backed
up on a CD or DVD. You
can download music
from the iTunes Music
Store only once. If something happens to that music on your computer, you will have to pay for it
again to be able to download it
again. To protect your investment,
create a CD or DVD of all the music
you purchase. The easiest way is to
put the Purchased Music playlist on
disc. If something happens to your
computer, you can restore your purchased music from the back-up disc.

FIGURE 18.8

Discus is a good tool to create disc labels if you use a Macintosh computer.

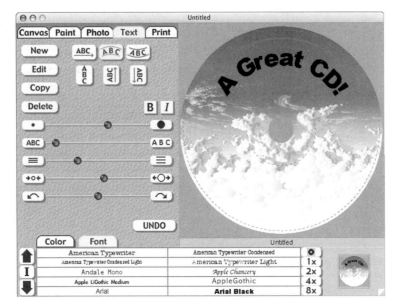

To print labels, you'll also need a printer and CD labels to print on. For best results, you should use a color printer, but black-and-white labels can look stylish, too.

Printing Disc Inserts

Fortunately, iTunes can help you create cool disc inserts so that you can label the jewel case in which you store your discs.

For best results, associate artwork with the songs that you put on a CD. When you create and print a disc insert, the artwork associated with the songs on the disc will become part of the insert. See Chapter 15, "Labeling, Categorizing, and Configuring Your Music," to learn how to do this.

To create a disc insert, perform the following steps:

note

To get more information about AudioLabel CD Labeler, go to www.audiolabel.com. To get more information about Discus, visit www.magicmouse.com.

1. Select the **playlist** for which you want to create a disc insert; obviously, this should be the same one that you used to burn the disc you are labeling.

2. Choose **File**, **Print**. You'll see the Print *"playlistname"* dialog box, where *playlistname* is the name of the playlist you selected in Step 1 (see Figure 18.9).

3. Click the **CD Jewel Case Insert** radio button.

4. Use the **Theme** pop-up menu to choose the type of insert you want to print. Some of the more useful options are explained in the following list:

   - *Mosaic* prints a mosaic of the artwork associated with songs in the playlist on the front and a list of the songs on the back. This is a color insert.

   - *White Mosaic* is similar except is prints on a white background.

   - *Single cover* places a single graphic on the front; the graphic of the selected song is used. It also includes a list of songs on the back.

   - *Large playlist* doesn't include any artwork, but does place the list of songs on the label. As you can tell by its name, it is intended for large playlists that have too many songs to be listed on the backside of the other insert types.

5. Click **Page Setup**. You'll see the Page Setup dialog box.

6. Configure the **page setup** to match the paper you are using for the insert. If you are using paper designed specifically for this purpose, you might have to experiment a bit to know which selection best matches the insert paper you are printing on. Unfortunately, iTunes doesn't support specific CD insert paper by brand and insert number as a dedicated disc label application does. Maybe in a future version....

tip

Most CD labeling applications contain templates for specific labels (identified by brand and label number) that you purchased. By choosing the right template for the labels you use, the labels you print will be the same as the labels you design.

note

If you choose a mosaic label and the songs included in the playlist have only a single piece of artwork (such as if they are all from the same album), that graphic will fill the front of the label.

FIGURE 18.9

Use the Print
dialog box to
choose the type
of jewel case
insert you want
to print.

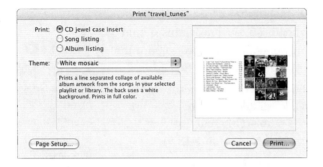

7. When you have configured the page setup, click **OK**. You'll move back to the Print dialog box.

8. Click Print to print the insert.

7. Cut or tear out the **insert** and place it in the jewel case. Prepare to be impressed!

Printing Song and Album Listings

In some cases, you might not want to label a disc, but instead you might want to create a listing of songs on playlists or even in your entire Library. iTunes can help you do this easily.

tip

When you use the Album listing option, any artwork associated with an album appears on the list.

1. Select the **source** for which you want print a listing.

2. Choose **File**, **Print**. You'll see the Print "*playlistname*" dialog box, where *playlistname* is the name of the source you selected in Step 1.

3. Click the **Song listing** radio button to print a listing of songs in the selected source or the **Album listing** radio button to print out songs grouped by their albums.

4. Click **Print**. The listing will be printed to the printer you have selected (see Figure 18.10).

FIGURE 18.10

Printing song or album lists is useful to keep track of the music you have; in this case, I printed the album listing for a playlist.

The Absolute Minimum

Burning a CD or DVD is useful when you want to listen to music apart from iTunes or from your iPod or to back up your music collection on disc. It is a relatively simple process as you have seen in this chapter. As you burn, keep the following points in mind:

- There are three types of discs you can burn with iTunes: Audio CD, MP3, and data discs.

- To prepare your computer to burn discs, you use the Burning tab of the iTunes Preferences dialog box to check to see that you have a compatible drive.

- To burn a disc, create a playlist containing the content you want to put on disc, configure the settings for the burn session, and then burn the disc.

- If you can't get discs to burn properly, open the **Burning** pane of the iTunes Preferences dialog box and choose a lower burn speed on the **Preferred Speed** menu. Then try to burn the disc again. Sometimes, using a lower burn speed will correct problems in the burn process.

- The format for a burn session must be compatible with the format of the music you are using. The most likely case that might cause you problems is when you attempt to burn a CD in the MP3 format but the music you are attempting to place on a disc is in the AAC format (such as what you purchase from the iTunes Music Store). In this case, iTunes can't burn the disc because you are trying to place music that is in the AAC format on an MP3 disc. These are different and incompatible formats. If this happens, use the Audio CD or Data CD format instead. Or, if you simply must put AAC music on an MP3 disc, you can do it with the following steps. Set the **Import** preference to the MP3 format (use the Importing pane of the iTunes Preferences dialog box). Then, select the AAC tunes you want to put on an MP3 CD and choose **Advanced**, **Convert Selection to MP3**. This will create MP3 versions of the selected songs and place them in the Library. Find the MP3 versions (use the **Info** window) and place them in a playlist. Then burn that playlist onto an MP3 CD.

- While iTunes can't help you print disc labels, it does a great job with case inserts and listings.

Sharing iTunes Music over a Network

If two or more computers are connected via a network—and with the broad use of high-speed Internet connections, networks are becoming common even in homes these days—you can share the music in your iTunes Library with other people on the network. They can listen to that music as if it was stored in their own Libraries. Of course, assuming other folks on your network are also generous, you can listen to music they share with you as well.

If you want to share your music even with non-computer devices, you can use AirTunes and an AirPort Express to do so.

Understanding How iTunes Music Sharing Works

When iTunes computers can communicate with each other over a network, they can access the Library stored on each computer. This means that you can see music in other iTunes Libraries, and other computers can see the music stored in your Library (both cases assume that sharing is enabled on your computer).

When music is shared with you, it appears as a network source on your Source List—if more than one source is available, the Shared Music source will appear. When you share your music with others, your music appears as a network source on their Source List. In either case, the person using the computer can select the shared source and listen to it using the same tools used to listen to other sources, such as CDs and playlists.

Even better, Windows and Macintosh users can share music with each other on networks that include both kinds of computers.

To share music with others on your network, you configure iTunes to share its music, which is covered in the next section. To access shared music, you configure iTunes to look for music being shared with you; that is the topic of the "Listening to Music Being Shared with You" section, later in this chapter.

note

In case you are wondering, you can't share iTunes music over the Internet. You can only share on a local network, such as the one in your home or business.

note

This chapter assumes that you have a network set up and that the iTunes computers on that network can communicate with each other. Installing and configuring a network is beyond the scope of this book. If you need help, lots of good networking books are available to you.

Sharing Your iTunes Music with Others

Setting up an iTunes computer to share its music is a two-step process. The first step is to connect your computer to a network. The second step is to configure iTunes to share your music.

You can also use iTunes to see who is accessing the music you have shared.

Connecting an iTunes Computer to a Network

As I wrote in an earlier note, this is not a book on networking, so I can't provide the information you need to connect computers together on a network. However, to enable sharing over a network, you must be connected to a network, which makes sense because the computers have to have some way to communicate with one another.

note

Later in this chapter, you'll learn about the amazing AirPort Express wireless hub that you can use to broadcast your music to other devices.

The network over which you share iTunes music can be wired, wireless, or both, and it can include Windows and Macintosh computers. If you have such a network and your iTunes computers are connected to it, you are ready to share your music. Otherwise, you will need to build the network before you can share your iTunes tunes.

Setting Up Your Computer to Share Music

To allow other people to listen to the music in your Library, perform the following steps:

1. Open the **iTunes Preferences** dialog box and then open the **Sharing pane** (see Figure 19.1).

FIGURE 19.1

Using the Sharing pane of the iTunes Preferences dialog box, you can allow other people on your network to listen to your iTunes music.

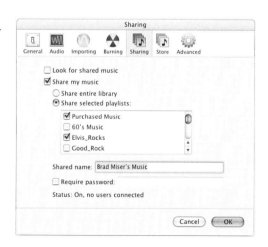

2. To enable music sharing on your computer, check the **Share my music** check box. The first time you do so, you will see a prompt reminding you that sharing is for personal use only; click **OK** to clear the prompt.

When you share music, you have two options for the music you share. You can share your entire Library or you can share only selected playlists.

3. To share your entire Library, click the **Share entire library** radio button.

    To share only specific playlists, click the **Share selected playlists** radio button and then check the box next to each playlist you want to share. You can scroll through the list of available playlists using the scrollbar located on the right side of the playlist list.

4. Enter the name of your shared music collection in the **Shared name** field. By default, this will be the name of your user account on the computer with *'s Music* added to it. However, you can enter any name you'd like. This name will be how others identify your music on their **Source List**.

5. If you want to require that people enter a password before they can listen to the music you share, check the **Require password** check box and enter the password they will have to use in the box.

6. Click **OK**. The music you selected to share will become available to others on your network.

7. If you require a password to let others access your music, provide them with the password.

Knowing Who Is Using Your Music

You can monitor how many people are using the music you are sharing by opening the Sharing pane of the iTunes Preferences dialog box (see Figure 19.2). At the bottom of the pane, you will see the current status of sharing (On or Off) and how many users are currently connected to your music.

FIGURE 19.2

At the moment, the Status information at the bottom of the pane shows that two users are sharing the iTunes music on this computer.

Listening to Music Being Shared with You

Two steps are required to listen to music being shared with you. The first one, which must be done only once, is to tell iTunes to look for any music being shared with you. The second one is to access and listen to that music.

Accessing iTunes Music Being Shared with You

To have iTunes look across the network and identify music that is available to you, open the **Sharing** pane of the iTunes Preferences dialog box (see Figure 19.3). Then, check the **Look for shared music** check box. Click **OK**. When you return to the iTunes window, you will see music that is being shared with you. If only one source is available, you will see the name of that source with a set of dark blue boxes and a musical note as its icon (see Figure 19.4).

FIGURE 19.3

When the Look for shared music check box is checked, iTunes will look for any music being shared with you.

If more than one source is available to you, you will see a source called **Shared Music** with an expansion triangle next to it. Click this triangle to expand the Shared Music source to see each of the music sources being shared with you (see Figure 19.5).

FIGURE 19.4

The source called Brad Miser's Music is being shared on the network.

FIGURE 19.5

Under the expanded Shared Music source, you can see that two computers are currently sharing music with this machine.

Listening to Shared iTunes Music

To listen to shared music, do the following steps:

1. Select the **source** to which you want to listen by clicking its icon. Your computer will attempt to connect to that music source.

2. If the source is protected by a password, you will be prompted to enter the **password** for that source. Do so and click **OK**.

   After you have entered the correct password, or if no password is required, the source's music will be shown in the Content pane (see Figure 19.6).

3. If the shared source has one or more playlists, you can view the playlists for that source by clicking the expansion triangle next to the source's name. When it expands, you will see the playlists it contains. In Figure 19.6, you can see that the Brad Miser's Music source has been expanded so that each of the playlists being shared appears.

note

If a music source requires that you provide a password to listen to it, you will see the padlock icon in the lower-right corner of the source's icon.

FIGURE 19.6

The Brad Miser's Music source is selected and its songs appear in the Content pane.

4. Select a playlist under the shared source, and its songs will be shown in the Content pane (see Figure 19.7).

5. Play **music** on the shared source just like music in your Library—by selecting **it** and clicking **Play**. Other playback tools, such as sorting the Content pane to change the order in which songs play, also work just as they do when you are listening to the music in your Library.

note

If only selected playlists on a source have been shared, when you select the source, you will see all the songs in the shared playlists rather than all the music in that machine's Library (which is what you see if the entire Library has been shared).

FIGURE 19.7

The shared source Brad Miser's Music has a number of playlists available; the Good Rock playlist is selected.

Sharing Your Music Anywhere with AirTunes and an AirPort Express

Sharing music with other computers is very cool, but what if you want to listen to your music someplace that doesn't have a computer? Using an AirPort Express wireless hub and iTunes's AirTunes feature, you can share your music with audio devices, such as a home stereo.

You can use an AirPort Express for a lot more than just sharing your iTunes music. It is a full-featured wireless hub, not that you would ever guess so because it is so small. It also enables you to wirelessly share USB printers and so on. The focus of this section is sharing iTunes music with a noncomputer device; explore the AirPort Express documentation to learn about its other features.

The general steps to use an AirPort Express to share music with an audio device are the following:

1. Obtain and install an AirPort Express on your network.
2. Connect your AirPort Express to a home stereo, a set of powered speakers, or other audio device.
3. Use the AirPort Express Assistant to set up a new network.
4. Set iTunes to broadcast music to that network.
5. Listen to the music.

Obtaining and Installing an AirPort Express

You can purchase an AirPort Express at any retail location that carries Apple products, such as the online Apple Store (see Figure 19.8). At press time, an AirPort Express costs $129, which is quite a bargain considering its small size and excellent features.

FIGURE 19.8
An AirPort Express is a full-featured wireless hub that is just slightly larger than a deck of cards.

After you have obtained an AirPort Express, use the installation CD that comes with it to install the AirPort Express software on your computer.

Connecting the AirPort Express to an Audio Device

As you can see in Figure 19.8, on the bottom of the AirPort Express are three ports. You use the Ethernet port to connect the device to a cable modem, DSL modem, or wired network so you can use the AirPort Express as a hub. You use the USB port to wirelessly share a USB printer. You can use the Line Out port to connect the AirPort express to any audio device that has an input port.

After you have installed the AirPort Express software, connect the Line Out port on the AirPort Express to the Line In port on an audio device. For example, connect a set of power speakers' output cable to this port. Or, use a mini-jack to RCA stereo cable to connect the AirPort Express's Output port to an input port on a receiver.

Then, plug the AirPort Express into a wall outlet. It will become active and you'll see its activity lights turn on.

That is all the installation that is required. How simple is that!

Setting Up a New AirTunes Network

To broadcast your music to an AirPort Express, you first set up a network for that device.

1. Launch the AirPort Express Assistant. On a Windows PC, choose Start, All Programs, AirPort, AirPort Express Assistant. On a Mac, open Applications, Utilities, AirPort Express Assistant. The Assistant will open and you'll see an information window explaining what you can do.

2. Click Continue. Depending on how your current wireless network is set up, you might see prompts that ask you to configure your current wireless connection. These prompts should be self-explanatory so work through them until you see the Introduction screen in the Assistant.

3. Click the Set Up a New AirPort Express radio button and click Continue

4. If you have an existing wireless network, click Connect to My Current Wireless Network. If not, click Create a New Wireless Network. The rest of these steps assume you are creating a new network; using an existing

network isn't much different. The computer will scan for the AirPort Express and you will see all available AirPort Express units on the Network Setup screen.

5. Click Continue to use the AirPort Express that was found. If multiple Express units are found, select the AirPort Express you want to use and click Continue. The Assistant will begin configuring the AirPort Express for the existing network. When it finds the network, you will be prompted to connect to it and the Network Setup screen.

6. Enter the name of the network you are creating along with a name for the AirPort Express, then click Continue.

7. Continue following the instructions in the Assistant until the AirPort Express is fully configured. The exact steps you will use depend on your specific network configuration. Fortunately, the Assistant makes it pretty easy in most situations. When the Assistant has completed its work, your AirPort Express will be ready to use.

tip

You can broadcast to multiple AirPort Express units at the same time. For example, you could connect one to a stereo in a basement and another to one in the living room.

Configuring iTunes to Broadcast to a Network

After your AirPort Express has been configured, you set iTunes to broadcast to it.

1. Open the Audio pane of the iTunes Preferences dialog box (see Figure 19.9).

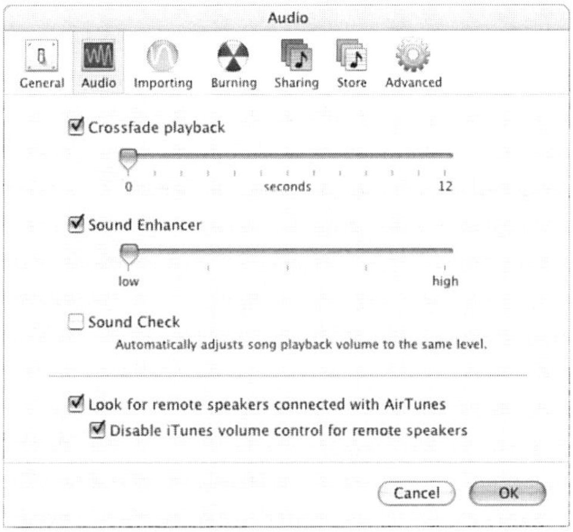

FIGURE 19.9

Use the Audio pane of the iTunes Preferences dialog box to configure AirTunes.

2. Check the Look for Remote Speakers Connected with AirTunes check box.

3. Check the Disable iTunes Volume Control for Remote Speakers check box if you don't want the position of the Volume slider in iTunes to impact the volume of the audio device to which you are broadcasting. Generally, this is a good option so that you don't accidentally change the volume at the remote device when you are using iTunes.

4. Click OK to close the Preferences window. You'll return to the iTunes window.

Listening to the Shared Tunes

Now, you can listen to your iTunes music from the remote audio device.

1. Choose the remote device on which you want to play music on the Speaker pop-up menu that has appeared in the lower-right corner of the iTunes window (see Figure 19.10). The name you choose should be the name of the AirPort Express connected to the device on which you want to play the music.

FIGURE 19.10

By choosing Express_1, music I play will be heard on the audio device (in this case, a pair of powered speakers, connected to the AirPort Express called "Express_1").

Speaker pop-up menu (appears when connected to AirPort Express)

2. Play the music you want to hear, such as playlist, CD, your Library, and so on. You'll see a message telling you that iTunes is connected to the selected speakers in the Information area. When that process is complete, music will begin playing over the device to which the AirPort Express is connected.

3. Use the audio device's volume control to adjust the volume. (If you didn't check the Disable iTunes Volume Control for Remote Speakers check box, you can also control the volume with the iTunes Volume slider).

Because the music source is iTunes, you control music playback from the computer streaming music to the AirPort Express, such as to start or stop it, change the playlist, and so on. You can control only the volume from the audio device, such as by muting it, increasing it, and so on.

To play iTunes music on the computer again, choose Computer on the Speaker pop-up menu.

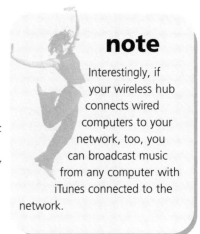

note

Interestingly, if your wireless hub connects wired computers to your network, too, you can broadcast music from any computer with iTunes connected to the network.

The Absolute Minimum

The ability to share your music with other computers on your network and being able to listen to the music on other people's computers is pretty cool, don't you think? Following are some points to keep in mind to help your sharing:

- In order to share music, the computer sharing it must be turned on and cannot be in Standby (Windows) or Sleep (Mac) mode. If the computer goes to one of these modes or is turned off, the shared music will no longer be available.

- Similarly, iTunes must be running for music to be shared. If you quit iTunes while sharing music, the music you were sharing will no longer be available to others.

- When it comes to sharing, iTunes doesn't care whether a machine is a Windows computer or a Mac. You can share music or listen to shared music from either platform.

- When you access shared music, you can only listen to it. You can't add it your Library, put it in playlists, change its information, put in on a CD, or other tasks that you can do with the music in your own Library.

- You can share your music with up to five computers at the same time.

- If you access music that was purchased at the iTunes Music Store, you must validate that you have permission to listen to that music by authorizing it. Music that you purchase from the iTunes Music Store can only be used on five computers at a time, and someone sharing music you purchased counts as one of those five. To be able to listen to shared music at all, you must be able to provide the account and username under which it was purchased. You'll learn about this in more detail in Part III, "The iTunes Music Store."

In this chapter

- Take care of iTunes, and it will take care of you.

- Be safe, not sorry, by backing up your music.

- Get help with those very rare, but possibly annoying, iTunes problems.

Maintaining iTunes and Solving Problems

As an application, iTunes is so well designed that you aren't likely to have many problems with it. And that is a good thing because who wants problems? However, you can minimize iTunes problems by keeping the application updated to the current release. You should also keep your music collection backed up just in case something bad happens to your computer.

In the rare event that you do have troubles, you can usually solve them without too much effort.

Keeping iTunes Up to Date

iTunes is one of Apple's flagship applications, especially because it is the only current Apple application that runs on both Macintosh and Windows computers. Because of this, Apple is continuously refining the application to both make it even more trouble free and to enhance its features. You should keep your copy of iTunes current; fortunately, you can set up iTunes so it maintains itself.

Keeping iTunes Up to Date on Any Computer Automatically

Setting up iTunes so that it keeps itself current automatically is very simple. Open the **General** pane of the iTunes Preferences dialog box. Then check the **Check for iTunes Updates Automatically** check box (see Figure 20.1). Click **OK**.

Once per week, iTunes will connect to Apple's servers and check for updates. When it finds an update, you will be prompted to download and install it on your computer.

The benefit of this is that you don't have to remember to check for updates yourself. There isn't really
a downside because you have the opportunity to decline to install the update if you don't want it installed. Also, you can always choose to do a manual update if that is your preference.

> **note**
>
> For automatic updates to work, you need to allow iTunes to connect to the Internet when it needs to. Check the **Connect to Internet When Needed** check box on the General tab of the iTunes Preferences dialog box to grant iTunes permission to do this.

FIGURE 20.1

Using the General pane of the iTunes Preferences dialog box, you can have iTunes keep itself current.

Keeping iTunes Up to Date on a Windows PC Manually

You can check for an iTunes update manually any time you think one might be available or if you prefer to do manual updates for some reason. You can check for iTunes updates manually on a Windows computer by choosing **Help**, **Check for iTunes Updates**. iTunes will connect to the Internet and check for a newer version of the application. If a new version is available, you will be prompted to download and install it. If a newer version is not available, you will see a dialog box telling you so.

> **caution**
>
> In order for iTunes to perform an automatic check for a newer version, it must be stopped and started once during the week. In other words, if you never quit iTunes, it won't ever perform the automatic check.

Keeping iTunes Up to Date on a Macintosh

Because both Mac OS X and iTunes are Apple products, iTunes is one of the applications tracked by Mac OS X's Software Update feature.

If you have set Software Update to check for updates automatically, it will check for iTunes updates according to the schedule you set. When it finds an update, you will be prompted to download and install it.

To manually check for updates, choose **Apple**, **Software Update** (see Figure 20.2). If an iTunes update is available, you will see it in the **Software Update** window. You can then select it and download it to your Mac.

> **note**
>
> If the computer you use doesn't have a consistent connection to the Internet (perhaps you use a laptop and only connect to the Internet occasionally), you'll need to use the manual update process to keep iTunes current because there is no way to make sure it checks for updates during the times you have an Internet connection.

FIGURE 20.2

On a Mac, you
can use Software
Update to keep
your version of
iTunes current.

Backing Up Your iTunes Music Library

Hopefully, you have and use a good backup system to protect all your files, including your iTunes Library. If so, you get extra points from me and can skip the rest of this section.

If you don't use a backup system to protect yourself, shame on you. However, you can earn some points back by at least backing up your music collection to CD or DVD. You can do this by creating a playlist containing the music you want to back up. Then, you burn that playlist to a CD or DVD. That will place a copy of your music on disc so that you can recover it should you ever need to. For detailed steps to burn discs, see Chapter 18, "Burning Your Own CDs or DVDs."

note

Unless you have a very limited music selection, backing up your music on CD isn't practical. However, if you only have a CD writer available, you should at least back up any music you purchase from the iTunes Music Store or download from the Internet. That will protect the music you get from those sources. You can always reimport music from the original audio CD sources if you have to.

If the playlist you select contains more songs than will fit on a single CD or DVD, you will be prompted to see whether you want iTunes to place the playlist on multiple discs. If you allow this, iTunes will keep burning discs until all the songs in the playlist have been placed on a disc.

Solving iTunes Problems

iTunes is about as trouble-free as any application gets; this is especially amazing because iTunes offers so many great features. However, even the best application is bound to run into a few hiccups.

Because the odds of me including in this book the specific problems you might experience are small, it is more profitable for you to learn where you can access help with problems you might experience. So, I've included the solution to one problem you are relatively likely to encounter here. Then, you'll learn how to get help for other problems should you experience them.

Solving the Missing Song File Problem

One problem you might encounter occasionally has nothing to do with iTunes not working properly. This problem occurs when something happens to the file for a song in your Library. When this happens, iTunes doesn't know what to do because it can't find the song's file. To show its confusion, iTunes displays an exclamation point next to any songs whose files it can't find when you try to play them or do anything else with them for that matter (see Figure 20.3).

To fix this problem, you have to reconnect iTunes to the missing file. Here are the steps to follow:

tip

When you back up your music, make sure you use the data format option, not the Audio CD or MP3 formats. This preserves the original format of the songs, such as AAC for those that you purchased from the iTunes Music Store.

caution

iTunes depends on QuickTime to work. If you remove QuickTime from your system, iTunes will stop working. You'll have to reinstall QuickTime or run the iTunes Installer to get it working again.

note

The most likely cause of the missing file problem is that a song's file has been moved or deleted outside of iTunes.

1. Double-click a song next to which the exclamation point icon is shown. You will see a prompt telling you that the original file can't be found and asking if you would like to locate it (see Figure 20.4).

Missing file icon

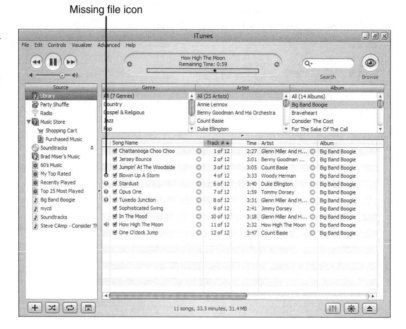

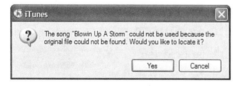

2. Click **Yes**. You will see the **Open** dialog box.

3. Move to the song's file, select it, and click **Open**. You'll return to the iTunes window, and the song will begin to play

If the problem was that the file had been moved, you might want to cause iTunes to place it back within the iTunes Music folder to keep your music files nicely organized. To do this, choose **Advanced**, **Consolidate Library**. In the resulting prompt, click **Consolidate**. iTunes will place a copy of any missing songs you have reconnected manually back into the proper location (within your iTunes Music folder).

note

If you can't find a song's file (probably because it has been deleted), you will have to reimport that song into your iTunes Library. (Because you have backed up your music, this isn't a problem. Right? Right!)

Getting Help with iTunes Problems

When you run into a problem that you can't solve yourself, the first place to go for help is Apple's Support Web site.

If you use iTunes on a Windows computer, go to http://www.apple.com/support/itunes/windows/. This page provides solutions to common problems, and you can search for specific problems you might experience (see Figure 20.5).

caution

I warned you before, and will do so again, that if you lose a song that you have purchased from the iTunes Music Store, you have to pay for it again to download it again. See why you should back up your music files?

FIGURE 20.5

If you use iTunes on a Windows computer, check this Web site when you have problems.

Mac users are certainly not immune to problems either. For help with those, check out `http://www.apple.com/support/itunes/` (see Figure 20.6).

You can also access Apple's general support resources at `http://www.info.apple.com/`.

Of course, the usual Mac support sites, such as `macfixit.com`, are also good sources of information about iTunes problems.

note

You can also write to me with iTunes questions. My email address is `bradmacosx@mac.com`.

FIGURE 20.6

Mac users can get help here.

The Absolute Minimum

Heck, who wants to spend time solving problems with a music application when the whole point is to spend time listening to and working with music? Not me, that's for sure. Fortunately, iTunes is designed and implemented so well that you aren't likely to experience any problems. If you do, help is available to you on the Web and from other sources.

- Of course, you can lower the chances that you will ever have problems with iTunes by keeping the application up to date. Fortunately, you can set iTunes to do this automatically.

- Just in case the worst happens, keep your music safe by keeping it backed up separately from your computer, such as on CD or DVD.

- You aren't likely to need to solve many problems. You might occasionally run into the "missing song file" problem. Fortunately, you learned how to solve that one.

- If you experience problems with iTunes, you can access the application's help system. You can also get help from the Apple Support Web page or by writing to me.

PART III

The iTunes
Music Store

Touring the iTunes Music Store

The iTunes Music Store might just be the best thing to happen to music, well, since iTunes and the iPod anyway. The iTunes Music Store gives you online access to hundreds of thousands of songs and thousands of albums by thousands of artists (that's a lot of thousands!). You can search for or browse for music in many different ways. When you find music that interests you, you can preview it to see if it seems to be up your alley. If it is, you can immediately buy it and download it into your iTunes Library. This all works so well because access to the iTunes Music Store is built in to iTunes so that you can make the most of the store using the iTunes tools you already know so well.

Why the iTunes Music Store Rocks

There are many reasons the iTunes Music Store is great. To get you pumped up, here are a few:

- **The one hit wonder**—You know what I mean—that group or artist who put out one great song and that's it. Before the iTunes Music Store, if you wanted to own such a song, you usually had to buy a CD with 11 less-than-good songs to get the one you wanted. Not so with the iTunes Music Store. You can buy individual songs, so you only pay for the music you want.

- **Try before you buy**—You can preview any music in the store to make sure you know as much as possible about a song before you actually buy it.

- **It's legal**—Unlike many other sources of online music, the iTunes Music Store contains only music that is legal for you to buy and download.

- **It's convenient**—Because you access the iTunes Music Store through iTunes, shopping for music is very easy and convenient.

- **You can find the music you want**—You can search for specific songs or you can browse entire genres, artists, and more.

- **Immediate gratification**—Because music is immediately downloaded to your computer, you don't have to wait for a CD to be delivered.

- **It's cheap**—Individual songs are only $.99. When you buy a CD's worth of songs, the price gets even lower and is usually less than you would pay elsewhere. Plus, there are no shipping costs.

> **note**
>
> Ever hear a song on a commercial or TV show you like? You can often find and buy such a song in just a few minutes.

- **Music allowances**—You can create music accounts that enable someone to purchase music up to a certain amount per period (such as per month). This is a great way to put a cap on the amount someone spends on music in the iTunes Music Store. Because it is so fun and simple to buy music this way, it is easy to get carried away. You might even want to put yourself on a music allowance.

- **iMix your music**—You can publish your own lists of songs, called an iMix, that other people can view and use to build their own Library. You can also access other people's iMix lists.

- **Pick and choose**—Because you can buy individual songs, you can pick and choose among songs from a specific artist. Even when you like an artist, sometimes collections from that artist might have only a few songs you like. Rather than getting stuck with several you don't like, you can buy only those you do like.

How the iTunes Music Store Works

Through the rest of the chapters in this part of the book, you will learn how to use the iTunes Music Store in detail. For now, read through the following sections to get an overview of this amazing tool.

Getting an Account

In order to purchase music from the iTunes Music Store, you need an account (you don't need an account to browse the store or preview music). This account lets you charge music you purchase and prevents you from having to enter your information each time you visit the store. After you create and configure your iTunes Music Store account, you can sign in to the store automatically so that you don't need to think about it again.

> **tip**
>
> You can use your iTunes Music Store account to log in to the store from any iTunes-equipped computer.

Accessing the Store

Accessing the store is as easy as clicking the **Music Store** source in the iTunes **Source List** (see Figure 21.1). The iTunes Music Store fills the Content pane, and you can begin browsing or searching for music.

Browsing or Searching for Music

You can use the iTunes Music Store's tools to browse for music by genre, artist, or other attributes. This is a good way to explore the store to look for music you might be interested in but are not aware of. You can also search for music using the iTunes Search tool, which becomes the Search Music Store tool when the Music Store Source is selected (see Figure 21.2).

Music Store source

FIGURE 21.1

When you shop at this store, you don't need to worry about parking.

FIGURE 21.2

You can use the familiar iTunes Search tool to search for music in the iTunes Music Store.

Previewing Music

When you find a song in which you are interested, you can play a preview of it. The preview typically consists of 30 seconds of the song. This can help you decide if the song is really one you want.

Buying and Downloading Music

When you find songs you want to add to your iTunes Library, you can buy and download them with a few mouse clicks. The music you buy is automatically placed in a special playlist called **Purchased Music** (see Figure 21.3).

What Happens to Music You Buy

When you purchase music, it is automatically placed in your iTunes Library. From there, with a few minor exceptions, you can do the same things with iTunes Music Store music as you can with music from CDs you purchase.

FIGURE 21.3

As you can see, I have had no trouble finding music to purchase from the iTunes Music Store.

What Can You Do with Music You Buy from the iTunes Music Store?

The answer to this question is, just about anything you can do with any other music in your iTunes Library. Of course, "just about" means that there are some limitations on the music you get from the iTunes Music Store. However, you aren't likely to ever find these very limiting (unless you are trying to do something you shouldn't be doing anyway). So, following are the exceptions that make iTunes Music Store music slightly different from the music you import from a CD:

- **You can listen to music you purchase from the iTunes Music Store on up to five computers at the same time**. For most people, this isn't a limitation because they don't have more than five computers anyway (maybe one at work and a couple at home). Even if you have more than five computers, it is easy to authorize and deauthorize computers to enable them to play iTunes Music Store music as needed.

- **You can burn to disc the same playlist containing iTunes Music Store up to seven times**. So, you can create up to seven copies of the same CD or DVD. You aren't ever likely to really want to create that many copies of a disc, so this isn't really much of a limitation either. Besides, all you have to do is change one song in a playlist and then you can burn the changed playlist onto up to seven more discs.

note

Although the iTunes Music Store has an enormous amount of music available in it, it doesn't contain music from every artist. Some music companies have chosen not to place their music in the iTunes Music Store—for now. The inventory in the iTunes Music Store is continually increasing, and because of its dramatic success, my guess is that most of these holdouts will eventually join the party.

- **You are supposed to use the music you purchase for personal use only**. Of course, this is the same limitation for the audio CDs you buy, too.

That's it. You likely will never encounter one of these limits in your regular use of iTunes Music Store music.

The Absolute Minimum

The iTunes Music Store is one of the best things to happen to music, ever. Personally, in the first few months the iTunes Music Store was available, I purchased more music than I did in several of the previous years. That's because I have fairly eclectic tastes and don't often want to purchase full CDs because I like only a few songs by some artists. That said, I have purchased a number of full CDs as well. Since the iTunes Music Store opened, I haven't ventured into any other online or brick-and-mortar music retailer very often. My guess is that once you start using the iTunes Music Store, you, too, might find it to be the only music store you need.

- When you shop in the iTunes Music Store, you can try any song before you buy it!

- To shop in the store, you need to set up an account. This can be done in just a few minutes, and you set up your account using iTunes.

- To visit the iTunes Music Store, simply click the **Music Store** source.

- You can browse and search the store for specific music that you want to hear.

- After you buy music and download it into your Library, you can do all sort of things with it, such as listening to it (duh), adding it to playlists, burning it to CD, and so on.

Configuring iTunes for the Music Store

Before you bust through the iTunes Music Store's doors, it is a good idea to configure iTunes for the store so that when you do get there, you can focus on finding and buying cool tunes to add to your collection. And that is the point of this chapter—to help you understand your shopping options and then to create and configure your iTunes Music Store account.

Understanding Your Shopping Options

When it comes time to buy in the iTunes Music Store, you have two basic options: 1-Click or Shopping Cart. The 1-Click option works best when you have a broadband connection to the Internet. The Shopping Cart method works well for everyone but is primarily intended for people using a slow connection, such as a 56K dial-up account.

1-Click Shopping

This method is aptly named. When it's active, you can click the Buy Album button to purchase an album or the Buy Song button to purchase a song (see Figure 22.1). The item you elected to buy (a CD of songs or a single song) is immediately purchased and downloaded to your iTunes Library. The process requires literally one click (which is where the name came from, I suppose).

FIGURE 22.1

The Buy Album button enables you to purchase and download an album with a single mouse click.

If you have a broadband Internet connection, such as cable or DSL, this is a useful option because it makes buying music so fast and easy. You can click a button, and the purchase and download process will take place in the background while you do something else, such as look for more music.

If you have a slow connection, such as a dial-up account, this is probably not a good option for you. Because downloading songs will consume your connection's bandwidth, you won't be able to do anything else while music is being downloaded. So, you will have wait until the download process is complete before continuing to shop. Therefore, you should probably use the Shopping Cart method instead.

Shopping Cart Shopping

When you use this method, music you select to purchase is moved into a Shopping Cart, which serves as a holding area for the music you want to purchase. When you find music you want to buy, you click the Add Album or Add Song button. The item whose button you click is moved into your Shopping Cart, which appears on the Source List underneath the Music Store source. When you select the Shopping Cart, you will see the music you have added to it (see Figure 22.2). From there, you can purchase the music, at which point it is downloaded to your computer and placed in your Library.

FIGURE 22.2

The Shopping Cart holds the music you are interested in.

If you have a slow Internet connection, the Shopping Cart method is useful because you can place music in the cart and then continue shopping for music in the store without being hampered by the music being downloaded to your computer. When you are done shopping, you can pop back to the cart and purchase the music in which you are interested.

Although the Shopping Cart is designed for slow connections, you can use this method with a fast connection in the same way. The benefit of this is that you can gather a collection of music without actually purchasing it. When you are ready to check out, you can move to the cart and select the music you do actually want to buy.

Configuring Your iTunes Music Store Account

To purchase music in the iTunes Music Store, you need to have an account and configure that account on your computer.

Obtaining an iTunes Music Store Account

If you already have an account with AOL, the Apple online store, or .Mac, then you already have an account with the iTunes Music Store because it can use any of those accounts.

If you don't have one of these accounts, you can obtain an account in the iTunes Music Store by following these steps:

1. Select the **Music Store** source. The Music Store will fill the Content pane (see Figure 22.3).

Account button

FIGURE 22.3

To sign in to the iTunes Music Store, you click the Account button.

2. Click the **Account** button, which is labeled Sign In when you are not signed in to an account. You'll see the Account Login dialog box (see Figure 22.4).

3. Click the **Create New Account** button. You will return to the Content pane, which will be filled with the first of the three screens you use to create an account.

4. Read the **information** on the first screen and click the **Agree** button. (The information on the first screen contains the terms of service to which you must agree if you want to use the iTunes Music Store.)

5. On the next screen, enter an **email address**, which will be your account's username (called an Apple ID), and password. Then enter a **security question**, **your birth date**, and select any **information** that you want to be emailed to you. Then click **Continue**.

6. On the third screen, enter your **credit card information** and **address** and then click **Done**.

7. If you are prompted to enter any additional information, do so and click the **Continue** or **Done** button. When the process is complete, you will see a completion screen. You will then be logged in to your new account (see Figure 22.5). Click **Done**. You will return to the iTunes Music Store and you can start shopping.

note

Apple uses extensive security measures to protect your credit card information. These measures are similar to those used by other online shopping sites. Information you provide via your iTunes Music Store account, such as your credit card number, is encrypted when it is communicated to Apple. It is highly unlikely that anyone would ever be able to obtain this information for nefarious purposes.

FIGURE 22.5

When you see this screen, you are ready to shop.

Logging In to Your iTunes Music Store Account

To be able to purchase music from the iTunes Music Store, you must log in to your iTunes Music Store account first. To log in to an existing iTunes Music Store account, perform the following steps:

1. Click the **Account** button (this will be labeled **Sign In** when you aren't signed in to your account). You'll see the Sign In dialog box (see Figure 22.6).

note

If you just want to browse for, search for, or preview music, you don't have to be logged in to your account.

FIGURE 22.6

You can sign in to your iTunes Music Store account by entering your Apple ID or AOL account information in this dialog box.

2. If you use an Apple ID to sign in to the store, click the **Apple** button (this is selected by default). If you use an AOL account to sign in, click the **AOL** button.

3. Enter your Apple ID in the **Apple ID** field or your AOL screen name in the **AOL Screen Name** field.

4. Enter your password in the **Password** field.

5. Click **Sign In**. You will be logged in to your account. When you return to the iTunes window, you will see your Apple ID or AOL screen name in the Account field. After you are signed in, you can shop for tunes.

note

If a different account is currently logged in, you must log out of that account before you can sign in to another one.

When you click the AOL button, the Apple ID field becomes the AOL Screen Name field.

Logging Out of Your iTunes Music Store Account

To sign out of your account, click the **Account button**, which shows your Apple ID or AOL account name when you are logged in to your account. The Sign In dialog box will appear. Click **Sign Out**. You will return to the Music Store and the Account button will again be labeled Sign In.

tip

If you can't remember your password, click the Forgot Password? button. You will move to a Web site that will help you retrieve your password.

Changing and Viewing Your iTunes Music Store Account

Times change and sometimes so does your personal information, such as your address or the credit card you want to use in the iTunes Music Store. If such changes occur in your life, you can change your Apple ID account information by using the following steps:

1. Click your **iTunes Music Store account name**, shown in the Account button, as if you want to sign out. The Sign In dialog box will appear.

2. Enter your **password**. (Your account name will be filled in already.)

3. Click **View Account**. The Content pane will be replaced by the Account Information screen. On this screen, you will see various buttons that enable you to change your account information.

4. To change your account information (such as your address), click the **Edit Account Info** button and follow the onscreen instructions to change your information.

5. To change your credit card information, click **Edit Credit Card** and follow the onscreen instructions to change your credit card information.

6. To view your purchase history, click the **Purchase History** button. The screen will be filled with a detailed list of all the transactions for your account (see Figure 22.7). Review the **list** and click **Done**.

> **tip**
>
> A few other buttons appear on the View Account screen that you aren't likely to use. The Terms and Condition button displays the current terms and conditions for the store. The Privacy Policy enables you to view Apple's privacy policy, and the Reset Warnings button resets all the warning dialogs so that you see them again the next time they become relevant.

FIGURE 22.7

Yes, I do use the iTunes Music Store, as my purchase history shows.

7. When you are done making changes, click **Done**. You will return to the Music Store.

Setting Up a Music Allowance

You can create a music allowance for an iTunes Music Store account. This enables someone using that account to purchase a certain amount of music per month. This is really useful if you have kids who you want to be able to buy music at the store, and you want to provide a limited amount of credit for them to use.

note

If you use an AOL account to access the store, you change your account information using the AOL software.

If the person to whom you are going to provide an allowance already has an Apple account, you will need his or her Apple ID and password. Alternatively, you can create an account for that person when you assign an allowance to him or her.

To create a music allowance, perform the following steps:

1. Access the **Account Information screen** for your account (see the previous section for the steps to do this).

2. Click **Setup Allowance**. You'll see the Set Up an iTunes Allowance screen.

3. Enter your **name** in the **Your Name** field.

4. Enter the **recipient's name** in the **Recipient's Name** field. If you are creating an allowance for yourself, enter your own information as the recipient's information.

5. Choose the **amount of money** the recipient will be able to spend each month in the **Monthly Allowance** menu—this amount will be applied to the recipient's account on the first day of each month. You can choose an amount from $10 to $200 per month.

6. If the recipient already has an Apple ID, enter the Apple ID in the two **Apple ID** fields (one is a verification field). If the recipient does not have an Apple ID, click the **Create an Apple Account for Recipient** radio button and enter an **Apple ID** for that person in the two fields. Again, if you are creating an allowance for yourself, choose the existing account option and enter your account information.

note

If the recipient doesn't spend an entire month's allowance, it carries over to the next month.

7. If you want to provide a personal message about the allowance, write it in the **Personal Message** field.

8. Click **Continue**. You'll see a screen that summarizes your purchase.

9. Review the information on the screen. If it is correct, click **Buy**. If not, click **Back** and make any needed changes; you'll then return to this screen and click **Buy**.

   If the recipient already has an Apple ID, you will see a screen that confirms that the allowance has been completed. Let the recipient know the good news—money is available in the iTunes Music Store!

   If you instructed iTunes to create an account for the recipient, you will see the Create an Apple Account screen. Complete the **information** on that screen and click **Create**. You will see an information screen. Read the information to make sure it is complete and then click **Buy**. You will see a screen that confirms that the allowance has been completed. Let the recipient know what his or her username and password are, and the shopping can begin!

   Click **Done** to complete the process or click **Set Up Another** if you want to set up another iTunes allowance. When you return to the Account Information screen, click Done to return to the iTunes Music Store.

> **note**
>
> If you know some music lovers who use iTunes, you can create gift certificates for the iTunes Music Store so the gift recipient can purchase music there. These work very similarly to allowances, except that gift certificates are for a set amount and expire when that amount has been spent. To start this process, click the Gift Certificates button on the Apple Account Information screen.

The recipient will receive an email containing information about the allowance (or gift certificate) you set up, including the username and password (if you created one for this person). When recipient signs in, his or her current balance will be shown next to the username in the Account box. This balance always reflects the amount left for the current month. When the recipient has spent all of this, the account won't be able to purchase more music until the next month.

To manage your allowances, return to the Apple Account Information screen. This screen will now contain the Manage Allowance button, which enables you to change current allowances or to create new allowances.

Choosing Your Shopping Preferences

The final step in preparing to shop is to configure your shopping preferences. To do so, follow these steps:

1. Open the iTunes Preferences dialog box.

2. Click the **Store** tab to open the Store pane (see Figure 22.8).

FIGURE 22.8

You can customize your iTunes Music Store experience using the Store pane of the iTunes Preferences dialog box.

3. To show the iTunes Music Store source, which is the default condition, check the **Show iTunes Music Store** check box. If this box isn't checked, the Music Store won't appear in the Source List.

4. Choose your shopping method by clicking either the **Buy and download using 1-Click** radio button or the **Buy using a Shopping Cart** radio button.

5. If you want songs that you buy to play as soon as you download them, check the **Play songs after downloading** check box.

6. If you use a slow Internet connection and want song previews to download completely before they play, check the **Load complete preview before playing** check box. This will enable the preview to play without pauses that might be caused by your connection's speed (or lack thereof).

7. Click **OK**. If you select the Shopping Cart method, the Shopping Cart will appear inside the Music Store source. You are now ready to shop!

The Absolute Minimum

Shopping at the iTunes Music Store is better than any music store I have ever seen. Here are some more shopping points to keep in mind:

- When you shop in the iTunes Music Store, you can choose the 1-Click or Shopping Cart method.

- To shop in the store, you need to obtain and configure an account.

- After you have an account, you configure iTunes to shop according to your preference.

- Almost all the music you buy from the iTunes Music Store has artwork associated with it. You can view the artwork by clicking the Show Artwork button.

- The music you buy from the iTunes Music Store is in the Protected AAC audio file format. This is the same AAC format in which you can import music into your Library, but it also includes some protections against copyright violations.

- The best thing about music you buy from the iTunes Music Store might be that you don't have to unwrap a CD. I hate trying to pry them out of their plastic wrapping!

Shopping in the iTunes Music Store

Now that you have an account in the iTunes Music Store and have configured iTunes to use it, it is time to start shopping. You can access the music in store, browse or search for music, preview it, and then buy the music you like—all with just a few mouse clicks and keystrokes. To shop in the iTunes Music Store, you use the following general steps:

1. Go to the store (no parking required).
2. Browse or search for music.
3. Preview music.
4. Buy music.

I've assumed you already have an iTunes Music Store account, which you need to have before you can purchase music from the iTunes Music Store. If you don't have an account yet, read the previous chapter.

Going into the iTunes Music Store

You learned how to do this step in the previous chapter, but I included it again in this chapter just for completeness's sake. To move into the store, select the Music Store source on the Source List. The iTunes Music Store will fill the Content pane (see Figure 23.1). If your account is shown in the Account button, you are signed in and are ready to go. If not, click the **Sign In** button to sign in to your account (see Chapter 22, "Configuring iTunes for the Music Store," for help).

As you move around the store, know that just about everything in the iTunes Music Store window is a link, from the album covers to the text you see to the ads showing specific artists. Just about anywhere you click will move you someplace else.

tip

Unlike brick and mortar stores, when you shop in the iTunes Music Store, you can forget the muzak because you can listen to other sources in your Source List while you are shopping. If you look closely at Figure 23.1, you can see I was listening to *The Lord of the Rings* soundtrack while I shopped.

Remember that you can make the Source List narrower by dragging its Resize handle to the left. This can be helpful so that you can see more of the iTunes Music Store without scrolling.

FIGURE 23.1

Shopping at the iTunes Music Store won't make your feet tired.

Browsing for Tunes

Browsing for tunes can be a great way to discover music you might be interested in but don't know it. You click through the store to explore in various ways; when you aren't looking for something specific, browsing can result in lots of great music of which you might not have even been aware.

Browsing the iTunes Music Store Home Page

You have several different ways to browse for music from the iTunes Music Store Home page.

You will see several special sections titled **New Releases**, **Exclusives**, **Pre-Releases**, **Just Added**, and **Staff Favorites**; these categories of music are relatively self-explanatory (for example, Just Added contains music that is new to the iTunes Music Store). To scroll through the music available in these areas, click the scroll arrows or buttons (see Figure 23.2). When you do so, you will see the next set of albums in that category. If you see an album that interests you, click it. You

will see the details of the album on which you clicked (see Figure 23.3). Once you get to something that interests you, you can preview and purchase it.

You can also browse the iTunes Music Store Home page by using the various lists presented on the screen, such as the **Today's Top Songs**, **Today's Top Albums**, **Featured Artists**, **Celebrity Playlists**, and **iTunes Essentials**. To browse a list, you can click its title or on any of the songs or artists in the list. For example, to see the most downloaded albums on a given day, click the title text of the **Today's Top Album** list. You will see a screen that shows the albums that have been downloaded most on the day you visit the store (see Figure 23.4). You can click an album to view its contents.

In the upper-left area of the Home page, you will see a list that enables you to access special areas, including **New Releases**, **Just Added**, **Audiobooks**, **Music Charts**, and so on. Just click a link to move to the related area.

Also on the Home page are a number of ads that change over time. These ads feature specific artists, the current sales promotion, and so on. Just click an ad to move to its topic.

Scroll buttons

FIGURE 23.2

You can browse the categories on the Home page by using the scroll tools.

Scroll arrows

FIGURE 23.3

Notice that browsing an album in the iTunes Music Store looks very similar to other iTunes sources; even better, it works in the same way too.

Forward Current browse path

Back Home Page

Selected album

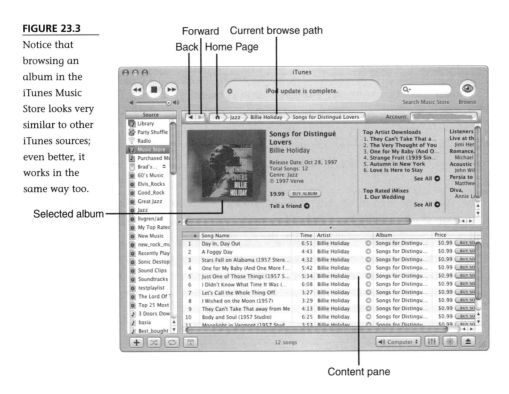

Content pane

FIGURE 23.4

The Today's Top Albums list is a good way to see what other people are finding on the iTunes Music Store.

Browsing by Genre

Browsing by genre is a good way to find music by its style. Start from the Home page and choose a genre on the Genre menu. The Home page will be refreshed, presenting music only in that genre (see Figure 23.5). The tools on the Home page will be the same; the content of the music you see will be entirely focused on the genre of music you are browsing.

tip

You can browse the iTunes Music Store by clicking the iTunes Browse button. The Browser pane will appear above the Content pane just as it does when you are browsing your Library. You can browse the store in the same way too. For example, click a genre to see all the music of that genre in the store.

FIGURE 23.5

If you like jazz, as I do, browsing the Jazz genre is a great way to find new music.

Searching for Specific Tunes

Browsing for music is fun, but it can be time consuming and might not lead you to the music you want. When you want something specific, you can search for music using the iTunes Music Store Search tools. The two kinds of searches are basic search and power search.

When you do a basic search, you search by one search term. Basic searches are fast and easy, but can sometimes bring back a lot of songs that you aren't interested in. When you perform a power search, you can combine several search terms to make searching more precise.

note

When you browse by genre, think of the resulting page as the "Home page" for that genre.

Performing a Basic Search

Because you already learned how to search with iTunes, you already know how to perform a basic search in the iTunes Music Store because this type of search works in the same way. To perform a basic search, follow these steps:

1. Select **Music Store** as the source. You will see the iTunes Music Store Home page.

2. Click the **Magnifying Glass** icon in the iTunes Search tool and choose the **attribute** by which you want to search (see Figure 23.6). The options are All, Artists, Albums, Composers, Songs, or Power Search (you'll learn about that one in the next section).

FIGURE 23.6

You can use this menu to choose the attribute by which you want to search for music.

3. In the Search box, type the **text** or **numbers** for which you want to search.

4. Press **Return** or **Enter**. The search will be performed and you will be presented with the results window (see Figure 23.7). At the top of the window are the top (with top meaning those that have been downloaded most frequently) albums relevant to your search. At the top-right side are the top songs related to your search. At the bottom of the window, you will see that the Content pane lists the specific songs that meet your search criteria.

tip

To clear a search, click the X button in the Search tool.

After you have performed a search, you can click the albums to view their contents, preview songs, purchase albums or songs, and so on.

FIGURE 23.7

In this search, I found all the music in the store with "Basie" as the artist.

Performing a Power Search

Sometimes a basic search just doesn't cut it. Fortunately, you can use a power search if you want to find something very specific. With a power search, you can search by more than one attribute at the same time, such as by artist and composer. To search with power, do the following steps:

> **tip**
>
> You can also perform a power search by choosing Power Search on the Search By menu (open it by clicking the Magnifying Glass icon in the Search tool).

1. From the iTunes Music Store Home page, click the **Power Search** link located in the upper-left corner of the window. You'll see the Power Search window (see Figure 23.8).

2. For the first attribute for which you want to search, enter **text** or **numbers** in its box. For example, to search by artist, enter the artist's name in the Artist box.

3. Repeat **step 2** for each attribute for which you want to search.

4. If you want to limit the search to a specific genre, choose it on the **Genre** menu.

5. When you have configured the search, click **Search**. The window will be refreshed, and you will see the albums and songs that meet your search criteria (see Figure 23.9). In the pane immediately under the search tools, you will see the albums that meet your search criteria. Below that, you will see the songs that met your search.

FIGURE 23.8
Using a power search, you can perform searches based on more than one attribute.

Just like a basic search, after you have performed a power search, you can click the albums to view their contents, preview songs, purchase albums or songs, and so on.

FIGURE 23.9
Here I have searched for music with the artist "Chapman" in the Inspirational genre.

Previewing Tunes

One of the great things about the iTunes Music Store is that you can preview music before you buy. These 30-second previews help you be more sure that the music you are buying is really something you want. For example, you can compare alternate versions of the same songs, listen to songs by artists who are new to you, or listen for any other reason.

To preview a song, you select it in the Content pane of the iTunes Music Store and click the **Play** button or double-click the **song** (see Figure 23.10). The preview will begin to play, again just like a song on another source, such as a CD or playlist. You can preview as many songs as you'd like, and you can preview the same song as much as you want.

tip

The Content pane for the iTunes Music Store works just like the Content pane for other sources. For example, you can sort it by any of its columns. You can also change the columns displayed. However, you can't choose from as many columns as you can for other sources. Of course, you can't drag songs from the iTunes Music Store onto a playlist, as you can those in other sources, until after you purchase them.

FIGURE 23.10

When you browse an album or any other content on the iTunes Music Store, you can preview a song.

Buying Tunes

After you have found music that you want to add to your Library, you can purchase it. How you do this depends on which shopping method you selected: 1-Click Shopping or the Shopping Cart method (if you don't know what I am talking about, take a look at Chapter 23).

Buying Tunes with the 1-Click Method

The 1-Click method is aptly and literally named. It really does require only a single click. To purchase an album, you click the **Buy Album** button. To purchase a song, you click the **Buy Song** button. In either case, whatever you selected will be immediately purchased and downloaded to your Library (see Figure 23.11). (Because you entered credit card information when you configured your iTunes Music Store account, you don't need to provide any payment information—after you click the Buy button, the store automatically gets the information it needs to complete your purchase.) After the download process is complete, the music will be in your Library and it is now yours to listen to, put on a CD, and so on.

> **tip**
>
> When you log in to your account, you can indicate whether iTunes should remember your password for shopping purposes. If you allow this, you won't need to enter your password each time you purchase music. If you don't allow this, at some point in the process, you will be prompted to enter the password for the account you are currently signed on under to be able to complete a purchase.

FIGURE 23.11

In the Information area of the iTunes window, you can see that I am currently downloading the album shown because I clicked the Buy Album button.

Buying Tunes with the Shopping Cart Method

Whereas the 1-Click method requires a single click to purchase music, the Shopping Cart method requires all of two or three clicks to accomplish the same result—that being to add new music to your Library.

When you find music in which you are interested, click either the **Add Album** button or the **Add Song** button to add an album or song, respectively, to your Shopping Cart source. When you do so, you will see a message in the Information area telling you that the item you selected has been added to your Shopping Cart (see Figure 23.12). Continue adding music to the Shopping Cart as long as you'd like.

When you are ready to buy music, select the **Shopping Cart** source on the Source List. You will see the music you have added to the cart (see Figure 23.13). The total cost of all the items in your cart is shown at the bottom of the window. To remove an item from the cart, select it and press the Delete key (or click the Remove button which is the "x" in the Price column). After you confirm this action at the prompt, the item will be deleted from the cart, and the cost information will be updated. When the cart contains only the music you want to buy, click the **Buy Now** button.

The music in the cart will be downloaded to your Library. After the download process is complete, you can listen to it, put it in playlists, place it on CD, and so on. (Just like the 1-Click method, you don't need to enter payment information because that is stored as part of your iTunes Music Store account and is provided for you automatically.)

tip

If you don't see the Shopping Cart source, click the expansion triangle next to Music Store. Music Store will expand and you will see your Shopping Cart.

tip

You can also buy individual songs or albums in your cart without buying everything stored there by clicking the Buy or Buy Song button next to the item you want to purchase.

FIGURE 23.12
Here I have added a song to my Shopping Cart.

FIGURE 23.13
You can view the contents of your Shopping Cart and purchase the music it contains.

Linking Your Music Library with the iTunes Music Store

You have seen how closely the iTunes Music Store is integrated into iTunes. You can take this a step further by linking the music in your iTunes Library to the iTunes Music Store.

Enable this link by opening the General pane of the iTunes Preferences window and checking the Show Links to Music Store check box and clicking OK.

When you view music in your Library, you will see arrow links next to each song, artist, and album (see Figure 23.14).

FIGURE 23.14

Click a store arrow to view related music on the iTunes Music Store.

Store arrows

If you click an arrow link for an item, such as an artist, you'll move into the iTunes Music Store and will view music related to the arrow on which you clicked (see Figure 23.15).

FIGURE 23.15

I clicked on the store link next to Glenn Miller (as shown in the previous figure) that took me to all music in the iTunes Music Store related to Glenn Miller.

Using the iTunes Music Store links to the music in your Library is a great way to be able to quickly find music you might like.

iMixing It Up

iMixes are collections of music that people create and upload to the iTunes Music Store. You can view other people's iMixes and preview and purchase music contained in them just like albums. You can also publish your own iMix.

Working with iMixes

There are many iMixes available in the iTunes Music Store for your browsing pleasure. To check them out, click the iMix link on the iTunes Music Store Home page. You'll see the iMix window. This window shows the iMixes currently available. These are organized in various groups, such as Top Rated, Most Recent, and so on. You can browse the available iMixes until you find one that interests you.

To view an iMix, click it. The iMix will open and you can view and preview the songs it contains (see Figure 23.16). You can also purchase all the songs in the iMix (if the Buy or Add All Songs button appears) or just selected songs (by using the Buy or Add Song buttons). In this regard, iMixes are just like albums and other sources of music in the iTunes Music Store.

FIGURE 23.16

This iMix was
created by yours
truly.

You can rate iMixes by clicking a Rating radio button and then clicking Submit. This rates the iMix and its average rating will determine its listing in the Top Rated section.

If you want to share an iMix with someone, click the Tell a Friend and provide an email address for the person to whom you want to provide the iMix. That person will receive an email with the iMix and a link to it in the iTunes Music Store.

While you can't tell who created an iMix, you can see more iMixes created by an iMix's creator. To do so, click the See All iMixes by this user link.

Unfortunately, there doesn't seem to be any way to search for iMixes. You can only browse them.

Publishing Your Own iMix

Anyone who has access to the iTunes Music Store can create and publish her own iMix, including you. To put your greatest hits in the store, do the following steps:

1. Create a playlist containing the songs you want to put in an iMix. You can include as many songs as you'd like in the order that you want. Be aware that the final iMix will contain only those songs that are currently available in the store. If you include songs that aren't available in the store, it won't be a problem; songs not in the store just won't appear in the published iMix.

2. Click the music store link (the arrow) that appears next to the playlist on the Source list. You'll see a prompt explaining what you are about to do.

3. In the prompt window, click Create. iTunes will access the music store and create the iMix, which you will see in the iTunes window.

4. Enter a name and description for your iMix (see Figure 23.17).

FIGURE 23.17
This iMix is
ready to be
added to the
store.

5. Click Publish. The iMix you created will be added to the store. The iMix screen will be updated and you will see a status message about it at the top of the window.

6. To share your iMix with others, click the Tell a Friend button. Complete the resulting form; everyone you list will receive an email that shows the iMix you created along with a link to it in the iTunes Music Store.

note

Remember that your published iMix will contain only music in the playlist that you selected that is available in the iTunes Music Store (whether you purchased it there or not).

I'd love to see any iMixes you create. Please include me (bradmacosx@mac.com) in your distribution list.

The Absolute Minimum

You now have all the skills you need to find, preview, and buy music from the iTunes Music Store. If you are like me, you will be hooked after your first trip. Following are some pointers to help you shop like an iTunes Music Store master:

■ When you search and iTunes can't find any music that matches your search, it will prompt you with its best guess about what you meant to search for. For example, if you were searching for music from the group Lynyrd Skynyrd and searched for "lynnrd" (who can ever spell that name right anyway!), iTunes would present a prompt in the search results asking you if you meant to search for "Lynyrd" because it can match that to its database. If you click the search text in the prompt, iTunes will search for that term instead.

■ No matter which shopping method you use, the price for everything is listed next to the buttons you use to purchase the song or album or to add it to your Shopping Cart. Songs are $.99 each. The cost of albums varies, but in most cases, the price per song works out slightly less when you buy an album than when you buy the same music by the song.

■ Some albums are available only as a partial album; this is indicated by the term "Partial Album" next to the album. This means that you can purchase one or more of the songs on the album, but not all the songs on the album or the album itself.

■ Some songs are available only as part of an album. This means that you can only purchase the song by buying the album of which it is a part. Songs in this category are indicated by the text "Album Only" in the Price column of the Content pane.

■ Even if you have a fast connection, you might prefer the Shopping Cart method because you can use the cart as a holding area for the music you might want to buy. This gives you a chance to think about it before you complete the purchase. When you use the 1-Click method, however, as soon as you click the Buy button, the deal is done.

■ Turn on the iTunes Music Store links so you can easily find music available in the iTunes Music Store that is related to music in your Library.

■ Explore iMixes to experience collections of songs other people have created and publish your own iMixes to share your favorites with other iTunes users.

Working with Purchased Music

The title of this chapter is somewhat misleading because it implies there is a lot different about working with music you have purchased than with other music in your Library, such as music you've imported from audio CDs. Although there are some unique aspects of music you purchased from the iTunes Music Store, mostly you can use it in the same way as any other music you have added to your own iTunes Library. But, there are just a few things of which you need to be aware, and that is where this chapter comes in.

The most important difference between music you purchase from the iTunes Music Store and other music in your Library is that a computer must be authorized to play music from the iTunes Music Store. You'll learn about this concept later in this chapter.

Understanding What Happens When You Buy Music from the iTunes Music Store

When you download music from the iTunes Music Store, whether you use 1-Click or the Shopping Cart, that music is added to your Library (see Figure 24.1). From there, you can listen to it, add it to playlists, burn it to disc, move it to an iPod, share it, and so on. In other words, it becomes mostly like music you have added to your Library from other sources.

FIGURE 24.1

This music came from the iTunes Music Store; it doesn't look any different than other music in the Library and acts only a bit different.

Using the Purchased Music Playlist

Immediately after your first purchase from the iTunes Music Store, the Purchased Music source becomes available on your Source List (see Figure 24.2). This source is actually a special smart playlist that will capture all the music you purchase from the iTunes Music Store. You can always return to your purchased music by using the Purchased Music source.

You can use the Purchased Music playlist like other playlists. To see its contents, select **Purchased Music** on the Source list. The first time you select it, you will see a dialog box explaining the function of the playlist (see Figure 24.3). Read the information and click **OK** to move to the Purchased Music playlist.

note

One thing you can't do with the Purchased Music smart playlist that you can do with others is to edit its criteria. The Purchased Music playlist is what it is; you can't change it (not that you'd ever want to anyway).

FIGURE 24.2

The Purchased Music source is actually a special playlist that always contains all the music you have purchased from the iTunes Music Store.

FIGURE 24.3

I suggest you check the check box so you don't see this dialog box each time you use the Purchased Music playlist.

You can then browse the Purchased Music playlist, search in it, play it, and so on. Of course, you can also configure view options for it, sort it, and do the other playlist tasks with which you are hopefully familiar by now.

You can also move music from your Library that you didn't purchase from the iTunes Music Store into the Purchased Music playlist, but I don't recommend that you do so because that will dilute its purpose.

Understanding Authorization

The music you purchase from the iTunes Music Store is protected in the sense that it has certain limitations on what you can do with it. Fortunately, these limitations are not very limiting!

One of these limits is that you can only play iTunes Music Store music on up to five computers at the same time. To implement this limit, the computer on which you play iTunes Music Store music must be *authorized*. When you authorize a computer, iTunes will connect to the Internet and register that computer with the iTunes Music Store to play the music purchased under the user account you used to buy it.

To state this another way, you actually authorize the music for a specific user account on up to five computers at a time. When you authorize a computer, you authorize all the songs you have purchased under an iTunes Music Store account; you can't authorize some of the songs you buy on one machine and a different set on another computer.

note

You can store the music you purchase on as many computers as you'd like. Then you can easily authorize the machines on which you want to play the music and deauthorize the ones you aren't using at the moment.

When a computer is authorized, it can play all the music that has been purchased under an iTunes Music Store account. If it isn't authorized, you won't be able to play any of the music purchased under an account.

Fortunately, it is quite easy to authorize or deauthorize a computer, as you will see in the next sections.

Authorizing a Computer

The first time you purchase music on a computer, you must authorize that computer before you can play the music you purchase. After that, the computer remains authorized until you deauthorize it.

To authorize a computer to play purchased music, try to play the music you have purchased from the iTunes Music Store. If the current computer has been authorized, the music will begin to play. If it hasn't been authorized, you will see the Authorize Computer dialog box (see Figure 24.4). Enter the username and password that was used to purchase the music and click **Authorize**. iTunes will connect to the Internet and authorize the computer. When that process is complete, the music will play.

If you attempt to authorize more than five computers under the same user account, you will see a warning prompt explaining that you can have only five computers authorized at the same time. You must deauthorize one of the computers to be able to authorize the current one.

tip

The five-computer limitation does not apply to iPods or to CDs. You can use the music you place on these devices as much as you'd like to.

caution

You must be able to connect to the Internet to be able to authorize a computer. This can bite you if you want to play purchased music on a laptop while you are on the road and can't connect. If you didn't purchase music while using that computer, make sure you authorize the machine before you remove it from its Internet connection. If you don't, the purchased music on its hard drive will be only so much dead digital weight until you can authorize that computer.

FIGURE 24.4

You use this dialog box to authorize a computer to play music you have purchased from the iTunes Music Store.

Deauthorizing a Computer

To deauthorize a computer, choose **Advanced**, **Deauthorize Computer**. You will see the Deauthorize Computer dialog box (see Figure 24.5). Click the **Deauthorize for Music Store Account** radio button and click **Finish**. You will see another Deauthorize Computer dialog box. Enter the username (Apple ID or AOL screen name) and password for the account that you want to deauthorize on the machine and click **OK**. iTunes will connect to the Internet and deauthorize the computer. When the process is complete, you will see a dialog box telling you so. Click **OK**. The computer will no longer count against the five-computer limit for the user account. (It won't be able to play music purchased under that iTunes Music Store account either.)

note

Just because you are signed into your iTunes Music Store user account on a computer, it doesn't mean that computer is authorized. In fact, you can purchase music using the same user account on a computer that isn't authorized. You won't be able to play that music until you authorize your computer.

You can authorize a computer again by attempting to play purchased music and providing the user account and password for which you want to authorize the machine. As you can see, it is quite simple to authorize and deauthorize computers.

In order to authorize or deauthorize a computer, you must provide the username and password for the account under which music was purchased. This information also enables you to buy music from the iTunes Music Store. If you don't trust others who will be playing music you purchased, you should authorize their computers directly rather than providing your username and password to them.

FIGURE 24.5

You use this dialog box to deauthorize a computer.

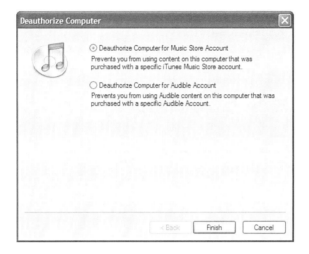

Moving Purchased Music to Other Computers

You can move any music between computers, but usually it is just as easy to import music from audio CDs to each computer on which you want to create a Library. However, if you have more than one computer, you might want to move music you purchased from the iTunes Music Store to the other computers so you can play it from there.

Understanding the Ways You Can Move Your Tunes

First, you need to move the song files from the computer on which they are stored (the machine from which you purchased the music) onto the machine you want to be able to play that music on.

In order to move files to another computer, you need to know where those files are located. From Part II, "iTunes," you know that iTunes keeps all the files in the Library organized in the iTunes Music folder (assuming you followed my recommendations and set the preferences to allow this). You can move to this folder to find the files you want to move.

note

You can purchase music on a machine that isn't authorized to play it. If you do this, you will see a warning dialog box that will explain that you won't be able to play the music on the machine you are using to purchase it until you authorize that computer. You can also store music purchased under different iTunes Music Store accounts on the same computer. To authorize the computer to play that music, you must authorize it for the iTunes Music Store account under which the music you want to play was purchased.

You can also find the location of song files by selecting them and choosing **File**, **Show Song File** or pressing **Ctrl+R** (Windows) or ⌘**+R** (Mac). iTunes will open a window showing the location of the files for the songs you have selected (see Figure 24.6).

FIGURE 24.6

When you use the Show Song File command, iTunes opens a window to show you where the song's file is located on your computer.

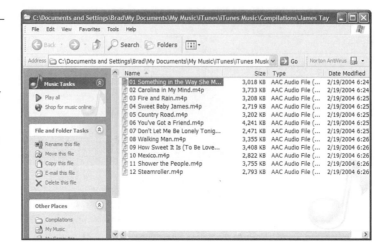

After you have located the song files, you need to make them available to the computer to which you want to move them. There are many ways to do this, including the following:

- Create a data CD or DVD containing the music you want to move. You can do this from within iTunes by changing the Burning preferences to use the Data CD or Data DVD format and then burning a disc. This process is very easy to do and works regardless of there being a network connection between the computers. The primary limitation is the size of the discs you use and the time it takes to burn the discs.

- Use a network to share files on the computer from which you bought music with the one to which you want to move the files. This method is simple and doesn't place a limit on the sizes of the files you move. You also don't need to spend time or money to burn discs. The downside is that you have to have the computers connected via a network.

tip

You can share music you have purchased with other computers on your network. However, for other machines to be able to play your purchased music, they must be authorized to do so and therefore count against the five-computer limit. Fortunately, as you have seen, it is simple to authorize and deauthorize computers, so you can keep up to five authorized quite easily.

- Create an audio CD of purchased music and import that into the other computer's iTunes Library. This is also an easy process, but you are limited to the amount of music that can fit onto an Audio CD.

- Move the song files onto a networked drive, such as a server. For example, if you use a .Mac account, you can use your iDisk to transfer files by copying them to your iDisk. This has the same pros and cons as moving files directly across a network.

> **tip**
>
> In Part I, "The iPod," you learned how to use an iPod as a portable drive. So, you can use an iPod to move music among computers.

- Copy the files onto a portable hard drive, such as a FireWire or USB drive. This is faster than and doesn't have the same space limitations as using a CD or DVD. Of course, the con is that you have to have such a drive available to you.

Lastly, you need to add the files that you are moving into the Library. This involves using the Add to Library command and then moving to and selecting the files you want to add.

Moving Purchased Music Files over a Network

The following steps provide an example of how to move files that are shared over a network and add them to the Library:

1. Share the files on the original machine with the network.

2. From within iTunes on the computer to which you want to move the songs, choose **File**, **Add to Library**. You will see the Add to Library dialog box.

3. Move to and select the files or the folder containing the files you want to add to the Library (see Figure 24.7).

> **note**
>
> On Windows PCs, you can choose the **Add to Folder** command, which enables you to select a folder to add. This works in the same way as adding files.

FIGURE 24.7

Here, I am accessing song files that are stored on a computer on the network.

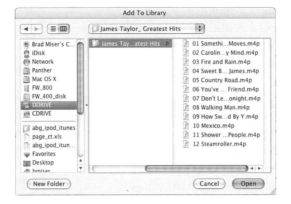

4. Click **Open**. The songs you selected will be copied into your Library (see Figure 24.8). If the music you moved into the Library was purchased on a different computer, you need to authorize the current computer to play that music (see the next section).

tip

The keyboard shortcut for the Add to Library command is **Ctrl+O** (Windows) or ⌘**+O** (Mac).

FIGURE 24.8

You can see that the files I selected in the previous figure are now in the Library.

You can create an audio CD from music you purchase from the iTunes Music Store and then import that music into a Library on another computer. Because the music is converted into the Audio CD format when you do this, it doesn't count against the five-computer limit for music you purchase from the iTunes Music Store. However, if you use this technique to play music you have purchased on more than five computers at the same time, you will violate the spirit and letter of the license agreement that you accept when you purchase music from the store. I recommend that you only use this method if this won't result in more than five computers playing this music at the same time. This can be particularly useful if one of the machines on which you will be playing music can't connect to the Internet, which is required for authorization to take place.

> **tip**
>
> Purchased songs that you move to a different computer won't be added to the Purchased Music playlist automatically. You can drag them onto that playlist from the Library if you want to put them there.

Viewing the Music You Have Purchased

You have a couple ways to see the music you have purchased.

The first way you have already read about. Select the **Purchased Music** source and you will see all the music you have obtained from the iTunes Music Store. (This assumes you haven't removed any songs from this playlist.)

The second way is to view the entire purchase history for a user account. To do so, perform the following steps:

1. While signed in under the user account whose history you want to see, click the **Account** button (you need to select the Music Store source to see this button). You will be prompted to enter the password for that account.

2. Enter the account's password and click **View Account**. The Content pane will be filled with the Apple Account Information window, which provides, amazingly enough, information about the user account.

3. Click the **Purchase History** button. The data will be retrieved, and the Content pane will show the music purchased during each shopping session (see Figure 24.9).

4. To view the detail for a shopping session, click its **Detail** button. The screen will be refreshed, and you will see a detailed list of all the music purchased during that session (see Figure 24.10).

Detail button

FIGURE 24.9
Your purchase
history will be
organized by
shopping
sessions.

FIGURE 24.10
You can also
view the detail
for any shopping
session.

5. When you are done viewing the history of your purchases, click the **Done** button; you'll need to click it twice if you are viewing a detail screen. You'll return to the Apple Account Information screen.

6. Click **Done**. You'll move back to the iTunes Music Store.

Backing Up Purchased Music

Because you don't have music that you purchase from the iTunes Music Store "backed up" on a disc (like you do for the music you have on audio CD), you should make sure you back up the music you buy. The easiest way to do this is to burn a disc from the Purchased Music playlist. Of course, if you have purchased more than can fit on a single CD or DVD, you will need to use multiple discs to back up the entire collection.

Consider creating a smart playlist whose criteria is based on the date you added music to your Library and for which live updating is enabled. When you purchase new music, update the criteria so that the added date is just before you made your most recent purchase. Then, all the music you purchased since that date will be added to the playlist. Burn that playlist to disc, and you will have backed up your new music that you purchased since the last time you did this.

The Absolute Minimum

The iTunes Music Store is very well designed and makes it quite easy to find and buy music—from individual songs from your favorite one-hit wonder to complete collections of classic artists. As you work with the tunes you buy, remember the following musical morsels:

- When you purchase music from the iTunes Music Store, it is downloaded into your Library.

- By default, all the music you purchased from the iTunes Music Store is stored in the Purchased Music playlist.

- To play purchased music on a computer, that computer must be authorized. You can have up to five computers authorized at the same time. You can deauthorize a computer by choosing the Deauthorize Computer command.

- To play purchased music on a computer that is different from the one on which you purchased it, you can move the purchased music to another computer. There are several ways to do this.

- There are a couple of ways to see the music you have purchased. One is to use the Purchased Music playlist. You can also use the Purchase History information for your iTunes account to see a list of all the music you have purchased from the iTunes Music Store.

- You should back up the music you purchase from the iTunes Music Store. The easiest way is to do this is to burn a CD or DVD of the Purchased Music playlist.

IN THIS CHAPTER

- Recover aborted music downloads.
- Solve the dreaded (not really) "Not Authorized to Play" problem.
- Fix problems with your iTunes Music Store account.
- Get help with the store.
- Ask for more music.

Solving iTunes Music Store Problems

You will see that this is a short chapter. The reason is simple: You just aren't likely to encounter that many problems when working with the iTunes Music Store. The store, just like iTunes and the iPod, is well designed and works flawlessly most of the time. If you do encounter a problem, this chapter will help you find the solution.

Recovering Music That Wasn't Downloaded Successfully

If the download process for music you purchased wasn't completed for some reason (for example, you lost your Internet connection in the middle of the process), you can restart the download process to recover music you have purchased but weren't able to download successfully.

To do this, choose **Advanced**, **Check for Purchased Music** (see Figure 25.1). You will be prompted to enter the user account and password for the account under which the music was purchased. Do so and then click Check.

The music you have purchased will be checked against the music that has been successfully downloaded. If music is found that hasn't been downloaded successfully, you will be able to download it again. If you have successfully downloaded all the music you have purchased, you will see a message stating so (see Figure 25.2).

note

No, you can't use this technique to download music you have purchased to more than one computer. When you successfully download music, that music is marked as having been downloaded. The iTunes Music Store doesn't care to which computer you have downloaded it. When you buy music, you are entitled to download it once and only once.

FIGURE 25.1

You use the **Check for Purchased Music** command to recover music you have purchased but weren't able to download for some reason.

FIGURE 25.2

When you see this message, you have downloaded all the music you have purchased.

Solving the "Not Authorized to Play" Problem

As you learned in the previous chapter, you can play music you have purchased on up to five computers at the same time. If you try to play purchased music and see the "This Computer Is Not Authorized to Play This Music" message, you need to authorize the computer before you can play the purchased music. If you already have five computers authorized, you will need to deauthorize one before you can authorize another. (If you need help doing these tasks, see Chapter 25, "Working with Purchased Music.")

The challenge can sometimes be remembering how many and which computers you have authorized. The "how many" part is easy. Just access the **Apple Account Information** screen for your account. The Computer Authorizations section will tell you how many computers are currently authorized to play music for the account (to learn how to access this screen, see "Viewing the Music You Have Purchased" on page **359**).

The "which ones" part is a bit more difficult. The easiest way to tell is to try playing purchased music from each computer you might have authorized. If it plays, the computer is authorized.

Also remember that computers with which you are sharing music also count against the five-computer limit. If you are unable to play music because of authorization, make sure computers on the network aren't the cause of you being over your authorization limit.

note

If you use iTunes on only one computer, you never have to even think about authorization because it is handled for you automatically. If you use five or fewer computers, it still isn't a problem because after you sign in to your account on each machine, you don't have to bother with it again. Only when you use six or more computers to play music you have purchased from the iTunes Music Store do you need to concern yourself with this topic.

caution

If you sell a computer or stop using it, make sure you deauthorize it first. Even if you wipe the machine's hard drive, it still counts as an authorized computer. If you no longer have access to an authorized computer, you will need to contact iTunes Music Store Customer Service to have that machine deauthorized.

Correcting Problems with Your iTunes Music Store Account

You can change information for your iTunes Music Store by accessing the **Apple Account Information** page and using its tools to make changes to your account, such as to change the credit card you use to purchase music. (For help using this page, see "Changing and Viewing Your iTunes Music Store Account" on page **329**.)

If something has changed from the iTunes Music Store side of the equation, you will be prompted to change your account information. The dialog box that appears will also enable you to access your Account Information page to make the required changes.

Getting Help with iTunes Music Store Problems

Hopefully you won't ever have any problems with the iTunes Music Store, and if you do, the information in this chapter should help you solve them. If not, don't despair because help is just a few clicks away.

To access the iTunes Customer Service page, choose **Help, Music Store Customer Service**. Your default Web browser will open and you will move to the **iTunes Customer Service** page for the type of computer you are using (see Figure 25.3). Use the links and information on this page to get help. For example, you can click the **Get Help with Computer Authorization** link to get help deauthorizing a computer to which you no longer have access.

FIGURE 25.3

This is the iTunes Customer Service page for Windows users.

Reporting Music You Can't Find in the Store

Although the iTunes Music Store is great, it isn't perfect. Its major flaw, which is a perfectly understandable one, is that it doesn't contain every song ever produced (as if that is even possible). The good news is that Apple is continually adding music to the store, especially as music producers and record companies see what a great way it is for them to distribute their music.

If you can't find the music you want to buy in the store, you can let Apple know about it. (Who knows, your contact may be the one that causes some specific artist or music to be added to the store!)

To request music, perform the following steps:

1. Open the **Customer Service page** per the instructions in the previous section.

2. Open the FAQ section and click the **Request a Song or Artist link**. iTunes will open and the Requests & Feedback section of the iTunes Music Store will appear.

3. In the Make a Request section, choose the type of request you want to make, such as **Song** or **Artist**, on the **My Request Is for A** menu.

4. Type what you want to request in the **Your Request** box.

5. Click **Send**. Your request will be submitted, and you will see a confirmation screen that explains that you won't get a personal response to your request. Hopefully, at some point, the music you requested will be added to the store.

The Absolute Minimum

The iTunes Music Store is a great tool to search for and add music to your iTunes Library. In fact, you might never purchase a CD again (okay, that's a bit dramatic, but you get the idea). Fortunately, the iTunes Music Store works very well, and you aren't likely to have any problems using it, which is a good thing.

Just in case, in this chapter, you learned how to do the following tasks:

- Recover music you didn't download successfully.
- Solve the "Not Authorized to Play" issue.
- Fix problems with your iTunes Music Store account.
- Get help from Apple.
- Request music you can't find in the store.

If you do have problems and none of the information in this chapter helps you, you can always write to me at bradmacosx@mac.com, and I will do my best to help you get back into your best shopping form.

Index

How can we make this index more useful? Email us at indexes@quepublishing.com

How can we make this index more useful? Email us at indexes@quepublishing.com

Requests & Feedback link
(iTunes Music Store), 393
Required Password check box
(Sharing pane), 314
resetting
Audio CD song order in iTunes,
207
iPod, 89, 160
resize pane handle (iTunes),
216-218
resize window handle (iTunes),
216-218
restoring iPod software,
157-160
Rewind button (iTunes), 200
rewinding music
in iPod, 57
in iTunes, 200
Rip to iPod software (iPod),
122
ripping. *See* importing
RockStar software (iTunes), 126

S

Sample Rate data field (iTunes
song tags), 246
screen (iPod), adjusting contrast, 87
screensaver software (iTunes)
Fountain Music, 129
G-Force, 130
LED Spectrum Analyzer, 130
vTunes, 130
WhiteCap, 130
Scroll bar (iPod menus), 43
Scroll pad (iPod), 55
Search tool
Artist field (iTunes), 240
iTunes, 192
iTunes Music Library, 239-240
iTunes Music Store, 339
searching
in iTunes Music Library, 239
clearing searches, 241
defining searches, 240
in iTunes Music Store, 339
basic searches, 362-363
clearing searches, 363
power searches, 364-365
security, iTunes Music Store
accounts, 349-351
Select button (iPod mini), 41
language selection, 40
turning on/off, 39

Select check box (iTunes), 203
Selected check box (iTunes),
203
selecting
CD format (CD burning), 301
gap lengths between songs
(CD burning), 301
in iPod
Equalizer presets, 85
languages, 89
music via playlists, 50
in iPod mini, 40-41
iTunes default actions, 201
songs for smart playlists, 278
Sennheiser PCX250
Headphones, 94
serial numbers (iPod
registration), 23
Set Up an iTunes Allowance
screen (iTunes Music Store),
353
Settings menu (iPod), 44
Setup Assistant (iPod), 32
Setup Status window (iTunes
Installer), 183
Share Entire Library radio
button (Sharing pane), 314
Share My Music check box
(Sharing pane), 313-314
Share Selected Playlists radio
button (Sharing pane), 314
Shared Music check box
(Sharing pane), 315
Shared Music source (Source
List), 312, 315
Shared name field (Sharing
pane), 314
shareware, 118. *See also*
freeware; software
sharing music
via iMixes, 372-373, 391
via iTunes, 311-318
Sharing pane (Preferences
dialog box)
Required Password check box,
314
Share Entire Library radio
button, 314
Share My Music check box,
313-314
Share Selected Playlists radio
button, 314
Shared Music check box, 315
Shared name field, 314
Status information field, 314

Sheldon iPod Case (ebags), 112
Shopping Cart (iTunes Music
Store), 347, 368-369
shortcuts (iTunes), 199-201, 218
Show Genre When Browsing
check box (General pane), 215
Show iTunes Icon in System
Tray check box (Preferences
dialog box), 208
Show Songs default action
(iTunes), 201
Show/Hide Album Art button
(iTunes), 193
Shuffle button (iTunes), 193
Shuffle feature
iPod, 82-83
iTunes
playlists, 273
Audio CD song order, 207
*Party Shuffle feature,
282-284*
Shure E2 Sound Isolating
earphones, 92
Shure E3 Sound Isolating
earphones with Extended
Frequency Response, 92
Shure E5 Sound Isolating
earphones, 93
Sign In dialog box (iTunes
Music Store), 350
signing in
iTunes Music Store, 350, 358
iTunes Music Store accounts,
348
Single Cover option (CD
inserts), 307
six-pin FireWire
iPod Macintosh connections,
31
iPod Windows PC connections,
28-30
six-pin to four-pin FireWire
adapters (iPod), 31
Size data field (iTunes song
tags), 246
sizing
Browser pane (iTunes), 239
iTunes windows, 216
in Macintosh, 218-219
in Windows PC, 216
Source List column (iTunes)
in Macintosh, 218
in Windows PC, 216
skipping songs in iTunes, 203
Sleep mode (iPod), 153

How can we make this index more useful? Email us at indexes@quepublishing.com

How can we make this index more useful? Email us at indexes@quepublishing.com